Studies in Military and Strategic History

General Editor: **Michael Dockrill**, Professor of Diplomatic History, King's College, London

Published titles include:

Brian Holden Reid
J. F. C. FULLER: Military Thinker

Stewart Lone
JAPAN'S FIRST MODERN WAR
Army and Society in the Conflict with China, 1894–95

Thomas R. Mockaitis
BRITISH COUNTERINSURGENCY, 1919–60

T. R. Moreman
THE ARMY IN INDIA AND THE DEVELOPMENT OF FRONTIER WARFARE,
1849–1947

Kendrick Oliver
KENNEDY, MACMILLAN AND THE NUCLEAR TEST-BAN DEBATE, 1961–63

Elspeth Y. O'Riordan
BRITAIN AND THE RUHR CRISIS

G. D. Sheffield
LEADERSHIP IN THE TRENCHES
Officer–Man Relations, Morale and Discipline in the British Army in the Era of
the First World War

Adrian Smith
MICK MANNOCK, FIGHTER PILOT
Myth, Life and Politics

Martin Thomas
THE FRENCH NORTH AFRICAN CRISIS
Colonial Breakdown and Anglo-French Relations, 1945–62

Simon Trew
BRITAIN, MIHAILOVIC AND THE CHETNIKS, 1941–42

Steven Weiss
ALLIES IN CONFLICT
Anglo-American Strategic Negotiations, 1938–44

Roger Woodhouse
BRITISH FOREIGN POLICY TOWARDS FRANCE, 1945–51

Studies in Military and Strategic History
Series Standing Order ISBN 0–333–71046–0
(*outside North America only*)

You can receive future titles in this series as they are published by placing a standing order.
Please contact your bookseller or, in case of difficulty, write to us at the address below with
your name and address, the title of the series and the ISBN quoted above.

Customer Services Department, Macmillan Distribution Ltd, Houndmills, Basingstoke,
Hampshire RG21 6XS, England

War and Empire in Mauritius and the Indian Ocean

Ashley Jackson
Research Fellow
Mansfield College
Oxford

in association with
King's College, London

First published 2001 by
PALGRAVE
Houndmills, Basingstoke, Hampshire RG21 6XS and
175 Fifth Avenue, New York, N. Y. 10010
Companies and representatives throughout the world

PALGRAVE is the new global academic imprint of
St. Martin's Press LLC Scholarly and Reference Division and
Palgrave Publishers Ltd (formerly Macmillan Press Ltd).

ISBN 0–333–96840–9

This book is printed on paper suitable for recycling and
made from fully managed and sustained forest sources.

A catalogue record for this book is available
from the British Library.

Library of Congress Cataloging-in-Publication Data
Jackson, Ashley.
   War and empire in Mauritius and the Indian Ocean /
   Ashley Jackson.
      p. cm. — (Studies in military and strategic history)
   Includes bibliographical references and index.
   ISBN 0–333–96840–9 (cloth)
      1. Mauritius—History, Military—20th century. 2. Mauritius–
   –History, Naval—20th century. 3. Mauritius—Strategic aspects.
   4. Indian Ocean Region—Strategic aspects. 5. World War,
   1939–1945—Mauritius. 6. World War, 1939–1945—Indian Ocean
   Region. 7. Great Britain. Royal Navy. 8. Decolonization—Mauritius.
   I. Title. II. Series.
      DT469.M47 J33 2001
      355'.009698'2—dc21
                                                2001024551

10 9   8   7   6   5   4   3   2   1
10 09 08 07 06 05 04 03 02 01

Printed in Great Britain by Antony Rowe Ltd, Chippenham, Wiltshire

Dedicated to Rosa Poppy Jackson and Abigail Jane Jackson

Contents

Acknowledgements

Thanks to the Hayter Fund, the Beit Fund, and the Modern History Faculty – all of the University of Oxford – for making it possible to visit Mauritius. Special thanks to two of the leading historians of Mauritius: to Raymond D'Unienville for supplying a wealth of information over the course of a year and for hospitality in Mauritius, and to Marina Carter for providing information and for translating articles from French to English and going some way towards compensating for the author's shameful mono-linguality.

I would like to thank the following people especially: Peter Twining for access to Sir Edward Twining's papers, Kate Tildesley of the Naval Historical Branch, Louis Hein de Charmoy, the President and Committee of the Mauritius Ex-Services League (BCEL), G. Andre Decotter and the Royal Pioneer Corps Association (Mauritius), the East African Forces Dining Club, Andrew Morton, Archivist at the Royal Pioneer Corps Museum, Monica Maurel for a copy of her father's diaries, Penny and Tony Ward of the British High Commission in Port Louis, Nicholas Bouchet, Michael Dockrill, and Terry Barringer of the Royal Commonwealth Society Library, Cambridge.

Too numerous to mention but equally thanked are all of the correspondents and interviewees in Britain, Mauritius, South Africa and America.

A. J. W. J.
Wadebridge, Cornwall
Woodstock, Oxfordshire

List of Abbreviations

AAPC	African Auxiliary Pioneer Corps
ADC	Aide-de-Camp
ADS	Assistant Director of Supplies
AMPC	Auxiliary Military Pioneer Corps
ARP	Air Raid Precautions
ATS	Auxiliary Territorial Service
AWOL	Absent without leave
BIOT	British Indian Ocean Territory
C-in-C	Commander-in-Chief
CB	Commander of the Order of the Bath
CBE	Commander of the Order of the British Empire
CDWA	Colonial Development and Welfare
CMF	Central Mediterranean Forces
CMG	Commander of the Order of St Michael and St George
CO	Colonial Office or Commanding Officer
CRE	Commander, Royal Engineers
CSM	Company Sergeant Major
DFC	Distinguished Flying Cross
DID	Detailed Issue Depot
DDT	Dichloro-diphenyl-trichloro-ethane (an insecticide)
DSO	Distinguished Service Order
EAAMC	East African Army Medical Corps
EAASC	East African Army Service Corps
EAC	East Africa Command
EAMLC	East African Military Labour Corps
FAA	Fleet Air Arm
FCB	Fabian Colonial Bureau
FCO	Foreign and Commonwealth Office
FMC	Field Maintenance Centre
FSS	Field Security Section
GHQ	General Headquarters
GOC	General Officer Commanding
GT	General Transport
HAA	Heavy Anti Aircraft
HCT	High Commission Territories
HMAS	Her Majesty's Australian Ship

HMIS	Her Majesty's Indian Ship
HMS	Her Majesty's Ship
HQ	Headquarters
HRH	His or Her Royal Highness
INC	Indian National Congress
IOL	India Office Library
IWM	Imperial War Museum
KAR	King's African Rifles
LAA	Light Anti-Aircraft
MBE	Member of the Order of the British Empire
MC	Military Cross
MDF	Mauritius Defence Force
MEC	Middle East Command
MELF	Middle East Land Forces
MLP	Mauritius Labour Party
MNBDO	Mobile Naval Base Defence Organization
MP	Military Police or Member of Parliament
MR	Mauritius Regiment
MTF	Mauritius Territorial Force
NAAFI	Navy, Army, and Air Force Institutes
NCO	Non Commissioned Officer
OBE	Order of the British Empire
OCT	Officer Commanding Troops
POW	Prisoner of War
PRO	Public Record Office
RAF	Royal Air Force
RAMC	Royal Army Medical Corps
RAOC	Royal Army Ordnance Corps
RASC	Royal Army Service Corps
RCS	Royal Commonwealth Society Library, University of Cambridge
RCS	Royal Corps of Signals
REME	Royal Electrical and Mechanical Engineers
RFA	Royal Fleet Auxiliary
RGA	Royal Garrison Artillery
RHL	Rhodes House Library, University of Oxford
RN	Royal Navy
RNAS	Royal Naval Air Station
RNVR	Royal Naval Volunteer Reserve
RPC	Royal Pioneer Corps
Rs.	Rupees

RT	Radio Telephony
RWAFF	Royal West African Frontier Force
SAS	Special Air Service
SEAC	South East Asia Command
SMF	Special Mobile Force
SOE	Special Operations Executive
TUC	Trades Union Congress
UK	United Kingdom
US	United States
VAD	Voluntary Aid Detachment
WO	War Office
WRNS	Women's Royal Naval Service
W/T	Wireless Telegraphy
'Y' Service	British organization for intercepting radio communications

Biographical Notes

Clifford, Captain the Honourable Sir Bede Edmund Hugh (1890–1969). Career in the Colonial Administrative Service, including a time as Imperial Commissioner in South Africa. Governor of Mauritius, 1936–42, then transferred to the Governorship of Trinidad and Tobago.

Mackenzie Kennedy, Sir Henry Charles Donald Cleveland (1889–1965). Career in the Colonial Administrative Service, spent mainly in Africa (Northern Rhodesia and Tanganyika), finishing as Governor of Nyasaland, 1939–42. Persuaded to take up the Governorship of Mauritius in 1942, where he remained until retirement in 1949.

Platt, General Sir William (1885–1975). Soldier in the British Army. Officer in Command of the Sudan Defence Force, 1938–41, prominent in the East African campaign, and General Officer Commanding-in-Chief East Africa Command from 1941 to 1945. Madagascar, Mauritius, and the Seychelles came under his command.

Shuckburgh, Sir John Evelyn (1877–1953). Transferred from the Indian Civil Service to the Colonial Office in 1921. Deputy Under Secretary of State for the Colonies 1931 until 1942. Appointed Governor of Nigeria in 1939, but the outbreak of war and retirement intervened. Narrator of the historical section of the Cabinet Office, 1942–48, and compiled the unpublished 'Colonial Civil History of the War'.

Smallwood, Major General Gerald Russell (1889–1977). Soldier in the British Army. British Military Mission to the Egyptian Army, 1937–39. Commanding troops in Madagascar in 1942, and Commanding Officer of East Africa Command's subordinate Islands Area Command, which included Madagascar, Mauritius, and the Seychelles.

Somerville, Admiral of the Fleet Sir James Fownes (1882–1949). Career in the Royal Navy. Commander-in-Chief East Indies, 1938–39. Commander of Force 'H' in the Mediterranean, 1940–42. Commander-in-Chief of the Eastern Fleet, responsible for the Indian Ocean, 1942–44.

Twining, Edward Francis (created Baron Twining of Godalming and Tanganyika) (1899–1967). Career in the Colonial Administrative

Service from 1929 after transfer from the Army. Transferred to Mauritius in 1939 as Deputy Director of Labour (later Director). Appointed Chief Censor and Information Officer on the outbreak of war. Responsible for the island's use as an intelligence-gathering outpost of Bletchley Park. Appointed Administrator of St Lucia, 1944–46, Governor of North Borneo, 1946–49, and Governor of Tanganyika, 1949–58.

Introduction: War and Empire

According to Captain Alfred North-Coombes, based on the Indian Ocean island of Rodrigues with a company of Mauritian soldiers guarding a British cable and wireless station, the greatest war excitement came on 3 March 1942 when the Cocos-Keeling Islands were shelled by an enemy ship, causing an interruption in the imperial cable link with Australia. This caused panic in Rodrigues, and 'at Oyster Bay was heard a humming, that was the sound of people praying aloud, even those who had never prayed before, that they would be saved from the Japanese. Rosaries were cut into pieces and shared with neighbours'.[1] Meanwhile, on Mauritius, 344 miles west across the Indian Ocean, 'one Indian widow, calling at the [Labour] Department with some copper utensils, said with pride "that she could spare them for England's hour of need"'.[2] Such minutiae demonstrate the truly imperial scope of the 1939–45 conflict, a war that generated a host of experiences common to both the people of Britain and the 60 million inhabitants of the British colonial empire.

In the Second World War Great Britain was loyally supported tooth and nail by the largest empire in human history. As the Governor of Uganda, Sir Alan Burns, said:

> In 1940, when we of the British Empire stood against the Axis, with our Allies overwhelmed by the Germans, and our own armies defeated, when our enemies exulted over our impending ruin, and even our friends had abandoned hope, this was the time when our Colonies stood by us – friends indeed, and true loyal friends.[3]

This loyalty is a primary fact that should never slip from view when the history of Britain and the war is considered.[4] Imperial participation in the war may not have been uniformly spontaneous, mutinies and resistance may have occurred, British prestige may have suffered irreparably through defeats on colonial soil, and demands for greater political autonomy may have been the price to pay for imperial participation, but none of this alters the fact that Britain was supported

1

overwhelmingly by its empire and emerged victorious with all its imperial territories in tow. Furthermore, it does not alter the fact that in 1945 the British empire remained the largest on earth, and that the shrunken, near-naked island of 1965 – divested of all colonies bar a few – was in an as-yet-unknown future, not, as now, in a predictable past. Teleological readings of the writing on the wall were not possible then. Though weakened by war, the simple fact of victory, a seat at the 'Big Three's' table, and an intact empire meant that the future looked bright. Challenges there were to be sure, but British policy-makers could look to the postwar world in sanguine mood and see an imperial Britain continuing to shape world affairs.

Though it is a modern trend to emphasize the weaknesses of empire, the ambivalence of imperial power, and the contradictions of the colonial state, its very real strength should not be overlooked. As Cain and Hopkins' claim that Robinson and Gallagher's portrait of imperial expansion driven by peripheral crises leaves empire detached from its metropolitan roots, so too does the empire need to be put back into the history of Britain and the war.[5] Whatever the weaknesses of British rule, the colonies were made to fight for Britain, and colonial manpower, womanpower and economic power were fully subordinated to the demands of the British world war effort orchestrated from Whitehall, the heart of imperial Britain.[6] Susan Briggs writes of the home front that 'the British advanced further during the Second World War towards a total mobilization of resources than the Germans did, although few people in Britain recognized it at the time'.[7] This was equally true on the imperial front, where Britain achieved a greater mobilization of overseas resources than any other belligerent power.

It is all too easy to overlook the imperial dimensions of Britain's war – perhaps they are so obvious that the wood is lost for the trees. The ways and places in which Britain fought the war were quintessentially products of her imperial past and imperial possessions, quite apart from their European roots and settings. The overwhelming importance of the sea lanes was the result of an industrial, agricultural and imperial heritage that had left Britain unable to feed itself and created the need for a global maritime presence. For example, the Indian Ocean, peppered with British islands and atolls, *had* to remain a 'British lake' if the empire was successfully to meet challenges in the East, to transport Allied aid to Russia, and maintain links with vital Middle Eastern battlefields and resources. The very fact of Britain's fight out of Egypt – that brought Tobruk, Montgomery and Alamein – was testament to its imperial past and present, as were other such calamities, battles and heroes – the fall of Singapore, the interventions in Iraq and Persia, the Abyssinian campaign, the invasion of Madagascar, Slim and his 'Forgotten Army' in Burma, and the American blood spilt to destroy Japanese forces in the British Pacific islands.

Our fathers and grandfathers, though perhaps little aware of it themselves as they reminisce about the Western Desert or the jungles of Malaya, were *imperial* soldiers, and alongside them though seldom sufficiently integrated into our picture, were hundreds of thousands of non-British soldiers drawn from a galaxy of imperial territories; not just the Australasians, Canadians and Indians of whom we are aware, but Palestinians, Torres Straits Islanders, Mauritians, Fijians, Batswana, Barbadians, Somalis and Straits Chinese, all by virtue of their common imperial bond. Memory of the Anzacs, the Canadians at Dieppe or the Indians and white South Africans serving with the Eighth Army, is embedded in popular awareness of the war, but there has never been knowledge, let alone memory, of smaller but no less important units. Their very names evoke the pageant of a dead empire; the Transjordan Frontier Force, the Somali Camel Corps, the Bermuda Volunteer Rifle Corps, the African Pioneer Corps, the Sudan Defence Force, or the Ceylon Volunteer Rifles (to name but a few).[8] Even colonial women served overseas in British uniform, like the 1000 Mauritians who arrived in Egypt in 1945 as members of the Auxiliary Territorial Service (ATS).

Whilst these distant subjects of Britain fought the enemy across the globe, people back at home – just like those in Britain – worried themselves sick over relatives at war, suffered the borderless privations of war's economic dislocations and 'did their bit' to grow more food, to raise money for Spitfires and to raise productivity for the war effort. It is vital to incorporate the home front, so familiar and reified a theme in Britain's war history, into the study of the empire at war. Even for the most remote colony, one could paint a picture similar to the familiar memory of wartime Britain – of rationing, blackouts, home guards, Air Raid Precaution (ARP) wardens and the ubiquitous voice of Churchill on the wireless.

Likewise, plans gestating throughout the war for a 'New Jerusalem' to herald the peace, and the Labour landslide that ousted Churchill in 1945, brought hope and expectation not just to the people of the home island, but to millions more around the world. 'Welfare imperialism' marked the postwar empire as much as the National Health Service marked Britain itself, and trades unions and development plans were to replace the law and order, balanced budget sternness of the prewar imperial order. Change was in the air and things would never be quite the same again.

It is a paradox beloved of imperial historians that Britain began to lose its empire at the time when it was most valuable to it. It was also the case that, in the terminal decades, the empire was more coherent, more *imperial*, than it had ever been before. Nowhere is the sense of the empire acting as a unit better illustrated than in the history of the Second World War, and one is drawn irresistibly to the image of a global Britain. This was a truly imperial war effort, stretching from the centres of British world power to the outposts of empire. Though the military forces of the empire sometimes performed indifferently, there is no doubt that the organization of the empire's war effort was quite remarkable. The empire was a vast manpower reservoir, a battleground and a base, and provided foodstuffs and strategic raw materials essential to the prosecution of war (in 1938, the British empire had the world's greatest output in 14 out of the 26 strategic raw materials).

War is a good time to study empire, because in war it became more imperial. As Keith Jeffery writes, 'only in war ... did the Empire approach the otherwise mythical status of a formidable, efficient, and effective power system, prepared to exploit its apparently limitless resources, and actually able to deploy forces throughout the world'. Studies of the empire and the war add weight to this claim, expressed somewhat differently by Robert Pearce. During the war Britain acted 'more imperialistically than ever before. In a sense this was the heyday of empire. Imperial control at last became a reality'.[9] As John Gallagher claims, the war marked the ultimate 'revival' of the empire.[10] The successful mobilization and utilization of colonial troops and home populations required consultation at every level, and study of the empire at war presents a cross-section view of the mechanics of British world power at work, from Cabinet, Parliament and Whitehall departments in the metropole, across the seas to proconsuls, their district administrations, local collaborators and their people on the periphery. Adding another layer to this structure of authority was the military, represented in London by the War Office, Admiralty and the Air Ministry. They were represented overseas in regional power centres like Cairo, home of Middle East Command (MEC), Colombo and Mombasa, variously the headquarters of the Eastern Fleet, and Nairobi, headquarters of East Africa Command (EAC). At the next level down, the military was represented locally by Officers Commanding Troops (OCT) and Naval Officers-in-Charge in garrison colonies like Mauritius.

Every British territory had a war experience, and this is telling in itself. All territories felt the beat of the world war, the trauma of sending troops overseas and of managing on a home front drastically altered by war. There were manifold political impacts – often new factors in old games – as wartime phenomena ran like larva down a mountainside's pre-existing channels. In Mauritius it was only natural that wartime factors like conscription and military service should flow into the political hot spots that clustered around issues of labour and race relations. The life and death question of food supply became prominent as many colonies – dependent like Britain on imports – found their sources cut off by shipping shortages and enemy submarines, or even conquered by enemy soldiers. What was bad for the imperial goose was bad for the colonial gander. Every corner of the empire had a military and resource production role to perform, and all contributed financially and felt the chill blasts of the war's economic impact. Wider worlds hoved into view. It was a mark of how much Britain needed the empire that the Second World War caused more imperial subjects than ever before to actually be told that there was an empire that they owed some kind of allegiance and tribute to, whether in terms of military enlistment, labour service, increased production or increased taxes. For the sake of King and empire, all had to tighten their belts or button up the uniforms of a quasi-alien army. Though during the war many of these imperial subjects 'didn't know what Government is and why anybody is fighting at all', they soon found out that, understood or not, it still had the power to touch them.[11] During the Second World War colonial governments felt the need to talk to and *include* their people within the imperial community, and to tell them that they were a part of something bigger than just their tribe, their village or their colony, and that this membership brought with it certain obligations. The war was arguably the first 'national experience' in the colonies, as the First World War had been for the Dominions.

Churchill for one never lost sight of the imperial dimension of Britain's war. He was a genuine imperial statesman who understood that Britain's place at the world's top table depended on it being an imperial power ('Hold Calais for the good of the British Empire', he signalled the defending commander during the Dunkirk evacuation). His 'rhetoric placed Empire unequivocally behind the cause of democracy and freedom, and, broadly speaking, there was an extraordinary acceptance and even enthusiasm for the war effort across the Empire'.[12] His speeches brought this imperial dimension into people's

homes, and, more importantly, to the people of the empire themselves. Again, reified images of Britain's war have wider resonances;
not just the suburban family tuning into the wireless to hear Churchill
address the nation, but the yard of a Mauritian home crowded with
people sitting on rocks and upturned tins in order to listen to the same
voice, or Batswana congregating at the chief's court to hear the new
vernacular radio broadcasts. War demanded involvement in empire,
united disparate populations in a variety of ways, and brought a
deeper penetration of imperial propaganda than ever before.

During the Second World War the co-operation or peaceful acquies-
cence of colonial populations was as vital to Britain as was the capacity
to defend the empire and the sea routes that were its highways. As
John Darwin writes, 'to survive at all as a political unit, the Imperial
system had two fundamental requirements: an effective means of
Imperial defence and the co-operation of political allies in all its
assorted colonial and semi-colonial hinterlands'.[13] Between 1939 and
1945 these two pillars were to groan under the weight of Britain's
global burdens, as the empire was whipped in by an imperial government pulling out all of the colonial stops in an effort to hold on to its
territory and defeat three formidable enemies. The horses could not be
spared if victory was to be achieved. It was not just land that was at
stake. As a maritime power Britain depended upon the seas to maintain contact with its empire, as well as the cable routes and the
airwaves that enabled the colonies to speak to the metropole. The war
was a battle of the high seas and of the radio frequencies as much as it
was a battle of the land.

This spectacle, this amazing feat of human organization and co-
operation that was the imperial war effort, was made possible by the
fact that Britain's was a liberal empire, albeit a liberal empire with
sharp, and occasionally bloody, teeth. Jeffery claims that the nature of
British imperialism, 'peacetime free press, civil rights, habeas corpus,
the cultivation of elites, and promises – however vague – of ultimate
self-government, paid enormous dividends during the war'.[14] The
elites remained loyal and collaborated in the mobilization of their
colonies for war.

However, this liberality also contained the seeds of imperial dissolution, as colonial authorities tried to pursue essentially contradictory
goals of altruism and control, and to use the postwar empire as a
buttress for the crumbling edifice of British national economic power
in a world where new ideologies vied for support, and where old-style
colonial rule could not be practised behind media-proof doors.[15]

Superpowers conceived of themselves as anti-colonial, though they were in fact conquest states themselves. A new generation of critics at home sought to ameliorate imperialism, and this fundamentally undermined it. The British sought to improve conditions in the colonies, and in conceding this need offered the forces of nationalism a legitimacy that could only grow more powerful.

Mauritius, the Indian Ocean and the Second World War

This study cannot be as grand in scope as these opening words. But it can be claimed that in focusing on one microcosm of the imperial war effort, the links that bind the war history of Britain to her former colonies will be illustrated. A breadth of vision beyond the monographical is sustained throughout. It appears to be overlooked in the early twenty-first century, with all its talk of globalism, that Britain has for long been global in her interests, never more so than when gripped in the years of 'total' war between 1939 and 1945. The First World War had been a dress rehearsal for a truly imperial war effort, and manoeuvres had been practised in eighteenth- and nineteenth-century wars when foes were asset-stripped of their colonies as European battles were carried across the globe.

In this study regional history is linked to the history of the world war and the metropolitan history of Britain, and to broad themes in the study of imperial history. The book is aimed at the military and naval historian as well as the imperial historian, seeking a greater fusion of military, naval and imperial history than is common. Taking as its focus a small British colony and its even smaller dependent islands scattered in the Indian Ocean, the effects of the war are examined, demonstrating that the people of the Indian Ocean were directly linked to the empire and the world at war. Kenya, Tunisia, Libya, Egypt, Madagascar, France, Palestine, Malta, Sicily and Italy all felt the tread of Mauritian soldiers' boots, and the colony was linked in other ways to Burma, South Africa, Australia, Central Europe, India and, of course, to Britain itself. The sea highways are a part of this story, as are the radio waves and submarine cables that were the connecting sinews of maritime empire. The chapters reveal the long-term strategic significance of the Indian Ocean and its islands, the military effort of Mauritius, the war's effects on the colonial home front, the vital role of colonial soldiers in supporting the British imperial forces in the Western Desert and beyond, the course of the war in the Indian Ocean, and the secret war of propaganda, censorship, code-breaking and intelligence-gathering. To defend an empire the British had to think imperially and their enemies might have had greater success if they too were able to effectively grasp the global magnitude of the struggle. As it was, the Germans and the Japanese recognized the crucial importance of the Indian Ocean theatre, but were unable to translate this into effective action. It was to be the British who held on to the Indian Ocean, and who successfully neutralized the threat from the major French base in the region, Madagascar.

Mauritius was first inhabited by the whites who lapped the shores of Indian Ocean islands as successive waves of European colonizers journeyed to the East, having been first visited by the Portuguese in 1505. The Dutch arrived in 1598 but left in 1710, the French arrived in 1715 and stayed, and the British took the island from the French in 1810, though did not settle in any number. The British conquered Mauritius for strategic reasons, and it remained a link in imperial communications and the control of the sea lanes, part of the eastern group of British colonies that at the end of the Napoleonic Wars also included Ceylon and the Straits Settlement in Malaya. Mauritius rapidly became an important part of Britain's tropical treasure trove, expanding its export of sugar to Britain and eclipsing the old West Indies sugar colonies. By the late nineteenth century it was second only to Ceylon in the colonial import-export league table. In 1852–54 its exports amounted to £1 256 624 and imports to £1 215 212. In 1882-84 these figures had risen to £2 685 709 and £2 875 666 respectively.[16] Trade slumped somewhat after this, however it recovered and then boomed during and after the First World War.

By the 1930s the island's population consisted of a white elite (c. 10 000), a Creole community (c. 115 000) descended from slaves imported to work the sugar plantations, and an Indian majority (c. 275 000), descendants of the migrants who maintained the labour flow once slavery had been abolished. There was also a Chinese community (c. 10 000).[17] The white community – often referred to as the Franco-Mauritians – were a social and economic elite, and had proved themselves over the years to be formidable opponents of local British rule. During the 1930s the non-white population became politically active beyond a narrow urban elite. The Mauritius Labour Party (MLP) was founded in 1936 and the island was shaken by strikes and riots that, along with those in the West Indies, alerted the attention of Colonial Office policy-makers. The war saw the increasing politicization of the Indians, and the British needed to bargain and negotiate with communities in order to elicit the degree of co-operation that the imperial war effort demanded. In this respect, the British had cause to regret the fact that the island's non-white population had never been effectively Anglicized despite 130 years of British rule, and blamed the influence of the Franco-Mauritians for the less enthusiastic response of some Mauritians to the imperial rallying cry.

'What on earth did *Mauritius* do during the war?', was a question frequently asked – in Britain and Mauritius – when conducting research. The answer is that it did a great deal and that an exposition of the colony's war history affords an excellent opportunity to appreciate how deeply the war affected even remote peoples, and how effectively Britain drew upon its imperial resources in the prosecution of the war. The home front, even in distant colonies, was deeply affected by modern 'total' war. The familiar national memories of wartime Britain could be matched in Mauritius; rationing (particularly after the loss of vital rice supplies from Burma), runaway inflation, profiteering, coastal blackouts, scrap-metal collections,[18] censorship, home guards, 'Dig for Victory' campaigns and ARP wardens.

Furthermore, the war exacerbated existing social and industrial tensions, resulting in serious rioting in 1943 that led to questions in both Houses of Parliament. It also led to unwelcome attention from British colonial critics – Labour MPs, the Fabian Colonial Bureau, the Aborigines Protection Society and even the India Office (always concerned about the plight of Indians elsewhere in the empire). Augmenting the pressure for change was the scrutiny of the local press and the Indian political elite in India and South Africa, in a period in which the *imperialization of opposition* to colonial rule was growing in significance and in power. As a result, constitutional reform could not be kept off the agenda, despite the wishes of local colonial officials and the Colonial Office in London. Wartime pressure and adverse publicity led to a quickening of the pace of constitutional change culminating in the groundbreaking 1948 election that saw the island's Indian majority enfranchised for the first time.[19] The war was a lot more than just a hiatus between the riots and unrest of the 1930s and the constitutional and political advances of the late 1940s, though this is how it is sometimes portrayed.[20]

As will be seen, opposition to empire and its local manifestations was imperial in the scope of its operation and organization, and there was never a time when imperious British proconsuls ruled dictatorially and without significant opposition. As D. A. Low notes, an imperial government subject to the criticism of Parliament had to be a 'flexible autocracy'.[21] The war and its immediate aftermath saw the publication of dozens of officially commissioned reports and inquiries into all aspects of the 'state of Mauritius', adding to the empire of knowledge so crucial to imperial rule, particularly in the new era of colonial development and welfare. Increasingly, metropolitan thinking extended itself to the colonies; the war saw the visit of many metropolitan experts, investigating health conditions, sanitation and education provision, and advising on the establishment of co-operatives and trades unions. It is no surprise that the new fashion of state-controlled development in Britain should affect planning for the future of the colonies.

In the piecemeal but nonetheless effective system of imperial rule, local elites and proto-parliamentary organizations played an important role in linking imperial demands with the capacity of colonies to deliver. In the Mauritian case an Indo-Mauritian elite and a powerful Council of Government helped mobilize support for the war and also articulated local grievances, acting as interfaces between the colonial government and the people.[22] The Council of Government consisted of British administrators and representatives of the Franco-Mauritian community elected by whites entitled to vote under the colony's 1886 constitution. Though its role was only advisory, it discussed legislation and acted as a forum for the expression of Franco-Mauritian opinion, and in 1940 an Indian and a Creole representative were appointed. The war was to be a catalyst for constitutional change that would see the island's non-white population enfranchised for the first time. In a liberal empire not based on immediate force, the collaboration of local elites was crucial. It could lead to political advance after the war in return for wartime support. Wartime hardship and privation exacerbated unrest and fertilized the seedbeds from which movements of protest could harvest support. Though usually wearing the hat of loyal opposition, the political elite could drive a hard bargain when it perceived the need to do so.

Mauritius (like all colonies) donated large sums of money to the imperial government for the prosecution of the war, in the form of outright gifts and interest-free loans. It provided the Royal Air Force (RAF) with a squadron of Spitfires, made an annual defence contribution to the Imperial Treasury, bought a Walrus sea plane and mess accoutrements for HMS *Mauritius*, and its schoolchildren paid for the first mobile canteens to appear on the streets of blitzed London in winter 1940. Direct taxation was introduced for the first time. The island's labour supply became regimented and – threatened with starvation because of its inability to feed itself and the evaporation of food imports from Australia, India, Burma and neighbouring Vichy islands – over a quarter of its sugar estate land was compulsorily converted to the production of foodcrops.

The war experience of Indian Ocean islanders was informed by their position in a dangerous ocean crucial to Britain's maritime supremacy and its defence by the ships of the depleted Eastern Fleet. Vital resources to and from India, Burma, Australasia and the Middle East war theatres had to be ferried across the Indian Ocean, and islands like Mauritius had a part to play in convoy protection and operations against enemy vessels. The convoy route through the Mozambique Channel ensured that Allied Lend-Lease supplies reached the Russians via the Persian Gulf. Control of the Persian Gulf was founded upon control of the Indian Ocean, imperative if the vital Middle Eastern oilfields in Saudi Arabia, Iran, Iraq, Kuwait and Bahrain were to remain open to the British (in 1939 Iran provided 24 per cent of Britain's oil, but from 1941 Middle Eastern output was sent direct to imperial forces in North Africa, Iraq and India).

Japanese submarines operated as far west as the East African coast, surveying the coastlines of Mauritius, the Seychelles and many other islands, and torpedoing HMS *Ramillies* and sinking a tanker in the recently captured Madagascan harbour of Diego Suarez in 1942. A powerful German submarine fleet operated in the ocean from the Japanese base at Penang. Before the British crushed the Italian forces in North and Northeast Africa in early 1941, the Italian Navy menaced the Indian Ocean sea lanes from its base at Massawa. After Pearl Harbor, and the end of effective British naval resistance in the Far East with the loss of HMS *Prince of Wales* and HMS *Repulse* in December 1941, the Indian Ocean was exposed to Japanese strikes westwards. Admiral Sir James Somerville's Eastern Fleet was withdrawn to Kenya after the fall of Singapore brought the enemy uncomfortably close to its Ceylon base, against which the Imperial Japanese Navy attempted a Pearl Harbor-like raid (at the time the Fleet was safe in the secret base at Addu Atoll in the Maldives).

In this strategically charged Indian Ocean, Mauritius and its dependent islands and archipelagos – particularly Rodrigues and Diego Garcia – had to be defended and made capable of aiding offensive action (Rodrigues had a population of 12 000, and there were about 1700 people in the other Mauritian dependencies). The Royal Navy turned Mauritius into a refuelling and repair base, and a base for Catalina flying boats. Diego Garcia was earmarked to become a major Fleet base. Fearing Japanese invasion, Mauritius became a country in uniform and was placed under Lieutenant General Sir William Platt's East Africa Command. Like every colony, the War Cabinet's Committee of Imperial Defence had ready a Defence Plan for Mauritius, involving coastal and air defences and a scorched earth policy in the event of invasion.[23]

Mauritius was linked to other familiar facets of Britain's war effort. Most obviously, it sent men to war. Thousands volunteered or were conscripted as construction workers for RAF and Royal Navy installations, infantry soldiers and military labourers. The Home Guard, the Coastal Defence Squadron,[24] the Mauritius Artillery, the Royal Pioneer Corps (RPC), the Mauritius Territorial Force (MTF), the Mauritius Civil Labour Corps, the Mauritius Signals Corps, the Mauritius Volunteer Air Force and even the Women's Volunteer Force vied for recruits.[25] Recruitment required conscription, and issues of race and racial discrimination were never far from the surface during this process. The RPC – in which over 4000 Mauritians served during the war under MEC – called into being a colonial army of over 100 000 military labourers without which the crucial British victories in the Western Desert could not have been achieved.

These locally raised forces were in addition to the imperial forces that were a feature of Mauritius as a garrison colony; units of the Royal Artillery and Royal Engineers had always maintained a presence on the island, manning the coastal defence batteries. On the outbreak of war the Mauritius Garrison consisted of a Heavy Battery of the Royal Artillery and a Fortress Battalion of the Royal Engineers, along with detachments from the Royal Corps of Signals (RCS), the Royal Army Medical Corps (RAMC), the Royal Army Service Corps (RASC) and the Royal Army Ordnance Corps (RAOC). A battalion of the King's African Rifles (KAR) was added in 1943, establishing a link that was to last into the 1960s. The battalion was sent as the Japanese threat loomed on the horizon. It was not the only wartime military link that was to last long into the postwar period, as Mauritius continued to send thousands of troops to the Middle East; shortly before the Suez Crisis in 1956 there were still 8000 Mauritians in the region.

Some Mauritians joined the metropolitan armies of the Allied powers. The Franco-Mauritian community sent men to join the Free French Forces and the British Army. Franco-Mauritians made a notable contribution to the Special Operations Executive (SOE), in the Indian Ocean and particularly in France. There were also Mauritians in the Special Air Service (SAS) and the RAF. Some of the Jews detained on Mauritius throughout the war joined the Jewish Brigade and the Czech Army.

Mauritius became a base for regional SOE operations. The SOE was established at Churchill's behest to 'set Europe ablaze' through sabotage and to organize resistance in enemy-occupied territories. However, it operated further afield too. Mauritius was the only colony to have in place an SOE team to harry the Japanese if they invaded. The team, part of a large SOE network in East and Southern Africa, was to establish wireless links with British forces, conduct acts of sabotage, and gather intelligence about Japanese strengths and intentions (for example, by using prostitutes as informers). Mauritius performed a valuable role in the secret war of code-breaking most famously associated with Bletchley Park. It was part of Britain's worldwide intelligence network, intercepting and re-transmitting Japanese and Vichy signals. It also played a part in propaganda broadcasting and military operations against neighbouring enemy islands loyal to the Vichy regime, and had a whole company of its soldiers captured at Tobruk in June 1942. Linking the colony to the Holocaust, nearly 2000 Jews who had fled from Central Europe were detained on the island for the duration of the war (as was the deposed Shah of Persia and the former Prime Minister of Yugoslavia). Further tied to the European war, the Franco-Mauritian settlers were divided along a Petain–de Gaulle fault line.

The Royal Navy had, of course, been a feature of Mauritian life since 1810 when it had fought and lost the Battle of Grand Port. With enemy threats to the Suez Canal and British losses in Southeast Asia during the Second World War, Mauritius regained some of its former strategic importance as a communications link, a garrison island and a naval base. It was used for naval and flying-boat operations, such as the searches for German submarine supply ships. In the 1970s satellite communications replaced the system of wireless relay stations that had kept the empire and its forces in touch, however until 1976 Mauritius continued to support a Royal Navy shore base and communications station.

Until the end of the 1960s the Indian Ocean remained a jealously guarded British preserve. The link remains to this day; before Mauritian independence in 1968, one of its dependencies, Diego Garcia in the Chagos Archipelago, was bought outright by the British Government and the population moved en masse to Mauritius (the deported islanders have recently won a case against the British Government in the High Court allowing them to return).[26] Diego Garcia formed the core of British Indian Ocean Territory (BIOT) and today, on lease, it is an American eavesdropping post and 'the most important military base outside of the US'.[27] Fifteen additional B-52 bombers were sent to Diego Garcia during the recent escalation in the Gulf, and more than 600 sorties were flown from the island during Operation Desert Storm.[28] The Americans had first visited the island and assessed its potential during the Second World War.[29] Thus an Indian Ocean island and its dependencies, from which France had pursued her rivalry with Britain in the eighteenth century, retains to this day a role in the changing world of British–American global defence and security. The centuries have transformed, but not broken, the link between war and empire in the Indian Ocean.

1
Mauritius and the Indian Ocean in Imperial Wars and Imperial Strategy: from the Eighteenth Century to the Interwar Years

The military, naval, and strategic significance of Mauritius and its scattered dependencies has a lengthy pedigree. This stretches from Anglo-French disputes like the Seven Years War (1756–63) and the Napoleonic Wars, through the period of two world wars, into the Cold War era and up to the present day. The history of the islands of the Indian Ocean demonstrates how profoundly being part of an empire could affect remote territories and how far Britain – especially in times of war – relied upon its colonies for military, naval, manpower, financial and intelligence resources. An oceanic and naval view is valuable for an understanding of the history of the British empire, though is seldom integrated into the work of imperial historians.[1]

The British empire – in Asia, the Caribbean, Africa, the Far East, the Mediterranean, the Middle East, the Pacific, the Indian Ocean and the Atlantic – had to be defended by imperial forces and make local contributions to its own defence. A doctrine of imperial defence based on sea power, imperial garrisons and the British and Indian armies had grown up piecemeal with the expansion of empire. Since the middle of the nineteenth century, the defence of this scattered empire had increasingly come to preoccupy imperial and military policy-makers in Whitehall. Despite the rise of air power and its use in imperial policing, on the outbreak of the Second World War it was maritime power based on capital ships that remained at the heart of imperial defence.[2]

On 3 September 1939 the Governor of Mauritius, Sir Bede Clifford, announced the coming of war to his colony in a wireless broadcast. His description of Mauritius as 'a remote island in the Indian Ocean' rankled in Whitehall because it gave precisely the wrong impression. This was a moment when imperial policy-makers were concerned to portray the empire as a tightly knit unit, emphasizing inclusivity rather than remoteness, the global protectiveness of British naval might and not the dangerous overstretch that left distant colonies at the mercy of hostile powers.[3] The Governor's choice of phrase raised hackles at the Colonial Office, which would have claimed that the affairs of Mauritius – whatever its location – received the same close attention as those of less 'remote' colonies. On the military side, it would have been claimed by the Admiralty and the War Office that with the ubiquitous projection of British sea power in the Indian Ocean, and given the fact that Mauritius was one of a select band of colonies to boast an imperial garrison, its remoteness did not leave it undefended. Elsewhere in Whitehall, the Treasury official, too, would have looked up from his ledger and scoffed at the suggestion that Mauritius was forgotten – he had the disputed invoices to prove it. As Viscount Samuel told the House of Lords, 'remote as is the geographical situation of the inhabitants of Mauritius, their progress and welfare are not matters of indifference to this House'.[4]

As a garrison colony and a part of the empire's worldwide communications web, Mauritian military resources were drawn upon whenever there was an imperial mobilization between Africa and the Far East; the Indian Mutiny, the Zulu War and the South African War all brought action for the island's imperial garrison, usually in the form of transhipment to distant trouble spots. In both world wars, Mauritius sent considerable numbers of locally recruited soldiers overseas, to Mesopotamia in the First World War, and Diego Garcia, Rodrigues, Madagascar, East Africa, North Africa, the Middle East and Europe in the Second World War. Mauritius was a frequent port of call for ships crossing the Indian Ocean, a coaling (later an oiling) station for the Royal Navy and in wartime a base from which to hunt the enemy by land and sea and to intercept enemy radio and cable traffic.

After the Second World War, Mauritius and its dependencies (particularly Diego Garcia) maintained their roles as bases for military communications, bomber and reconnaissance aircraft and as naval ports of call. The imperial garrison remained until the 1960s a battalion of the KAR providing the bulk after its swap with the 1st Battalion The Mauritius Regiment in 1943. The island played a part in the Cold War. The Indian Ocean remained a 'British lake' as part of Britain's contribution to western defence before the east of Suez retreat at the end of the 1960s. Thereafter the Americans shouldered the burden in the region, Diego Garcia (leased from Britain) becoming a major military installation.

The Indian Ocean washes the shores of many islands and atolls, most of which were British, and some of which formed the 'lesser dependencies' of Mauritius.[5] This was the Mauritian sub-empire within the empire, visited annually by an Assistant Magistrate and provisioned and garrisoned by Mauritius during the Second World War. Rodrigues lies 344 miles east of Mauritius, the Chagos Archipelago 1200 miles northeast, the Cargados Carajos group 250 miles north and the Agalega islands 580 miles north. The Seychelles group was governed by Mauritius until formed into a separate colony in 1903, and in the 1960s some of its islands were merged with Diego Garcia to form BIOT.

In the eighteenth century Mauritius was a colony of pivotal strategic importance in the British and French struggles for imperial mastery. In the nineteenth century, with the establishment of British hegemony and the construction of the Suez Canal, its strategic importance declined. But it did not become inconsequential and it continued to rank above many other colonies. The simple fact was that such places *needed* to be British, for if they were not they could be used by another, perhaps hostile power. The island had been taken exactly for this reason – to deny it as a base for French operations against British possessions and shipping in the Indian Ocean region. Likewise, during the Second World War it was better British than a base for hostile German or Japanese operations in an ocean the shipping lanes of which carried vital supply and troop convoys, escorted by the hard-pressed warships of the Eastern Fleet. Such bases gave the British *options*, not to mention defensive headaches. They were essential everyday rivets in the British world system based upon sea power. In the nineteenth century there were about 44 000 British troops – over a third of the British Army – in colonial garrisons. Just over half were in the 'fortress' garrison colonies – Malta, Gibraltar, Bermuda, Halifax, St Helena and Mauritius – 'stations that were considered particularly vital for defence purposes and designated "imperial fortresses"'.[6]

With the Indian Ocean considered a 'British lake' for decades after the Second World War, it was better to have and to hold than to offer potential footholds to other powers. As the British were forced by local opposition – and by international disapproval of the old ways of dealing with such opposition – to pull out of one base area after another, it was to such territories that the British looked to maintain a worldwide military capability. Thus, when Kenya became untenable as a base for MEC and Aden looked like going the same way, Indian Ocean islands like Mauritius were viewed in a new light. Mauritius and its outpost Diego Garcia remained staging posts on the sea lanes from the Cape to Ceylon. The opening of the Suez Canal in 1869 had diminished 'the important victualling and transit trade with ships going round the Cape of Good Hope', but it remained a link in the imperial chain the importance of which could wax when security in the Canal region waned.[7]

Technological advance added to the island's significance in the chain of imperial outposts that girdled the globe. After the eclipse of sailing vessels, steamships called at Port Louis as they cruised between Ceylon and the Cape.[8] The island and its dependencies (particularly Diego Garcia and Rodrigues) were important imperial communications stepping-stones. Indeed, it was partly because of their value as communications relay posts that they were viewed as worthy of imperial defence. The Cape to Australia cable ran via Mauritius, Rodrigues and the Cocos Islands. As Ronald Hyam writes, 'the spreading net of submarine cables added yet another potent strategic imperative. This was especially true of the main cable to India from Cape Town, which reached Mauritius in 1879, making the east coast of Africa more significant than ever'.[9] The development of wireless communications from the early 1900s was seen as a valuable addition to, not a replacement for, cable communications.[10] Mauritius duly became an imperial wireless base. In the Second World War it was an important station for intercepting enemy cable and radio signals as part of the successful British intelligence-gathering work associated with Bletchley Park, and for beaming propaganda into enemy territories. Mauritius provided a listening post for the British until the 1970s, and to this day Diego Garcia is an important American eavesdropping centre.

From the 1920s the growing importance of air communications and air power was seen by some as a means by which Mauritius could regain her pre-Suez Canal strategic importance.[11] The Second World War brought air communications to Mauritius for the first time following the British retreat from Singapore. Using Mauritius and other Indian Ocean islands as air bases gave the British a surveillance and offensive reach beyond that which could be achieved by the surface vessels of the Eastern Fleet. The island's international airport is the former Royal Naval Air Station at Plaisance, built during the war and named HMS *Sambur* (handed over to the RAF in 1945).[12] The RAF built a flying-boat base at Tombeau Bay for general reconnaissance and torpedo bomber operations, RAF Hurricanes contributed to the gathering of meteorological data essential to military operations, and the colony's Observatory was taken under military control for the same purpose.[13]

In his 'Colonial Civil History of the Second World War', Sir John Shuckburgh wrote that:

> Certain colonies, owing either to their potential value to the enemy, or to the location of a British Imperial base within their borders, required a standard of local defence, even in peace time, that could not be provided from the Colony's own resources. It was in these territories that Imperial garrisons were maintained ... It remained the duty of the local authorities to support and supplement them to the best of their abilities.[14]

Mauritius paid five-and-a-half per cent of its annual revenue to the Imperial Treasury as a contribution to the maintenance of the garrison on the island, and from the First World War recruited local forces to supplement the defensive capabilities of the garrison and to serve overseas.

Mauritius and imperial warfare from the eighteenth century

By the outbreak of war in 1939, Mauritius had been a military base of varying strategic significance for nearly 200 years. To this day Mauritius abounds with place names echoing distant imperial battles and the island's military past – Cannoniers Point, Gunners Quoin, Arsenal, Signal Mountain, Sebastopol and Balaclava. The ruins of coastal fortifications from the Dutch, French and British periods remain,[15] and the island's participation in two world wars is evidenced by coastal fortifications, its airport, war memorials (such as that by Churchill Bridge in Rodrigues), redundant naval fuel tanks and even a 'Boulangerie Spitfire' in Beau Bassin.

Memorial tablets in the neglected repose of the Anglican Cathedral in Port Louis speak of an earlier age when British regiments served a tour of duty as part of the Mauritius Garrison. The malaria that afflicted the island until the 1950s accounted for most of their fatalities (an eradication programme initiated by the Royal Navy in 1942 finally wiped out the disease). Among others, there are memorials for the 87th Royal Irish Fusiliers, the Northamptonshire Regiment, and Royal and Merchant Navy seamen. One tablet remembers Lieutenant Henry Cole, aide-de-campe to Lieutenant General the Honourable Sir G. Lowry Cole, Governor and Commander-in-Chief, who died in 1827 on a mission to Radaman, King of Madagascar, at a time when

Governors harboured ambitions of British expansion into the giant neighbouring island. General Charles Gordon, once commander of the Ever Victorious Army in China and later the martyr of Khartoum, was Commanding Officer of the Royal Engineers on Mauritius in 1881–82. In the eighteenth century the Indian Ocean was a key strategic arena in the wars between Britain and her European competitors. During the War of the Austrian Succession and the Seven Years War, it was a base for war in India. In the latter conflict Port Louis was the nearest base for French operations on the subcontinent, though its distance hampered its effectiveness. In 1781 Admiral Suffren arrived at Port Louis with a powerful fleet and 11 000 men.[16] Efforts were made to improve Mauritius as a naval base that could support large-scale expeditions. The island was important as an arsenal and a supplies depot during the Anglo-French wars; between 1780 and 1783 more than a hundred warships left the island supplied with arms, men and food as Port Louis became the French Indian Ocean headquarters after the loss of Pondicherry. With subsidiary bases in Madagascar, the Seychelles and Bourbon (Reunion), Mauritius was 'the stronghold, the naval base, and the seat of government' of France in the Indian Ocean.[17] After the loss of Mauritius in the nineteenth century, Madagascar became the main French base in the Indian Ocean, where garrison troops were stationed and a first-class anchorage was provided by the natural harbour at Diego Suarez. After the establishment of British hegemony in the Indian Ocean in the eighteenth century, Mauritius became a 'nest of corsairs' as French nationals continued to threaten British shipping.[18] It was from Mauritius that Robert Surcouf 'became the terror of English merchantmen in the Indian Ocean and a formidable opponent for the Royal Navy' during the Napoleonic Wars.[19] From 1796 to 1803 Mauritius was virtually independent of metropolitan France, and the Franco-Mauritian settlers financed and mounted expeditions against British ships, seizing 119 prizes between 1793 and 1802.

In 1810 the British suffered a naval reverse at the Battle of Grand Port off the southeast coast of Mauritius, the only French naval victory recorded on the Arc de Triomphe.[20] After a long blockade, the island was eventually taken by 10 000 Indian troops carried in 60 ships that landed in the north and marched on the capital Port Louis, the Indian Army again proving its value as a manpower reserve that projected British power far and wide.[21] Rodrigues had been captured in 1809 as a pre-invasion assembly point. At the Peace of Paris in 1814 Mauritius was retained by Britain, though the neighbouring island of Reunion –

also captured – was returned to France. This was a decision based entirely on strategic calculations; Mauritius had an excellent port from which the French had harried British East Indies trade and transit. Reunion did not, and was therefore surplus to British requirements. At the Peace of Paris 'Britain's own gains were limited to some West Indian acquisitions . . . and the colonial conquests which were of over-riding importance for worldwide communications within the empire – Malta, the Cape and Mauritius'.[22] Already possessed of the Cape and Ceylon, the capture of Mauritius guaranteed the sea route to India and thus secured British naval hegemony.

As the First Sea Lord boasted in the early years of the twentieth century, Britain held 'the five strategic keys that locked up the British world: Dover, Gibraltar, Suez, the Cape of Good Hope and Singapore'.[23] Mauritius was one of the smaller keys – the fortress garrison colonies. Malta, Bermuda, St Helena and Mauritius were 'stations that were particularly vital for defence purposes and desig-nated "imperial fortresses"'.[24] In 1832 the British garrison numbered 1600 troops.[25] At the end of the nineteenth century, 355 British soldiers garrisoned the island, though the number was usually greater (excluding locally raised forces).[26] The colony's Latin motto – granted in 1905 along with its coat of arms and used to this day – proudly proclaims the island to be 'the Star and Key of the Indian Ocean'.[27]

In most nineteenth-century imperial conflicts the garrison of Mauritius was affected in some way. The 'chief immediate result on Mauritius of modern wars has been that the garrison soldiers have more to do, and are frequently taken away from Mauritius as soon as possible'.[28] During the Indian Mutiny of 1857–58, most of the garrison went to India.[29] The imperial legions were summoned from diverse locations to suppress the Mutiny – the 35th from Burma, the 64th and 78th Highlanders from Persia, the 5th from Mauritius, the 90th and 93rd from Cape Town (both originally bound for Hong Kong and thence China for the Second Opium War).[30] The garrison was again reduced during the Zulu War in 1879, and mobilized during the Anglo-French tension stirred by the Fashoda incident of 1898.

The South African War of 1899–1902 saw the British garrison depleted, though the 2nd Battalion The Central African Rifles was sent to make up the difference; an assembly of 7 officers, 32 Sikhs, 878 African other ranks, 220 wives and 77 children.[31] Contemporary service privileges ensured that family life moved with colonial soldiers, though one man found carrying a baby on parade in Mauritius was considered to have gone too far.[32] As troops of the KAR were to discover on arriving in Mauritius in 1943 (see Chapter 5), African soldiers were not popular. In the face of local hostility the African battalion was moved offshore to Flat Island in 1899, and soon on to action in Somaliland.

The Mauritius Garrison was even mobilized during the Russo-Japanese War of 1904–05, as the Russian Baltic Fleet steamed east to meets its fate in the Straits of Tsushima.[33] Prior to the Russo-Japanese War, the French and Russian General Staffs had met to discuss plans for a war with Britain. In such an event, France was to take naval action in the Mediterranean supported by Russian action from the Black Sea Fleet, and Russia was to take action in the Pacific supported by French action from the Indian Ocean fleet based at Madagascar.[34] As in the Second World War, the Indian Ocean was a sea in which great powers sought to challenge British naval hegemony. If Britain's communications in the Indian Ocean were broken or the Suez Canal taken, the empire would be broken in two – these were the high stakes that British maritime power was forced to play for in times of world war.

Defence of the nooks and crannies of empire was entrusted to the Royal Navy, the British and Indian Armies (and later the RAF) and a host of long-forgotten imperial military units. At the time of the Russo-Japanese alert in Mauritius, for example, the main fort defending Port Louis was manned by No. 57 Company Royal Garrison Artillery (RGA), No. 1 Company Ceylon-Mauritius Battalion RGA and the Hong Kong and Singapore Battalion RGA. In maintaining order within the empire, Peter often had to be robbed to pay Paul, and the Mauritius Garrison was often stripped of troops, as late as the 1950s the KAR garrison battalion leaving to help suppress the Mau Mau rebellion in Kenya.[35]

The First World War

Throughout the First World War the island's participation was para-doxically greater than it had been during the colonial wars of the nineteenth century, even though its strategic significance had lessened since the imperial wars of the eighteenth century. Its participation prefigured the much greater demands of the 1939–45 war. In 1914–18 all colonies were expected to play their part in sending men and money to aid the mother country. New technology increased the vulnerability even of colonies far removed from the main theatres of war. The empire was engaged in a lengthy struggle with a great power possessed of far-flung imperial territories and a worldwide naval capability. Germany maintained cable and wireless facilities in its colonies that directed shipping and threatened the security of the 'southern British world'.[36] Germany also posed a submarine and commerce raider threat in all oceans, casting a shadow across the food supply situation in Britain and the colonies that relied on seaborne trade. From being a self-sufficient island in the early nineteenth century Mauritius had become absolutely dependent on imported foodstuffs as sugar spread to dominate the economy and the landscape. Mauritius embarked on a new chapter in its military-strategic history when a naval wireless facility was constructed at Rose Belle, ensuring 'uninterrupted communication with other countries and ships within radius'.[37] The station was closed in July 1921, but opened again in the Second World War.[38]

In October 1915 it was decided, as in past conflicts, to withdraw most of the thousand-strong British garrison. The soldiers were sent variously to Britain, India and Mombasa. The 59th RGA and the 25th Royal Engineers were the only units to remain.[39] Mauritius itself sent 1700 men overseas in the Mauritius Labour Battalion to serve with imperial forces fighting in Mesopotamia. The Battalion consisted of coloured Mauritians officered by white Franco-Mauritians and British regulars;[40] 520 Franco-Mauritians and British settlers served on the Western Front.[41] To compensate for the depletion of the Mauritius Garrison in the event of an attack, a Volunteer Defence Force was created by a Council of Government Bill based on the Ceylon Volunteer Ordinance. Enlistment for the Mauritius Volunteer Artillery and Engineers began in April 1916; 500 men were recruited, forming three infantry companies, an artillery company, an engineers company and an ambulance corps, costing £4460 per annum.[42] The electric searchlights installed at Fort George in 1895 were upgraded to the tune of £13 896 in 1915.[43]

German armed merchantmen and cruisers threatened British territories in the Indian Ocean. The German raider *Wolf* approached Mauritius and carried a small sailing ship off to Germany. The raider *Konigsberg* sunk a British merchantman and a cruiser before being run to ground in the Rufiji Delta in Tanganyika where specially drafted Royal Navy monitors were sent to sink her. The light cruiser *Emden,* operating at large in the Indian Ocean, made a call on Diego Garcia in October 1914 whilst trying to avoid British units searching for her after an epic voyage from Tsingtao in eastern China. At Diego Garcia the crew were welcomed by islanders unaware of the war; the twice-yearly steamer from Mauritius – the island's only link with the outside world – had yet to bring the news.[44] Captain Muller took advantage of this to beach his ship and scrape its keel.[45] The ship was sunk by HMAS *Sydney* in the Indian Ocean on 9 November 1914 after a rash bombardment of the British communications installation on the Cocos-Keeling Islands. In 1916 the Governor of Mauritius, Sir Hesketh Bell, sailed for St Brandon island (part of the Mauritian Cargados Carajos dependency) on board HMS *Talbot* in search of a reported German raider.[46] With the eventual removal of the German naval threat, Port Louis was reduced to the status of an undefended port in October 1917.

Given the island's dependence on the export of its sugar crop and the import of its food, it was:

> singularly fortunate in possessing a harbour so good and so well placed as to be a fortified and garrisoned Imperial coaling-station. The constant presence and coming and going of ships of war meant a safeguard at once against actual privation and against unrest arising from apprehension of privation. When the German raiders had been accounted for, the Indian Ocean was comparatively safe ... to the end the island was in no danger of starvation. Its staple product was in great demand, and the ships that fetched the sugar brought food ... [Mauritians] had more or less assured markets with abnormal prices.[47]

On the home front, the war brought a decrease in rice (the staple food of the majority of the population) imports from India, and efforts to grow maize as a substitute. Mauritius also relied upon imports of beef from Madagascar, and in turn Rodrigues relied upon supplies from its 'mother' country, Mauritius. The booming sugar industry guaranteed ample employment. Sugar was sold to Britain at higher than normal prices, and sections of the population prospered during the war years and in the postwar sugar boom. Revenue reached record heights. Between 1910 and 1915 average annual revenue from the sugar crop was rupees (Rs.) 40 million. From 1915–19, it was Rs. 70 million. Gifts of sugar and money were sent to Britain. Despite freight problems, the food situation was little affected in the early years of the war. However, the steady decrease in available shipping and ever increasing demand for what food there was meant that from 1916–17 freight costs rose, leading to rising food prices and profiteering. Greater regulation was needed and a new Food and Trade Control office was created to control supplies and to regulate distribution. All food prices were regulated and two beefless days a week were introduced. By the end of 1917 the area under food crops had increased by 50 per cent. Like all colonies, Mauritius supported the mother country financially throughout the war. Five-and-a-half per cent of the colony's annual revenue was paid to the imperial government as a contribution towards the upkeep of the Mauritius Garrison – a sum of around Rs. 500 000 (before 1934 the Mauritian rupee was the same as the Indian rupee). Though the garrison had virtually ceased to exist in 1915 with the removal of troops overseas, an increased contribution was repeated in 1915 and 1916 by a Council of Government keen to show its support for the war effort. In October 1916 the Governor announced that the Council of Government had voted a war contribution of Rs. 500 000 to Britain from surplus funds. Soon afterwards the sugar planters in the Chamber of Agriculture declared a gift of the same amount and suggested 'that this sum be applied towards the creation of a battle-plane squadron or the building of an airship'.[48] With this money 30 aeroplanes were presented to the British Government, 15 for the Navy and 15 for the Military Air Service. Three further planes were presented by a public subscription that raised Rs. 101 000. Apart from the annual contribution for the garrison, the Government of Mauritius contributed Rs. 1 028 000. In 1916 legislation was passed for a loan to Britain via a bonds scheme. The amount raised exceeded Rs. 8 million. In addition, private effort and war charities raised an estimated Rs. 3 578 000.

The interwar period to the eve of the Second World War

The military contribution of the colonial empire to the Second World War 'must be considered against the backdrop, and within the general framework, of Imperial Defence'.[49] The interwar years were a time of naval disarmament and though the age of the aircraft carrier was looming, national strength was still measured by the number of capital ships a nation had afloat. The concept of imperial defence remained anchored in the retention of sea power, the exercise of which required a chain of firmly held naval bases and implied the ability to move reinforcements at will and deny the enemy the opportunity of making overseas expeditions. There was little danger to Britain or the empire except from across the sea (the landward danger to Singapore was not adequately appreciated). Few colonies had land frontiers across which large-scale invasions could be launched. So the empire could be considered secure as long as command of the sea was maintained and sufficient force was available in each colony to withstand the initial invasion pending the arrival of reinforcements.

In Mauritius, from 1935 a locally recruited unit, the MTF, supplemented the imperial garrison. The primary task of this force was to man the coastal defences and provide a small infantry deterrent. Such colonial forces were also established with internal policing in mind. The defence of Mauritius, its dependencies and all the other British islands in the Indian Ocean ultimately rested on the Royal Navy. An annual event in the Mauritian social calendar was the official visit of the Royal Navy. Parties and ceremonial attended the visit, the ships were fully dressed and illuminated and tours given aboard. In 1939, the Governor of neighbouring Reunion was the guest of Governor Sir Bede Clifford, and 1400 people attended a garden party at Government House. With war in the air only two ships, HMS *Liverpool* and HMS *Gloucester* (flying the flag of Rear Admiral R. Leatham, Commander-in-Chief East Indies Station), made the visit. Usually at least two ships from the Africa Station and two from the East Indies Station (this Station lapsed in June 1942 when the Eastern Fleet was created) would attend. Observing the strict protocol that underpinned imperial relations, the Commander-in-Chief Africa Station, on board HMS *Neptune,* sent apologies for his absence.[50]

The object of the exercise was, of course, the showing of the flag on which the projection of British sea power depended. It was a visible reminder to the people of the colonies that the Royal Navy was a genuine defensive shield, not an abstract concept. Faith in this shield was stretched to the limits in the Second World War as seaborne air power transformed regional power balances, and Britain faced three powerful navies simultaneously. The sinking of HMS *Prince of Wales* and HMS *Repulse* in 1941 was a particularly tragic example of the Royal Navy's inability to provide this shield in all places at all times, and the Australasian dominions – not to mention all of Britain's Far Eastern possessions – were left at the mercy of the Japanese. But in the Indian Ocean, the Eastern Fleet held out.

The annual visit of the Royal Navy was an opportunity for local forces to be put through their paces. HMS *Liverpool* arrived off Diego Garcia on 23 May 1939 and steamed on to Rodrigues on 27 May, where the band was landed to entertain the locals and courtesy visits made by the Captain. Tours of the ship were conducted and it was floodlit at night. The ship then sailed on to Mauritius, where on 29 May exercises were carried out with the MTF. As the ship's Captain reported to the Admiralty:

A raiding force was landed by moonlight at Petite Riviere Bay at 0200 and met with no opposition until they had reached Port Louis and caused great damage. At 0616 arrived at the entrance buoy but had to wait an hour for the pilot who, like the defences on shore, was not expecting such an early arrival.[51]

Observing traditional Whitehall procedure, the Admiralty passed the Captain's report on to the Colonial Office for information and comment. The Colonial Office considered it an embarrassing report and an official minuted that 'perhaps the Defence Force would put up a better show if the enemy were not a friendly one ... [We] know part of the Defence Force was inefficient and had to be disbanded'.[52]

Though air power had significantly altered the realities and demands of sea power by the time of the Second World War, imperial defence did not change. The governing assumption remained that British sea power could prevent major attacks on the colonies. If it could not, then it was up to local formations such as the MTF to do their best to harry the enemy. Efforts had been made to improve local defence capabilities in the interwar period, and locally raised military forces were much stronger in 1939 than they had been in 1914. As Shuckburgh writes:

What was more important still, the Government of every Colonial ⎩ territory had on record in its secret archives a document known as the local 'Defence Scheme', that is to say a carefully prepared programme of action to be taken in the event of the outbreak of hostilities.[53]

In the case of Mauritius, this provided for a scorched earth policy in case of invasion, and was significantly altered in 1943 when the island and its dependencies were transferred to EAC. The Defence Plans were reviewed by the Overseas Defence Committee, a sub-committee of the Committee of Imperial Defence. In Mauritius, a Local Defence Committee helped the commanding officer supervise the plan.[54]

Although there were ordered plans in place for the defence of the colonies, the Second World War was to require an escalation in local and imperial defence measures as the British empire faced a much greater threat to its existence than in the First World War, together with the early collapse of its main military ally. The Indian Ocean was set to become a contested theatre for the first time since the Napoleonic Wars, and the British were to find – all over the world –

that there was an unbridgeable gulf between paper power and the realities of modern world war against three militaristic nations all of whom wanted a fight at the same time.

2
Defence of Empire and the Sea Lanes: the Royal Navy and the British Indian Ocean World

The Royal Navy was always an instrument of empire, even though it was never an adjunct of empire. As Nicholas Rogers argues, imperial historians have sometimes assumed that the navy was there because of the empire, whereas the navy was older than empire and traditionally saw its role as a world role befitting Britain's worldwide interests – interests bigger than those of empire alone.[1] However, even if empire was not the aim of naval actions, the fact was that empire often resulted from Britain's efforts at sea in support of its trade or in its numerous wars against continental powers.

Without the Royal Navy there could have been no British empire. Britain was a thalassocracy, a maritime nation that relied upon the Royal Navy to keep the sea lanes open so that the ships of all nations could traverse the globe on their lawful occasions. Many parts of the empire had been acquired for strictly naval reasons (for example, the Indian Ocean islands), and all parts relied upon the naval shield for protection and the maintenance of trade routes and communications. This was true for the largest imperial territories as well as for the smallest; despite a considerable military capability of its own, even Australia depended on Britain for its defence when a much stronger regional power – Japan – threatened. Though hindsight lends the sequence of events an air of inevitability now, in 1939 there really was no alternative guarantor of imperial security, particularly given American isolationism. Until the Second World War, Britain was the world's only superpower.[2]

It is remarkable to note how regions of the empire might be gained for one reason but held on to for others, as the fluid world of geostrategy altered imperial (and post-imperial) assessments of their value. For example Aden – annexed by the East India Company in

1839 to protect shipping from coastal pirates, provide a coaling station, and safeguard the overland route to India threatened by Egypt's Mehemet Ali – became a key base for Britain when the region was transformed by oil in the twentieth century, and an important hub in Britain's dominance of the sea and land routes to Asia (today the US enjoys naval rights in Aden). Cyprus, annexed by Disraeli to buttress Britain's position after the Russians had come close to taking the all-important Straits in 1878, remained an important imperial outpost long after air power and missiles had negated the earlier significance of the Dardanelles. In today's independent Cyprus, Britain still maintains a significant military base. During the Second World War the islands of the Indian Ocean – once a focus of eighteenth-century imperial struggles between Britain and France – became bases in a sea where British hegemony was challenged by new enemies. In the postwar and even the post-colonial period, their strategic value remained as the region became an area of Cold War tension. From wooden wall ships to nuclear submarines, the region's significance was transformed by changes in international affairs and technology.

The Royal Navy was important in the nineteenth-century acquisition of Indian Ocean islands, as it was in their retention in the twentieth century when British maritime hegemony was threatened.[3] It is necessary to understand the naval context and to see Mauritius and its dependencies as part of the British Indian Ocean world, connected to the empire in the Far East, East Africa and the Middle East. With this view, Mauritius was not 'a remote island in the Indian Ocean' as its Governor contended, but part of the British world system with a role to play in helping prop up that system when conflict arose. The waters of the world were integral to the British empire and the projection of British world power; as a port belongs to the sea as well as to the land, so too the empire.

Whilst some imperial historians have taken the navy for granted, others have ignored its importance. As Barry Gough writes, it is 'surprising that historians of the empire hardly ever take their scholarly investigations beyond these shores ... The role of the navy as an instrument of empire ... has hitherto been conceived as primarily a problem for naval historians. But can modern imperialism mean anything without analysis of the tools and methods used to enforce the law and executive authority?'.[4] This chapter analyses the naval situation in the Indian Ocean during the war, and the use made of British islands for defensive and offensive purposes.

Sea power and the challenge to Britain in the Indian Ocean

The Second World War 'could not be won in the Indian Ocean but it might very well be lost there'.[5] Willmott writes that the 'issue of defeat and victory was resolved elsewhere and by other means, and was never dependent upon events in the Indian Ocean', but its retention by the British and its continuous use as a convoy route was of crucial importance.[6] This was recognized by the Germans and Japanese, but both failed to take sufficient offensive action to overthrow British supremacy. Sir Robert Brooke-Popham, Commander-in-Chief Far East, recognized in December 1941 that overseas communications in the Indian Ocean were essential to the British war effort.[7] The fact that the ocean remained British was the product of Allied supremacy elsewhere, 'but both victory and supremacy in the Indian Ocean in 1945 were nevertheless very real'.[8] Keeping the Indian Ocean open was Britain's primary naval contribution to the war against Japan.

At the outbreak of war the problem for the British was that they were no longer able to maintain in Far Eastern waters a fleet capable of matching that of the strongest power in the region, Japan. Home waters and the Mediterranean took priority, there were not enough capital ships to go around after decades of naval disarmament, and the importance of the aircraft carrier had not been fully grasped by the Admiralty. As Liddell Hart wrote of Britain, 'sea-power, her mainstay, had been handicapped by the advent of air-power' as well as her lack of adequate ships.[9] Naval disarmament had stopped the American development of its bases at Guam and in the Philippines, and so the American fleet could no longer operate in the western Pacific. 'Hence the British Empire and Japan were now the only effective naval powers in that area'.[10] This did not augur well for the British in the Pacific, or, as a knock-on, in the Indian Ocean. The Royal Navy in the Far East was abjectly inferior to the Imperial Japanese Navy.[11]

But Britain's weakness was not fully exploited when war came. According to Nicholas Rogers, the Indian Ocean was:

> one of the great might-have-beens of history, for if the Japanese had taken the Indian Ocean a little more seriously, and the Germans the Levant (instead of regarding them as side-shows, as they both did) the Axis powers might have joined hands, Britain might have lost the whole (and not just the fringes) of its eastern empire, and the course of the war would have been very different.[12]

A great concern of Churchill and the Chiefs of Staff was that Japan would meet the Axis forces in the Indian Ocean, probably by the conquest of the Vichy island of Madagascar. If Rommel had taken Egypt and the Suez Canal, the danger would have been perilously close. German victory in the Middle East would have snapped the empire in two, and if Axis hands had been joined in the western Indian Ocean the balance would have swung decisively in their favour. But the selfishness of both powers, and army jealousies, prevented fruitful cooperation in this theatre.[13] For example, 'when Japan wanted to launch an offensive against Madagascar, which lay in the sphere claimed by Germany, it was stifled in the planning phase by massive German objections'.[14] There was Axis agreement that 'the way to victory lay in the meeting of German and Japanese forces in the Middle East and Indian Ocean. The leadership in both Germany and Japan, especially that of the two navies, saw quite clearly that control of the Indian Ocean was essential to Axis victory'.[15] Though Japan had plans for the invasion of Madagascar, and Hitler earmaked it as a destination for deported Jews, it was to be the British who took the initiative.

The retention of sea power remained at the heart of imperial defence during the 1930s, and this required a chain of firmly held bases and the capacity to move troops and supplies unhindered across the seas.[16] The assumption remained that British sea power could prevent major attacks on the colonies. This may have proved a sound assumption, had it not been for the fact that Britain was simultaneously to face three major naval powers (four, if Vichy France is counted). If Japan entered the war, the worried Australasian dominions had been promised the dispatch of a major force of capital ships, and there was of course the recently completed and fully manned 'impregnable' naval base at Singapore ready to provide for their defence.[17] Russia was not an ally until 1941, and before Operation 'Barbarossa' was one half of the Nazi-Soviet Pact. The enmity of Italy put additional strain on the Mediterranean and Red Sea areas, thereby depleting the Royal Navy's capacity to send ships to counter the Japanese. The removal of Italy from Northeast Africa cleared the western shore of the Indian Ocean, a 'matter of major significance when Japan entered the war later and there were Axis hopes of cutting the Allied lifelines through those critical waters'.[18] The Commander-in-Chief Eastern Fleet had formed 'Force T' to support the offensive against Italian Somaliland. Though French Somaliland, controlling the straits between the Gulf of Aden and the Red Sea, went Vichy, the local military commander,

General Paul Gentilhomme, joined the British forces fighting the East African campaign.[19] In the Far East, Pearl Harbor and the temporary crushing of American power was a catastrophic blow. Before May 1940 'the consequences of a collapse of France were never contemplated', and this unforeseen occurrence left major units of the French fleet and major naval facilities (like those in Madagascar) in the hands of the new Vichy enemy.[20] These disasters threw all of the intricate plans and calculations for aggressive and defensive imperial action into the fire, and left Britain 'trying to fight a five ocean war with, at best, a two ocean navy'.[21]

Some in Japan advocated the orientation of Japanese power towards the Indian Ocean so that a link with Germany could be forged.[22] For the Allies, this was potentially the most threatening Japanese war aim. The main block to the realization of this plan was the attitude of the Japanese army, anxious to avoid major land commitments in the Indian Ocean; it would not even grant two divisions for the invasion of Ceylon.[23] Furthermore, the Axis-Japanese alliance never functioned as smoothly as that between Britain and America. Though Japan could not attempt the invasion of India or Ceylon due to army refusals, it wanted to mount a major operation in the Indian Ocean against Madagascar. According to Weinberg, Japan's Indian Ocean exploits represented strategic defeats, despite tactical victories like the sinking of HMS *Repulse* and HMS *Prince of Wales*. Precious resources were expended, but the Eastern Fleet was not destroyed and Madagascar was not taken.

Britain was facing no lightweight foe in the German and Japanese navies. Following the Washington Disarmament Conference of 1921 Japan was the third largest naval power in the world. In 1939 the Japanese Imperial Navy had more aircraft carriers than Britain and America, and Japanese 'torpedoes in particular were the best of any navy's'.[24] After Pearl Harbor, Japan overran the British Far Eastern colonies in quick succession, and by the spring of 1942 Britain had been extinguished as a power in the Far East.[25] The next calamity to be feared was the invasion of India, as on 28 April 1942 Major-General William Slim received orders to withdraw Burma Corps to India, thus abandoning Burma to the Japanese.[26] By March 'Japanese warships had the run of the whole of the Bay of Bengal'.[27] But luckily for the British the raid on Ceylon had failed to catch the remaining British ships in port, and 'a strong squadron under Sir James Somerville' was mustered and based on the Maldives (at Addu Atoll). 'Though incapable of meeting the modern Japanese Fleet, [it] was strong enough to discourage any attempt to break out to the west'.[28] However, it was still considered necessary in 1942 to launch an invasion of Madagascar, for fear of a German or Japanese descent upon the island. The context of the Mauritian war was the threat posed in the Indian Ocean by Japanese victories in the Far East; the Italian naval threat; the operations of German and Japanese raiders and submarine fleets; neighbouring Vichy islands; and the weakness of the Eastern Fleet in an ocean crossed by vital convoy routes. On the security of the Indian Ocean rested the ability to supply the armies in the Middle East, to maintain the flow of oil from the region, to give aid to Russia via the Persian Gulf, to reinforce India, Burma and Malaya, and to come to the aid of Australia and New Zealand.[29] Oil from the Middle East was considered vital to the British war effort, and it has been argued that Britain could have been defeated if Hitler had diverted forces to take Iran. Southern Iran was by far the most important oil supplier in the region, with a refinery at Abadan (10 million tons per year, and 4 million from Iraq by pipeline to Tripoli and Haifa). The fact was that, though most British oil came from America, the shortage of tankers meant that, had the Middle Eastern supply been lost, the difference could not have been made up from other sources. Middle Eastern oil directly supplied the British forces in the Middle East and Indian Ocean regions. 'The loss of supplies would have seriously crippled, if not nullified, the British war effort'.[30]

In the aftermath of Japan's blazing entry into the war in December 1941, a major Indian Ocean offensive was expected by the British, and this transformed the war experience of Mauritius as the front line hoved into view. The Eastern Fleet was thrown back on the defensive, retreating from Ceylon to East Africa (to Kilindini near Mombasa), and signals intelligence became an increasingly important weapon given the Fleet's weakness.[31] 'With the Suez Canal virtually shut because of Axis operations in the region, supplies for Middle East Command depended on the 12 000 mile Cape route', and the halfway house island of Mauritius began to receive an increased amount of shipping bound to and from the east.[32]

The Indian Ocean was a vital convoy thoroughfare. In the first 12 months of the war 274 402 service personnel had moved through the territory of the East Indies Station (in June 1942 this station lapsed and all forces came under the Eastern Fleet).[33] By March 1941, 643 198 empire troops had traversed it, along with all manner of supplies – in a typical month the Eastern Fleet escorted ships loaded with troops, military vehicles, mules, barley, coal, diesel, sugar, gasoline, kerosene, tinned meat, ammunition, chrome ore, railway materials and salt.[34] In one month alone (October 1940) the Fleet safely escorted 127 ships (1 018 902 tons) northwards through the Red Sea, and 106 south-bound ships (868 241 tons). The Mozambique Channel, threatened by Japanese and German vessels often operating on intelligence gathered by Axis spies in the contiguous Portuguese colony, was an area of 'dense convoy traffic'.[35]

The Eastern Fleet

Whilst Britain was still at peace with Japan, the resources of the Royal Navy in the Indian Ocean and further east were stretched and often plundered as fighting in regions like the Atlantic and the Mediterranean took priority.[36] The territory covered by the Eastern Fleet was vast, as indicated by the disposition of the Fleet's ships. In March 1941 it was as follows: Red Sea Area twenty-one (including the Red Sea Dhow Patrol, countering the flow of contraband to and from Italian Eritrea); Persian Gulf Area five; Arabian Sea four; Indian Ports and Ceylon Area seven; Bay of Bengal one; Indian Ocean three; East African Coast (including Durban) nineteen; Mauritius Area two; and Seychelles Area one.[37] A year later, the Fleet consisted of five battle-ships, the pick being HMS *Warspite*, elderly (she had seen action at Jutland) but recently modernized, displacing 34 500 tons (fully loaded), 646 feet in length, and mounting eight 15–inch, eight 6-inch, and eight 4-inch guns.[38] The other four battleships were of the obsolete 'R' class (HMS *Ramillies, Resolution, Royal Sovereign* and *Revenge*, described by Churchill as 'floating coffins').[39] There were 3 aircraft carriers (HMS *Formidable*, HMS *Indomitable*, and HMS *Hermes*), though the 57 strike aircraft and 36 fighters they embarked were all inferior to those of the Japanese. There were 14 cruisers (though as of March 1942 only 6 had arrived – HMS *Dorsetshire*, HMS *Cornwall*, HMS *Enterprise*, HMS *Emerald*, HMS *Dragon*, and HMS *Caledon*), 16 destroyers and 3 submarines.[40] Not only was the Fleet inferior to that of the Japanese in terms of modernity, aircraft and gun range, but it desperately needed time to train as a unit.[41]

Japan's entry into the war fundamentally affected the operations of the Eastern Fleet. It 'saw Allied Sea Power in the Indian Ocean driven back on the defensive'.[42] Japanese conquests (Malaya, Singapore etc.) and the totemic sinking of HMS *Prince of Wales* and HMS *Repulse* off Malaya were mighty blows to Britain's naval power and its claim to be able to protect the empire. The sinkings removed the one remaining force which, after Pearl Harbor, could have seriously interfered with the operation of the Japanese Navy. 'In the first three days of war against Japan the enemy had thus obtained complete naval superiority from India to the Pacific'.[43]

As O'Neill writes:

> By March [1942] Japanese warships had penetrated into the Indian Ocean. Rangoon fell as a consequence. The Andaman [and Nicobar Islands] were occupied; and before the month was out Japanese warships had the run of the whole of the Bay of Bengal. But by a miracle of reorganization and mobility the Admiralty had assembled a strong squadron under Sir James Somerville. It was based on the Maldives [Addu Atoll]; and its strength measures the importance attached to the protection of the communications round the Cape ... The squadron, though incapable of meeting the modern Japanese Fleet, was strong enough to discourage any attempt to break out west.[44]

Admiral Sir James Somerville had previously commanded Force 'H' in the Mediterranean (where he had been responsible for the attack on the French fleet at Mers-el-Kebir). As Commander-in-Chief Eastern Fleet he was instructed to keep the Fleet 'in being', a recognition of the fact that it was perilously weak and unlikely to be reinforced in the foreseeable future.[45] However, the enemy determined to prevent even its survival. 'The Japanese High Command decided that the time had come to destroy once and for all British naval power in the Indian Ocean'.[46] Admiral Nagumo, commanding the most powerful fleet afloat, approached Ceylon, expecting to catch the British in Colombo harbour on 5 April 1942. But Somerville's Eastern Fleet 'had disappeared into the broad wastes of the Indian Ocean', making for the secret safety of Addu Atoll in the Maldives, a hurriedly constructed base unknown to the Japanese.[47] So the raids on Ceylon (Colombo and Trincomalee) – the only significant surface venture into the Indian Ocean by the Japanese – were not a calamity for the British, even though Nagumo had 'sent out the first eleven'.[48] The heavy cruisers HMS *Cornwall* and HMS *Dorsetshire* were sunk on 5 April, and four days later the carrier HMS *Hermes* and her escort destroyer HMAS *Vampire* went down, all victims of Japanese bombers.[49] In addition, a further destroyer (HMS *Tenedos*), a corvette (HMS *Hollyhock*), a merchant cruiser, 25 merchantmen and 59 aircraft were destroyed. Panic had been created in Southern India, the port installations rendered unusable and air power in Ceylon virtually eliminated. But the Indian Ocean was still British and the Eastern Fleet largely intact. Luck was involved, as Somerville departed Addu Atoll with his whole Fleet intending to meet the Japanese, only to turn back because his old battleships needed refuelling. Therefore, of his main units it was just two cruisers and HMS *Hermes* caught by the overwhelming Japanese air superiority. Japanese success would have 'cut off British communications and supplies from the East', posed 'a grave menace to the Royal Navy in the Red Sea and the Persian Gulf', and raised 'the nightmarish possibility that Axis and Japanese forces could meet at Suez'.[50]

The Fleet had already retreated following the fall of Singapore, to be based at Colombo. A main reason for Singapore's surrender, according to the Commander-in-Chief Eastern Fleet, was that there was 'no naval base capable of housing and maintaining the Eastern Fleet anywhere near its possible sphere of operations'. Both Colombo and Trincomalee were too small to hold the whole Fleet. This was why secret work was undertaken to develop Addu Atoll (the southernmost of the Maldives) into a defended port capable of taking the whole Fleet.[51] Underwater and anti-aircraft defences were constructed and an aerodrome built (on Gan Island). The Fleet could not be kept 'in being' by remaining at Ceylon because of its inferior firepower, lack of aircraft and lack of adequately defended bases. The need for a second retreat became overwhelming after the raid on Ceylon. So the Fleet, along with the intelligence-gathering organization previously located at the shore base HMS *Anderson* in Colombo, retreated across the Indian Ocean to Kilindini in Mombasa.

Admiral Somerville realized that his Fleet could not resist a concerted Japanese attack in the Indian Ocean. As he wrote in his diary on board HMS *Warspite*, on 8 April 1942, 'our present naval and land-based air forces are quite inadequate to dispute this command'.[52] He sent his older ships, the four 'R' class battleships (along with the 'C' and 'D' class cruisers and six destroyers), to Kilindini for their own safety and to protect Middle Eastern and Persian Gulf communications and transport. HMS *Warspite*, the carriers and the cruisers continued operating at large in the Indian Ocean, using Colombo, Bombay, the Seychelles, Mauritius and occasionally the East African ports as bases. It was hoped that its itinerant existence would prevent enemy detection.[53]

Throughout 1942 and into 1943 the Eastern Fleet was on the defensive in the Indian Ocean, where the 'threat to our maritime control was all too clear'.[54] Ironically, the Japanese withdrew from the theatre just when success was most likely – at the time of the Eastern Fleet's retreat across the Indian Ocean to East Africa following Nagumo's raid on Ceylon. Nagumo's carriers returned to Japan after the raid, many soon to be destroyed at the Battle of Midway in June 1942. Though not fully appreciated at the time, this decisive battle 'destroyed all possibility of successful Japanese naval aggression by eliminating the Imperial Navy's carrier force'.[55] After Midway, the Indian Ocean 'was a sea too far' for the Japanese.[56]

In 1943 the Eastern Fleet continued to be asset-stripped, 'to a point where offensive action [was] out of the question'.[57] The last of the Fleet's carriers was moved elsewhere, as was the modern cruiser HMS *Mauritius*, as the Fleet became a 'floating reserve for operations elsewhere'.[58] However, weakened or not, the Fleet still had the demanding task of keeping the Indian Ocean open for business. Before the arrival of the long-hoped-for extra ships that enabled offensive action in the Pacific, it had to 'continue to keep sea routes open, ensuring that the rising tide of supplies and equipment reached the Middle East, India and Ceylon safely'.[59] The Chiefs of Staff believed that even in its enervated state the Eastern Fleet could prevent disruption of British traffic in the Indian Ocean. According to Churchill and the Admiralty, its main role was to deter Japanese operations in the region.[60]

British fortunes began to turn in 1943, and in September of that year the Commander-in-Chief Eastern Fleet's headquarters returned to Colombo from Kilindini. Things improved largely because of Japanese defeats at the hands of the Americans and because Madagascar had been secured by British invasion. By the start of 1944 the enemy simply did not possess the wherewithal to mount a serious challenge in the Indian Ocean.[61] Japanese long-range submarines departed from the Indian Ocean after June 1944, and it was the Germans who maintained the submarine threat in the region. As the fortunes of the Allies rose and the Japanese were forced back to their island home, the Eastern Fleet was built up in preparation for a significant British return to Far Eastern and Pacific waters, and the Indian Ocean was used to train the light fleet carriers. Victories elsewhere freed British ships for the war against Japan, like the crippling of the German ship *Tirpitz* and the sinking of *Scharnhorst,* and the surrender of Italy that eased the situation in the Mediterranean. In January 1944 Admiral Somerville's Fleet was given a shot in the arm when the modern battleships HMS *Renown,* HMS *Queen Elizabeth,* HMS *Valiant,* and the carrier HMS *Illustrious* arrived (carrying over 60 aircraft, including the Fairey Swordfish torpedo planes that had attacked the Italian capital ships at

Taranto).[62] In August 1944 a further carrier, *Victorious,* arrived at Ceylon. Fourteen cruisers and 24 destroyers also went East, as the Admiralty proposed to build up its forces in the Indian Ocean to 146 vessels.

The Eastern Fleet could begin to look towards offensive operations for the first time, however there were still scares, as when the Japanese Fleet moved to Singapore in February 1944 (though only to escape destruction). With Somerville's raid on Sabang in April 1944, 'the Eastern Fleet at last struck a true offensive blow against the Japanese'.[63] The Fleet had been joined temporarily by the carrier USS *Saratoga* and her destroyer escort. Further raids were launched against Port Blair in the Andamans and again on Sabang. In August 1944 Somerville was succeeded by Admiral Sir Bruce Fraser, his appointment coinciding with the structural reorganization of the growing British naval presence in Eastern waters; the Eastern Fleet was abolished and the East Indies Station re-created. The main strength of the Eastern Fleet went to form the new British Pacific Fleet, of which Fraser became the first Commander-in-Chief. The Pacific Fleet joined the Americans when the war at sea against Japan had effectively already been won, 'like a once-great actor making a cameo performance near the end of his career'.[64]

Island naval and air bases in the Indian Ocean

War necessitated the development of bases throughout the Indian Ocean, as well as the protection of the islands and atolls of the British Indian Ocean world.[65] Steps were taken to safeguard lines of communication and build a chain of naval and air bases and refuelling stations between South Africa and Ceylon. The Seychelles, Mauritius and Diego Garcia were used as 'fuelling and minor operational bases for naval craft and for flying-boats to enable air reconnaissance to be extended to areas out of range of Ceylon'.[66] As will be seen, Mauritius became an island in uniform. Such islands needed to be defended whilst capable of aiding offensive action:

> A large programme of works of a greater or smaller nature was also undertaken at Kilindini, Diego Suarez on Madagascar, the Seychelles and Mauritius, all of which had been very deficient in, if not wholly without, base facilities when Japan entered the war ... all needed protection to enable them to be used as fuelling bases.[67]

The strategic significance of Indian Ocean islands went up as the threat of Japan waxed, and down when it waned, particularly from early 1944.[68]

The Second World War brought to Mauritius a 'renewed military importance'.[69] Resonating with nineteenth-century echoes, the Committee of Imperial Defence's Mauritius Defence Plan stressed the island's continued strategic importance given its position on the trade route and – in the event of the Suez Canal being seriously threatened during war (as it was to be) – the increased amount of shipping that would enter Port Louis harbour (already 500 000 tons per annum). Equidistant from the Cape and Ceylon, Mauritius was well situated to protect commerce along this vital sinew of empire. Mauritius was also considered important because of its close proximity to the first-class French naval base at Diego Suarez. Port Louis was a defended naval anchorage with minor repair facilities and a port of refuge for merchant ships. The island retained its importance on the all-British cable communications route.

As a wireless station and interception post Mauritius was to prove its great value during the war for Royal Navy shipping in the Indian Ocean; the wireless station at Rose Belle was reopened in 1939 and had a range of 800 miles by day and 1500 miles by night. An Imperial Wireless Chain had been developed after the First World War and Royal Navy vessels were all equipped with wireless equipment, some with advanced technological facilities such as radar (radio detection and ranging) and ASDIC (Allied Submarine Detection Investigation Committee).[70] The Naval Officer-in-Charge Mauritius was chiefly concerned with the running of the Mauritius Transmitting Station. Together with other bases in the region, the Admiralty was to spend a projected £855 000 on 'Plan R', the wireless and radar enmeshment of the Indian Ocean.[71] Also operating on the island was the Wireless Interception Service, linking Mauritius to the code-breaking endeavours of Bletchley Park, and cable censorship. British success in countering German and Japanese submarine and raider operations in the Indian Ocean was greatly aided by the superiority of Allied intelligence gathering.

Mauritius was, of course, also a base for Royal Navy ships patrolling the ocean, escorting convoys and for sea and air searches for Axis ships and submarines. The threat to Allied shipping in the Indian Ocean and the need to use islands as bases against enemy raiders and submarines led to defensive works and the installation of coastal and anti-aircraft guns. After the calamitous fall of Singapore, Mauritius was built up as a base for the Royal Navy and the RAF. Grand Port Bay was much larger and deeper than Port Louis harbour, so was chosen as the main naval base. The Royal Navy built repair and fuelling facilities, and at Grand Port there was a flying-boat base for anti-submarine work and a fuelling base for the main Fleet. The Eastern Fleet's fuel requirements were stored at Durban, Mombasa, the Seychelles and Mauritius.[72] On Mauritius, 20 000 tons of fuel for all classes of ships was supplied by the Asiatic Petroleum Company.[73] More than 600 tons of reserve ammunition was stored inland. Port Louis was a refuelling base for cruisers and smaller vessels (the biggest warships were refuelled by pipeline) and a repair base for destroyers and smaller vessels.[74]

Plaisance, near Mahebourg and Grand Port, was the site of a Royal Naval Air Station (RNAS) constructed by the Civil Labour Corps (a force of Mauritians conscripted to provide military labour). The aerodrome had an all-weather concrete, non-skid runway, 2000 by 50 yards, capable of taking aircraft up to 90 000 lbs.[75] This new base, HMS *Sambur*, was designed for a disembarked Fleet Air Arm (FAA) squadron, a squadron of RAF fighters, and as a base for 'land-based General Reconnaissance Torpedo Bombers'. A small force of Hurricanes gathered meteorological data and the colony's Observatory was put to military use.[76] Local launches manned by the Mauritius Volunteer Air Force (Marine Crafts Section) refuelled Catalinas and other flying boats in Mauritian territorial waters. On the other side of the island, at the mouth of Rivière du Tombeau near Port Louis, a seaplane base was constructed for the RAF and used primarily by Catalina flying boats (American-built seaplanes, 64 feet long, 18 feet high, with a wing span of 104 feet, weighing 34 000lbs).[77] They were important in Admiralty surveillance of the Indian Ocean, searching for enemy vessels and giving the Navy a wider vision. War brought Mauritius its first air communications with the outside world. By 1944 a regular air service was up and running to Diego Suarez and South Africa. When the RAF left the island the aerodrome was run by the Mauritius Volunteer Air Force until July 1947 when a Government department was formed to take it over. Air France soon stopped at Mauritius, as did the East African airline Skyway and the British Overseas Airways Corporation (BOAC).[78] Today the former Royal Navy aerodrome is the island's international airport, Sir Sewoosagur Ramgoolam Airport.

Mauritius and the other British islands of the Indian Ocean became forward defensive outposts of a withdrawn frontier. They were also vital bases for hard-pressed ships needing fuel and rallying points when on patrol for enemy vessels or on convoy escort duties. As the

Army recognized, the islands provided EAC with outposts in the region, but also presented problems of reinforcement in the event of an emergency.[79] British islands in the region had their defences upgraded. Secret work, successfully concealed from the Japanese was undertaken on Addu Atoll in the Maldives to make it a defended port capable of taking the whole Fleet. With the Fleet's withdrawal from Ceylon, however, the project fizzled out and was eventually abandoned. With the Fleet's retreat to Kilindini, work on Addu Atoll was scaled down, and the Seychelles, Mauritius and Diego Garcia (a Mauritian dependency in the Chagos Archipelago) assumed a new importance as fuelling bases (Diego Garcia also as a harbour for the Fleet's non-capital ships). Improvements to their defences were given priority second only to those of the Kilindini headquarters.[80] The first defence upgrade for Diego Garcia came with the provision of 6-inch coastal guns (installed by a defence battery of the Indian Army).[81] The island was also a wireless and cable communications centre and a base for Catalina reconnaissance planes. In some parts of Diego Garcia land was requisitioned for military purposes, such as the construction of an aerodrome for a general reconnaissance or torpedo bomber squadron. At the RAF camp 400 'coolies' were employed. By June 1942 Somerville could write that Mauritius and Diego Garcia had adequate anti-submarine defences in place.[82]

Air attack was also a possibility, requiring anti-aircraft guns. After the Battle of Midway the Scale of Attack estimate was reduced from 200 planes, the 14-inch guns of a battleship and a brigade group of infantry, to the operations of submarines, midget submarines and armed cruisers.[83] Underwater defences for the harbours of Addu Atoll and Diego Garcia were undertaken and mines were laid.[84] For this task, Royal Marines Mobile Naval Base Defence Organization (MNBDO) personnel were transferred from 'Port T' (Addu Atoll) to Diego Garcia, escorted by HMS *Glasgow*.[85] MNBDO 'were formed to occupy and defend naval bases overseas'.[86] The supply ship *Zambezia* sailed from Diego Garcia to Mauritius in January 1941 carrying military personnel, as Mauritius was responsible for providing troops for the defence of its dependencies. However, these troops did not impress the Commander-in-Chief Eastern Fleet, who wrote that the 'coastal defence [on Diego Garcia is] manned by Mauritian troops and I have received numerous reports which show that these troops are inadequately trained and of poor physique'.[87] An Indian infantry company was to replace them.[88] The Indians were joined by two Hong Kong and Singapore Royal Artillery Coastal Defence batteries.[89] Diego Garcia was considered 'likely to be a depressing station in any circumstances'.[90] By March 1942 coastal defences had been installed by MNBDO and indicator nets laid in the entrance to the harbour.[91]

The Mauritian dependency of Rodrigues housed a wireless and cable installation, and Somerville gave the Seychelles high priority as a base for his ships. So provision was made to improve the harbour defences of the Seychelles and Rodrigues.[92] Rodrigues was also garrisoned by a Company of the MTF, a mixed British and MTF Royal Artillery Coast Battery, and the 200 men of the Rodrigues Volunteer Force.[93] Two 6-inch naval guns from HMS *Gnat* were sent to the Seychelles and installed at Port Victoria, manned from January 1941 by troops of the Ceylon Garrison Artillery.[94]

Air operations in the Indian Ocean (excluding FAA) were the responsibility of the Air Commander-in-Chief South East Asia Command (SEAC). His headquarters were at Colombo and he kept in close touch with the Commander-in-Chief Eastern Fleet and Air Headquarters East Africa. The Air Commander had at his disposal a force of ten flying-boat squadrons and nine land-based medium- and long-range squadrons.[95] Aircraft were sent to patrol areas where submarines and supply ships were known or suspected to be operating. 'The range of flying boat reconnaissance was extended by operating them from anchorages in outlying bases such as the Maldive Islands [Addu Atoll and Gan], Chagos Archipelago [Diego Garcia], the Seychelles, and Socotra [a British island off the Horn of Africa]'.[96] There were also flying-boat bases built at Port Blair (Andoman Islands), Nancowry, Sabang (North West Sumatra) and Mombasa.[97]

British air cover in the Indian Ocean was limited but increasingly necessary as the Eastern Fleet struggled to patrol a vast ocean. Flying-boat bases became more important as the amount of manpower and material traversing the ocean increased, whilst the Eastern Fleet's supply of escort ships diminished. In March 1942 the Defence Committee approved three Catalina squadrons for the Indian Ocean. In August 1943 the flying boats in the Eastern Fleet's region were disposed of thus: Eastern Area 26; Northern Area 18; Western Area 24; Southern Area 23; Australia 2; and Middle East 5.[98]

Flying boats undertook many patrols in search of enemy vessels. Even 'negative' reports from Catalinas were useful to the Commander-in-Chief Eastern Fleet.[99] Aircraft were particularly useful among the unpopulated islands and outcrops of the Indian Ocean that could shelter enemy vessels. For example, on 8 August 1941 a Catalina from Mauritius flew to the Seychelles via Agalega, Fortune Bank and

Coetivy.[100] On 12 June Catalinas flew from the Seychelles to Diego Garcia searching the western and southern edges of the Saya de Malha bank. Aircraft carriers were also used to mount searches. On 15 June 1942 HMS *Illustrious* flew off seven Swordfish aeroplanes for a reconnaissance of the Chagos Archipelago, and HMS *Formidable* flew off four Albacores for the same purpose.[101] On 22 October HMAS *Australia* left Colombo for Mauritius to conduct a search around the Kerguelen and Crozet islands that were being used as supply bases for enemy raiders. These distant outposts of the French empire's sub-Antarctic archipelagos – 3000 miles west of Australia – were ideal hiding places for enemy vessels; between 1773 and 1893 only one French ship had visited the islands![102] HMAS *Australia* laid mines to welcome enemy ships should they return. Early in the war the Commander-in-Chief Eastern Fleet organized extensive searches for the German pocket-battleship *Graf Spee* (prisoners from the ship were later to be held in Mauritius).[103] The areas around the Seychelles and the Chagos Archipelago were searched, as well as the waters to the south of Madagascar where she had destroyed the *Africa Shell*.[104]

The submarine and raider threat

Both German and Japanese submarines were very active in the Indian Ocean during the war; it was by no means the Atlantic alone that was menaced by U-boats, and islands like Mauritius risked being cut off from their sources of supply. During the war, 385 British, Allied and neutral ships totalling 1 789 870 tons were sunk in the Indian Ocean. Enemy submarines sank approximately 250 of these ships.[105] The twin peaks of losses in the Indian Ocean were March 1942 (65 ships lost) and April 1942 (31 ships lost), and large-scale losses were sustained throughout 1943 and 1944. Of course this activity led to a dramatic downturn in trade for islands like Mauritius – rice supplies were cut off, as was inter-island trade in the western Indian Ocean. The population, particularly the poorer sections, was affected by food shortages and malnutrition (see Chapter 7).

Indian Ocean operations were the main German interest in the Japanese war effort in 1942, though Midway prevented the Japanese from conducting their promised offensive. Having no submarines spare for a major campaign, from December 1942 the Japanese provided a base for German submarines at Penang in the captured British territory of Malaya. This developed from the summer of 1943. Initially 11 submarines were sent from bases in occupied France with a supply submarine and supply ships. Unlike the British who had imperial bases around the world, Germany had to rely upon floating supplies. The German submarine force in the Indian Ocean, though achieving notable successes, was not strong enough to seriously threaten large amounts of Allied shipping. The last significant successes were in early 1944.

From 27 June to 6 July 1942, 16 ships were sunk or attacked in the Mozambique Channel.[106] In the June–August 1943 period, German submarines sunk 35 ships in the Cape–Mozambique Channel area. September brought a respite from offensive operations as the submarines refuelled from the tender *Brake* 450 miles south of Mauritius.[107] From then until the end of 1943, 21 ships were sunk in the Indian Ocean, mostly by Japanese submarines.[108] In January 1944 German U-boats returned from their Penang base to patrol the Ceylon–Gulf of Aden–Mauritius area. From January to March 1944, 29 vessels were sunk in this area, 'the highest shipping losses sustained in any theatre of war in that period'.[109] The shortage of escort forces available to the Commander-in-Chief Eastern Fleet meant that more would have been lost but for Enigma intelligence that made it possible to attack the German supply ships, the *Charlotte Schleimann* and *Brake*. Intelligence could also give British forces early warning of the approach of enemy vessels. In September 1943 broken intelligence informed the Admiralty that seven large German U-boats had recently arrived in the Indian Ocean.[110] In June 1944, ten specially modified 740-ton U-cruisers arrived, known as the Monsoon Group. All together they could have seriously threatened Allied shipping in the Indian Ocean, however three were sunk on their voyage out, and two more had to sacrifice their fuel so that five could continue the voyage.[111]

U-boat successes could lead to heavy loss of life. In February 1944 the *Khedive Ismail* sailed from Mombasa destined for Ceylon, carrying 11th East African Division's 301 Field Artillery Regiment. The ship was torpedoed and 900 East African soldiers lost their lives.[112] Ships bound for and leaving Mauritius were sunk, often by submarines lying in wait outside Port Louis harbour. In June and July 1942 Group A of the Japanese 8th Submarine Flotilla hunted in the vicinity of Mauritius.[113] At 11.15 pm on 2 July 1943 the *Hoi How* – whose passengers included the Colonial Secretary's daughter, Joan Moody (sailing to join the WRNS in East Africa), soldiers and seven Mauritian intelligence workers joining the British military administration in Madagascar – was hit by a torpedo and sunk within one-and-a-half minutes, 105 miles west-northwest of Mauritius.[114] Of 154 passengers, only five survived. The commander of U-181 surfaced to question the handful of 'dago' survivors.[115] This commander, Wolfgang Luth, was one of the most senior and most decorated U-boat commanders and shortly after sinking the *Hoi How* was promoted to command the 12th U-Boat Flotilla.[116] He was the second most successful U-boat ace of the war, sinking 228 429 tons of Allied shipping.[117]

On 14 March 1942 the *Yulworth Castle* was sunk by a torpedo near Ascension Island, loaded with 10 000 tons of sugar, aloes and rum from Mauritius. Two weeks after the *Hoi How* went down, two more ships were torpedoed about 350 miles southwest of Mauritius. At 6.30 am on 29 July 1943, SS *Cornish City* was torpedoed without warning. Also in July the *Empire Lake* and *Fort Franklin* were sunk in the region. On 4 August 1943 the *Dalfram* was sunk 80 miles west of the island, and three days later the *Umvuma* went down only 10 miles from Port Louis – witnessed by people on the island. The SS *Clan Macarthur*, carrying equipment for the naval base on Mauritius, was sunk approaching the island on 11 August. An intelligence leak was feared and the Jews who were working on Admiralty property were the first to be suspected.[118] On 17 August the *Empire Stanley* was sunk. The submarines U-181 and U-197 were responsible for all of these losses, according to *Lloyd's Register of Ships*.[119]

Despite these successes, enemy submarine activity between Malaya and East Africa was not enough to overthrow British hegemony in the region. According to Carl Boyd, the Axis powers were unable to subordinate selfish goals and co-operate for mutual advantage in the Indian Ocean. Fortunately for the Allies, submarines were the 'stepchild' of the Imperial Japanese Navy. Though often commanded by daring officers, the overall strategic use of submarines was not the Imperial Navy's strongest suit.[120] Germany reluctantly increased its commitment in the Indian Ocean when it became clear that the Japanese, mortally wounded at Midway, were a spent force in the region.[121] The December 1941 Tripartite Agreement had demarcated spheres in the Indian Ocean, but this went by the board as German vessels roamed across the whole ocean. From August 1942 Germany realized that it could not rely on Japan to stop the flow of British materials crossing the Indian Ocean, and so intervened.

Few British islands escaped Japanese submarine-borne reconnaissance in search of units of the Eastern Fleet. The latest I-class submarines were fitted with aircraft or midget submarines.[122] Five submarines of the 4th Submarine Flotilla had assembled at Penang at the end of April 1942 and crossed the Indian Ocean, refuelling at sea from two supply ships. Their aircraft reconnoitred East African ports as far south as Durban. Reunion, Rodrigues, Diego Garcia, the Seychelles, Kilindini and Mauritius were all surveyed in 1942–43.[123] On 29 May 1942 an aircraft was spotted over Diego Suarez and in the evening a midget submarine torpedo attack damaged the battleship HMS *Ramillies* and sank a British tanker anchored in the harbour.

The Indian Ocean was also an important transport route for the Germans and the Japanese. Although the sinking of the supply ships *Brake* and *Charlotte Schleimann* ended the enemy's use of surface vessels in the region, special cargoes continued to travel west to east by way of submarines. These cargoes were mainly the fruits of German technological research sent to Japan for its own weapons development programmes and beleaguered industrial base. Items included large gun prototypes, ground radars, drugs, sample aircraft, a complete British Mosquito fighter, industrial diamonds, lead, mercury and steel balls. Of course, the tonnage that could be shipped by submarine was small and the Allied offensive against enemy submarines and their supply ships further curtailed the amount of material successfully completing the journey. In preventing this traffic from threatening the Allied war effort, Ultra intelligence was all important.[124]

In the early years of the war it was enemy surface raiders, like *Graf Spee* and *Admiral Scheer*,[125] and commerce raiders ('merchant ships converted into warships with concealed armament'),[126] rather than submarines that were the main threat to British shipping. German strategy sought to cut British merchant shipping routes. Prominent commerce raiders operating in the Indian Ocean were the auxiliary cruisers *Schiff 33/Pinguin* and *Schiff 16/Atlantis*. Hiding from the ships of the Eastern Fleet they would reappear to sink Allied vessels (*Pinguin* was the most successful German raider in terms of tonnage sunk).[127] By the time the *Pinguin* was sunk by the heavy cruiser HMS *Cornwall* off the Seychelles on 8 May 1941, it had sunk or captured 32 ships.[128] There were 541 men lost in the sinking of the *Pinguin*, including 200 prisoners (82 men survived).[129] HMS *Cornwall* had sailed to Saya de Malha with HMS *Glasgow* in search of the raider, and after the sinking both steamed to Mauritius to refuel. On 20 May 1941 HMS *Cornwall* left Mauritius for Durban for repairs to damage received in the engagement.[130] An Italian raider, *Ramb 1*, was also sunk in the Indian Ocean, by HMNZS *Leander* on 27 February 1941.

The *Atlantis* had an epic run before being sunk near Ascension by HMS *Devonshire* on 22 November 1941. Raiders evaded detection by changing names and adding false superstructure to disguise their identity. This presented the Admiralty with a mammoth problem; 'it became evident that, to put a stop to this practice, it would be necessary for the Admiralty to compile a plot giving the position of every merchant ship known to be at sea anywhere in the world' (this was known as the check-mate system, fully operational by May 1943).[131] In such a task, shipping intelligence such as that provided by the Wireless Interception Service on Mauritius was vital. Ultra intelligence was central to the sinking of the *Atlantis*. Between sailing from Germany in March 1940 and being sunk, *Atlantis* sank or captured 22 ships and circumnavigated the globe. Codes were intercepted ordering *Atlantis* to refuel U-126, and HMS *Devonshire* was ordered to find her.[132]

Two Japanese surface raiders *Hokoku Maru* and *Aikoku Maru* operated in the Indian Ocean in late 1942. This produced the only surface engagement seen in the Indian Ocean during the war. The raiders weighed 10 400 tons each and were armed with eight 6-inch guns. They caught an Indian minesweeper, HMIS *Bengal* and the Dutch ship *MV Ondina*. Both were badly damaged in the unequal contest but managed to sink one of the Japanese ships. The crews then reboarded their ships and managed to work them to friendly ports.[133]

Patrols and convoys

Mauritius and its dependencies were visited by merchant ships crossing the Indian Ocean and by Royal Navy ships refuelling, rendezvousing, re-arming, resting or refitting. Offensive operations were often co-ordinated air and sea searches. Broken enemy intelligence was used whenever it was available, though the British had to be cautious in its employment so as not to alert the enemy to the fact that the security of their secret signals had been compromised.

Operation 'Canned' was a co-ordinated air and sea search to find the German ship *Charlotte Schleimann*, a 7747-ton support ship from which German submarines refuelled. Admiral Sir James Somerville personally made the plans for the operation.[134] The ships taking part in the exercise assembled at Mauritius between the 19 and 21 January 1944, their names neatly reflecting the links between Britain and its colonial empire. HMS *Newcastle*, *Kenya* and *Suffolk* arrived from Ceylon. HMS *Nepal* and *Canton* came from Durban and HMS *Bann* and *Battler* from the Arab Sea. HMS *Gambia* and *Illustrious* were also involved. To supplement the Mauritian Catalina force, two flying boats were transferred from Air Headquarters East Africa to the new

Tombeau Bay base on 17 January. Squadron Leader J. Stacey was ordered to Mauritius on 15 January by the Air Vice Marshal of No. 222 Group RAF Ceylon to establish communications and weather conditions. Altogether, seven Mauritius-based Catalinas took part in the operation, locating the *Charlotte Schleimann* for the destroyer HMS *Relentless* to attack on 11/12 February 1944.[135] After the operation the ships returned to Mauritius to refuel. Fuelling arrangements had been made in advance so that by 17 January there was sufficient fuel for the force available at Port Louis. RFA *Olynthus* had been sent ahead with 10 000 tons of furnace oil. In-shore tanks with pipelines to the ships could supply 10 000 tons of furnace oil and 1200 tons of diesel oil. At Diego Suarez a further 15 000 tons of furnace oil and 750 tons of diesel oil was available.

Operations 'Covered' and 'Stingaree' in the following month were undertaken to destroy the German tanker *Brake,* reported 450 miles south of Mauritius.[136] This was the other ship that refuelled submarines of the Monsoon group.[137] As with the interception of the *Charlotte Schleimann,* Ultra intelligence was used, as were Catalina flying boats based on Mauritius. They worked in co-operation with *Newcastle, Roebuck, Battler, Suffolk* and *Quadrant,* sent from Durban to Grand Port to prepare for the operation. The *Brake* was sunk by the destroyer HMS *Roebuck* in March 1944, some 100 miles southeast of Mauritius.[138]

Another major task of the Fleet was the location and interception of enemy convoys. In October 1941 Mauritian-based Catalinas went in search of a Vichy convoy en route from Madagascar to Saigon.[139] In January 1944 Operation 'Thwart' was mounted to intercept blockade runners sailing from Japan to Europe and reported southeast of Mauritius.[140] In September 1941 operations 'Ration' and 'Snip' were aimed at the interception of a French convoy attempting to run the blockade of Vichy territories in the Far East, the Indian Ocean and Europe. HMS *Hermes, Enterprise* and *Mauritius* searched around Diego Garcia then patrolled Saya de Malha and the Mauritian dependencies of the Cargados Carojos group.[141] Two Catalinas from Diego Garcia were sent on a 12-hour search in conjunction with the surface force. Naval intelligence benefited greatly from messages intercepted on Mauritius, helping the Royal Navy maintain the blockade of the Vichy islands that contributed to their capitulation. Intelligence supplied by the Naval Officer-in-Charge Mauritius led to the interception of a valuable Vichy convoy consisting of *Bernadin de St Pierre, Le Conte de Lisle* and *Sontay.*[142]

On 9 March 1941, HMS *City of Durban* left Mauritius for Operation

'Supply', followed by HMAS *Leander* and HMAS *Canberra*.[143] The operation was directed against the four remaining Italian submarines, as the Commander-in-Chief East Indies feared that as pressure on the Italian Navy in Massawa increased, Italian warships and submarines might try for a 'death or glory' strike on British bases or convoys in the Red Sea.[144] After the operation HMAS *Leander* returned to Mauritius on 22 March 1941.[145] She left the next day for a patrol off Madagascar in the hope of intercepting the Vichy ship *Ville de Verdun* on its journey from Saigon to Madagascar.[146] Its presence was revealed by signals intelligence intercepted on Mauritius. On its passage HMAS *Leander* intercepted the Vichy ship *Charles Louis Dreyfus* bound for Diego Suarez from Reunion, and it was sent to Mauritius under armed guard where it was requisitioned by the Governor as a war prize and its mixed cargo auctioned.[147]

Shipping protection was another of the duties of the Eastern Fleet, as troopships and freighters plied the ocean's convoy routes. The ship *Talamba* carried 810 Mauritian and 300 Seychellois troops of the Pioneer Corps from their home islands to Suez, escorted by destroyers of the Eastern Fleet.[148] The ship formed part of convoy WS6 (the 'WS' prefix stood for 'Winston's Specials' and was used to identify troop convoys) that consisted of 31 ships, amounting to 267 827 tons.[149] It carried a total of 23 115 troops destined for the Middle East. A draft of Mauritian troops left Port Louis in the SS *Tinhow* to join convoy RS5 at Durban on 17 August 1940.[150] The convoy, escorted by HMS *Kandahar*, was destined for Britain via the Cape and Suez.

As in the First World War, convoys were the most successful way of protecting merchant shipping from enemy submarines and raiders. The Admiralty was always hard pressed to find the necessary cruisers and destroyers with which to escort convoys in all the world's oceans, particularly after interwar defence cuts. After its capture in 1942, Diego Suarez in Madagascar was used as a convoy assembly port where merchant ships could gather and join the warships which were to protect them on their journeys across the Indian Ocean. Sometimes special convoy measures were required. The world's two largest passenger ships, *Queen Mary* and *Queen Elizabeth*, were used as troopships from January 1942, with their troop capacities raised from 6000 to 15 000. They were primarily used for the transport of American troops to Britain (55 crossings of the Atlantic from January 1942 to December 1943).[151] However, in June 1942 the *Queen Mary* was operating in the Indian Ocean and the Commander-in-Chief Eastern Fleet had to find fast modern ships to escort her from Cape Town to Suez with 9000 troops on board. HMS *Mauritius* was sent, with HMS *Devonshire* taking over on 16 June 1942 whilst HMS *Mauritius* headed for its namesake colony to refuel. The following day she left Mauritius to join Convoy WS19, relieving HMS *Shropshire*. Such was the work-a-day routine of keeping the Indian Ocean open to Allied shipping.

Madagascar and Reunion

At the Fall of France in May 1940, the French empire divided between Petain and the Vichy regime on the one hand and de Gaulle and the Free French on the other. As the war progressed, the holdings of the former waned and of the latter waxed, as British empire and Free French forces won successes against Vichy French colonies, and as French governors saw which way the wind was blowing and moved to the Allied cause. Rather than declaring war en masse against the Vichy colonies, the British preferred to 'pick off' individual colonies as and when manpower, supplies and transport allowed.[152] An operation to take the port of Dakar (Operation 'Menace') – which threatened Atlantic sea routes – failed in 1940; in July 1940 the British attacked the French western Mediterranean squadron harboured at Mers-el-Kebir in Algeria (Operation 'Catapult'), killing 1300 French sailors. Churchill could not risk the fleet falling to the Axis and tipping the naval balance in the region decisively against the Royal Navy. A campaign against Vichy forces in Syria and Lebanon succeeded in 1941; in 1942 British and Free French operations secured the surrender of Reunion; and in the same year Operation 'Ironclad' saw the successful conquest of Madagascar.[153]

Though not a celebrated campaign, the victory in Madagascar provided the British with what at the time was a rare and significant victory. The British feared losing the harbour of Diego Suarez to the Japanese, and viewed with gravity the signs of co-operation between Vichy and the Japanese regarding Madagascar.[154] Madagascar was seen as the key to keeping the Indian Ocean British and protecting the vital lines of supply and communication that traversed it. Mauritius was important in operations against the Vichy islands on three counts. Firstly, Mauritius was able to feed the Admiralty and EAC with intelligence gathered from all the cables using the line that ran between Reunion and Madagascar via Mauritius (Cable and Wireless were instructed to restore the Mauritius–Reunion–Tamatave cable link),[155] and from intercepted wireless signals. Secondly, Mauritius was the operational headquarters for SOE operations against the Vichy islands of Reunion and Madagascar.[156] A major contribution was made by the Mauritian SOE agent Percy Mayer (and his wife), who for many months submitted valuable reports from Madagascar providing vital pre-invasion intelligence. Mayer was behind the February 1942 attempt to bribe the commander of the French naval garrison at Diego Suarez, an attempt justified by SOE reports that the naval forces in Madagascar were profoundly Anglophobic and pro-Vichy. The stream of intelligence he provided led to his decoration by the King.[157] From Mauritius, Lieutenant Peter Simpson-Jones of SOE was put on to Reunion to try and rally the island to the Allied cause.[158] Finally, Mauritius was the location of covert radio stations run by the British colonial authorities, SOE and the Free French, subjecting the populations of both islands to sustained Allied propaganda.[159]

Madagascar and Reunion would not simply fall to the British and Free French at the first huff and puff. The Vichy government in France was understandably opposed to the loss of any of its imperial territory. As Martin Thomas writes:

> The empire was a physical embodiment of what limited independence remained to the Vichy regime. Preservation of imperial control helped Vichy governments withstand Germano-Italian pressure for concessions in metropolitan France, and was pivotal to Vichy's claim to be more than the mouthpiece of a defeated nation.[160]

Madagascar and Reunion were considered 'aggressively Vichy', and the British consul departing from Madagascar in November 1940 'estimated that the Governor had completely crushed what remained of Free French support within Madagascar'.[161] Governor Annet was a devout Petainist. A new governor, Cayla, was reported to the Admiralty as being 'very anti-British'. The British had a good picture of the situation in Madagascar through intelligence intercepted on Mauritius. For example, it was reported that there were 6000 troops on the island and rumours of the arrival of 200 planes from North Africa were picked up by the Chief Censor's Office on Mauritius.[162] Madagascar and Reunion were focal points for Vichy ships attempting to run the British blockade, which from July 1940 had caused 'a collapse of exports, price shortages, and often chronic shortages of rice'.[163] An increasing body of evidence collected on Mauritius (from cable censorship and intercepted wireless signals on Reunion and

Madagascar) showed the intention to run merchant vessels to metro-politan France and other parts of the Vichy empire.[164] Vichy France did not have the naval wherewithal to defend and provision its colonies around the world. The Eastern Fleet stopped 'most vessels sent to reprovision Indo-China'.[165]

Adding weight to calls for an invasion of Madagascar was the strong suspicion that the island was being used as a base for Axis vessels and that further rights might be granted to the Japanese. In 'March 1942 "Magic" intelligence revealed that Germany was pressing the Japanese to occupy the island'.[166] Japan had already occupied Vichy territory elsewhere. It had 'proved none too difficult to browbeat the French in Indo-China into granting facilities for Japanese troops and aircraft there, notionally for use against China. This came in September 1940'.[167] In July 1941 Japan had sent substantial forces to Indo-China, a springboard for action further south against the Dutch East Indies. Though by the summer of 1942, following the Battle of Midway, the Japanese Navy 'was in no position to take further offensive action anywhere', foresight was not a benefit enjoyed by the British in early 1942.[168] At that time a stubbornly 'hostile presence in Madagascar became intolerable to the British government after the devastating loss of Singapore'. If Vichy had conceded it to the Japanese, 'Allied control of the western Indian Ocean would have been jeopardized as surely as the British empire in South East Asia was endangered by the French capitulation in Indo-China'.[169]

A powerful voice urging British invasion of Madagascar was that of Jan Smuts, Prime Minister of South Africa. He wrote to Churchill:

> I look upon Madagascar as the key to the safety of the Indian Ocean and it may play the same important part in endangering our security there that Indo-China has played in Vichy and Japanese hands. All our communications with our various war fronts and the Empire in the East may be involved.[170]

For him, as for the people of the Indian Ocean, the rising sun was on the horizon and a Japanese invasion appeared a distinct possibility. In Mauritius a 'Japanese attack as a side-show to an occupation of Madagascar, was regarded as inevitable'.[171] Prewar Japanese penetration of Southern Africa was recalled, as was the use made of Diego Suarez by Japanese warships during the First World War.[172] South African fears of Japanese invasion made Mauritian concerns seem reasonable. In South Africa the Union Defence Force garrison was co-ordinated into complementary 'land and sea' units, with defensive resources invested in Inland and Coastal Area bunker zones. With much of the eastern seaboard dangerously low-lying and exposed, operational plans were revamped to thicken South Africa's coastal and strategic port defence measures – batteries, aerial reconnaissance, mobile radar systems and light naval force expansion for anti-submarine and anti-mine warfare.[173] Barbed wire appeared on the Durban beaches to repel the invaders.[174] Before the successful British imperial invasion of Madagascar, Smuts thought that a Japanese attack on South Africa was likely.[175] Scores of Allied ships were sunk around the South African coast by Japanese and German submarines, raiders and mines.[176] In 1942–43 rural millenarian movements spread rumours of a Japanese invasion that would liberate Africans from 'white slavery'.[177] Smuts promised that if the Japanese invaded, the country's African population would be armed.

So there were compelling reasons for a pre-emptive strike against Madagascar. British and imperial troops invaded in May 1942 in Britain's first major amphibious assault, commanded by Major-General Robert Sturges, supported by a strong naval force under Rear Admiral E. N. Syfret, Commander of Force 'H', the powerful Mediterranean force previously commanded by Somerville. Syfret brought with him the battleship HMS *Malaya*, the carrier HMS *Illustrious* and the cruisers HMS *Hermione* and *Devonshire*. The invasion fleet also contained units borrowed from Somerville's Eastern Fleet, the carrier HMS *Indomitable* and the 'R' class battleship HMS *Ramillies*. The Eastern Fleet was too run down to undertake the operation single-handedly without seriously jeopardizing its shipping protection duties. Captain Paul Maerten, commanding French naval forces in Madagascar, had about six warships on station, two colonial sloops and four to six submarines.[178] This force, together with the available air force, was quickly disabled or surrendered.

Most of the participating British soldiers were diverted from a convoy of troops bound for Colombo. Royal Marine Commandos were used in the initial landings, along with other British and South African forces (the KAR led the later extension of the invasion across the island). The invaders were faced by 8000 French colonial troops. The surprise attack went in on 5 May 1942 and took Diego Suarez successfully. After that, the British were faced with the problem of whether to take the rest of the island if the Vichy Governor refused to surrender, and when to bring in the Free French authorities. The attack on HMS *Ramillies* and pressure from General Smuts – who was unconvinced that control of Diego Suarez alone secured Madagascar – led to later attacks on Majunga and Tamatave, and the capital Tananarive.

In March 1942 a British SOE mission was sent to reconnoitre Reunion and to organize elements hostile to the Vichy regime. In charge of Operation 'Bluewater' was Royal Navy Lieutenant Peter Simpson-Jones. He arrived in Mauritius in January 1942 from Durban, transporting radio transmitters in sealed canisters in the ship *Tegelberg*. Whilst in Mauritius his cover was Operation 'Blanket' – the vetting of signals coming out of Madagascar. There was the need to establish in Reunion a network able to inform the British about defensive measures, the economic and political climate and to prepare acts of sabotage if the enemy moved into Reunion.[179] Simpson-Jones needed someone who knew Reunion, so the British intelligence officer Greaves called upon Pierre Arnulphy and his step brother Sylvio Fanucci. They were deposited on Reunion by the Mauritian Government's tug *Portia*, taking the precious transmitters with them. The SOE operation on Reunion was compromised when Simpson-Jones and his team were attempting to rejoin the *Portia*, which had been signalled to come and collect them. The boat was commanded by Arthur Stamberg (another British intelligence officer) but Simpson-Jones and his team did not appear for the rendezvous, having been either arrested or drowned.[180] Simpson-Jones, surviving members of his team and his Reunion collaborators, were arrested and sent to Madagascar to be dealt with by higher Vichy authorities.[181] Fortunately events overtook them and they were released when the British took the town later in the year.

A successful attempt to detach Reunion from Vichy was made later in the year. In November 1942 the Free French super-cruiser *Leopard* left Simonstown for Mauritius to lead the operation, arriving off Reunion on 27 November.[182] *Leopard* was under the orders of the French National Committee in London and had been diverted on its way to Australia to rally the island to the Free French. It refuelled at Port Louis and then sailed for the capital St Denis, where it intended to land marines and capture the Governor. On board was de Gaulle's Mauritian representative, Hector Paturau, and Capagory, de Gaulle's choice of Governor to replace the Vichyite Aubert. Aubert, believing that he was faced by three cruisers and 3000 troops, retired to Hellbourg in the mountains with diehard supporters and 400 men.[183]

The commander of the *Leopard* wanted British troops available, and the Governor of Mauritius told the Colonial Office that he could send two companies of the MTF. HMS *Hawkins* was on standby to ferry reinforcements from Madagascar to Reunion. But assistance was not needed, as the Governor accepted the Free French terms; the *Leopard* 'secured its accession to the Free French on the 30th by the persuasive effect of 200 shells fired into the battery at Point Galets, where the defenders put up considerable resistance'.[184] The toppled Governor was removed to Mauritius.

With the capture of Madagascar, the waning of the Japanese and German naval threat in the Indian Ocean, and the corresponding increase in ships released from other theatres to join the Eastern Fleet, the threat to British hegemony in the region finally passed in 1944–45. In March 1944 a general reduction in the scale of defences for Mauritius, Addu Atoll and Diego Garcia was approved. In April all naval personnel were withdrawn from the latter. The role of Diego Suarez as a fleet and convoy assembly port lapsed.[185] The Admiralty's plans to defend the Indian Ocean ground to a halt as the Japanese naval threat dissolved, the Fourteenth Army beat the Japanese out of Burma, and the Allies advanced in Northern Europe. Yet the outcome could have been very different, and on the islands of the Indian Ocean civilian populations had been mobilized to provide for the defence of their homelands, the subject of the next chapter.

3
Defending the Home Front: Local and Imperial Defence Measures

Governors throughout the empire were left in no doubt by the Colonial Office that, when war broke out, their primary duty was to do all in their power to provide for the security of their territories and to ensure their greatest possible self-sufficiency. Supplies of foodstuffs and essential goods were likely to be cut off as shipping was either sunk or requisitioned, and imperial garrisons, where they existed, were likely to be depleted or withdrawn. To this end, efforts had been made to stockpile supplies in the colonies before the outbreak of war. Britain was not the only part of the empire that relied on imports to feed itself and exports to pay for them. Mauritius was almost a hundred per cent dependent upon imported foodstuffs, and the production and export of sugar was its overwhelming commercial activity.

Though the Royal Navy was the mainstay of colonial defence, imperial military and naval forces were supplemented by local forces and local defence initiatives. All colonies sought to cater for their own defence whilst supplying raw materials and soldiers for the imperial war effort. From the outbreak of hostilities, the Indian Ocean was an active theatre of war. For Mauritius, the threat of enemy attack became much greater with Japan's entry into the war. As well as training local men to serve as soldiers, passive and active measures were needed for air defence as the aircraft carrier brought a new threat to parts of the empire that previous enemies could not reach. As in Britain, the colonial home front could not but be deeply involved in the empire's world war effort.

Sir John Shuckburgh highlighted the war's demands on the colonial home front:

The maintenance of locally raised forces was no longer the only defensive requirement that Colonial Governments had to meet. It had become one of many: the total character of modern warfare demanded a high state of preparedness on the part of the civil as well as of the military side of the administration. Measures for passive air defence, for the control of food and other commodities, for censorship, for internal security and for development of economic resources, had all to be taken in hand. The purely military measures, which in earlier days would have been regarded as the sole criterion of preparedness for war, had ceased to be sufficient.[1]

The mobilization of home fronts called for an unprecedented regimentation of society that put pressure on the colonial state and exacerbated racial tensions. In Mauritius, rationing and 'dig for victory' propaganda marked the home front, as they did in Britain. ARP sirens were a common sound and Home Guards a common sight as Mauritius was imperilled by enemy bombers and the prospect of invasion.[2] Church bells were silenced from January 1942, only to be used in the event of an invasion. In his broadcast announcing the outbreak of war the Governor exhorted the MTF, the Naval Reporting Service and the police to have 'alert' as their watchword for they were charged with the defence 'of this important link in Empire communications'.[3]

During the war, the British maintained the simple notion of total empire loyalty. Whilst this went too far towards suggesting that all colonial peoples enthusiastically supported Britain's cause and cheerfully shouldered new burdens, it accurately reflected the fact that the elites who Britain saw as representing colonial peoples were loyal and that overt acts of disloyalty were rare. 'With enthusiastic loyalty the colony placed its men and materials at the disposal of His Majesty', wrote Governor Sir Bede Clifford to the Colonial Office. The colony was 'solidly behind the war' and was busily raising money for the war effort – in the Governor's words, it 'assumed the additional financial and other burdens of war with equanimity'. The Governor was keen to create and sustain the impression of questionless loyalty to the empire in its hour of need, even if this required a little embellishment of the facts; in the draft stage of his speech, the reference to the colony's assumption of wartime burdens 'with equanimity' had replaced the crossed out phrase 'without pleasure'.[4]

On the outbreak of war the Committee of Imperial Defence's Defence Scheme was put into operation in all colonies. The War

Cabinet recognized that – initially at least – the greatest contribution the colonial empire could make to the war effort was to produce as much as it could and reduce import demands to the barest minimum. For Mauritius this meant producing more sugar, conserving existing supplies and reducing the use of shipping and other services requiring imperial manpower, particularly by increasing the amount of food produced for local consumption. To this effect, the Government of Mauritius had built up a large supply of petrol, coal and rice when war looked increasingly inevitable after the Munich crisis. Later, when food imports were cut off (with the loss of Burma and the lack of merchant shipping), sugar planters were legally obliged to convert over a quarter of their land to foodcrops.

In Mauritius and its dependencies a range of local initiatives sought to provide for home defence given the threat of enemy attack. The imperial element in defence comprised the guns of the coastal artillery, provision of a battalion of the KAR, the installation of an SOE team and the construction of bases for offensive RAF and Royal Navy use. Though reliant on British naval hegemony as the ultimate guarantor of its security, this could not be counted on, especially when Britain faced three major enemies simultaneously. The entry of Japan into the war, and the consequent withering of British naval strength in the East, left colonies like Mauritius exposed.

The threat to Mauritius and the imperial response

When the European war broke out Whitehall thought it unlikely that anything more than the odd enemy cruiser would operate in the Indian Ocean, and for this – should the Royal Navy not get there in time – Mauritius had coastal defence guns manned by imperial troops backed by the infantry of the MTF. Even after the fall of France considerably altered the security situation in the region it was considered that an attack from enemy forces in Madagascar and Reunion was unlikely.[5] However, this rather relaxed assessment was before Pearl Harbor and the dramatic rise of a potent new threat to the scantily guarded British territories and spheres of interest stretching from East Africa to Shanghai and Samoa. It was also before the true implications of air power had dawned upon an unprepared British world.

The Governor of Mauritius bombarded Whitehall with requests for new minesweepers, more troops, anti-aircraft guns, mortars, small arms and armoured cars, stressing the inadequacy of available forces for withstanding an invasion.[6] Feeling more of a sense of urgency than those back in Whitehall, the Governor told the Colonial Office of nearby submarine activity and stressed the strategic threats in the area, such as the neutrality of Portuguese East Africa and the aggressive stance of the Vichy islands.[7] Sir Bede Clifford's successor maintained the pressure, telling Whitehall that there was absolutely nothing to stop enemy submarines coming into the ports, laying mines, sinking ships and having a parlous effect on the export of sugar on which the economy depended. 'My chief anxiety is lest Port Louis harbour be denied to the Eastern Fleet', wrote Mackenzie Kennedy.[8] New minesweepers for the island had been ordered in May 1941, but over two years later had not arrived.[9]

When Japan entered the war, defence prospects became alarming. The island's 6-inch coastal defence guns were wholly inadequate as they were outranged by the guns of modern destroyers (let alone more powerful ships). These guns and two companies of indifferently armed local infantry, argued the Governor, were hardly likely to repel an attack.[10] The War Office's predicted Scale of Attack – before it became clear that Midway had seriously curtailed Japan's offensive potency – left no doubt that the forces on Mauritius had a lot expected of them. They might face a commando raid by 200 men; a full-scale brigade strength attack to evade or overcome coastal defences; an air attack by 150–200 planes; a boat or submarine raid on ships or port installations; and the bombardment of coast, ports or ships by the 14-inch guns of a battleship.[11]

In January 1942, the total manpower available on Mauritius (excluding the two companies of the MTF and imperial garrison troops) was: the Coastal Defence Squadron of 500 men and a dozen boats; 200 police (specially recruited for defence purposes, excluding the regular police force); 1200 Home Guards (about 100 armed)[12]; 520 unarmed Pioneers preparing for transfer to the Middle East; the Rodrigues and Diego Garcia infantry companies numbering 270; 26 motor vehicles, 25 motorbikes and 187 bicycles.[13] As the Governor wrote to the Colonial Office, echoing Churchill's famous speech, 'we will fight them on the beaches, but only one beach at a time, please'.[14]

After the Japanese reverses at the Battle of Midway, the estimated Scale of Attack was reduced. However, this did not happen suddenly, for it was not clear that the battle had so seriously impaired Japan's offensive strength. By the end of 1942 the possibility of offensive action by Vichy forces from Madagascar or Reunion had been removed by their surrender.[15] In July 1942 the War Office believed that the growing strength of the Eastern Fleet, the increased effectiveness of air reconnaissance from Ceylon and Indian Ocean bases, and combined operations in the Pacific, would protect the Indian Ocean. It was felt that the existing garrison was enough to dissuade the Japanese from attempting to invade Mauritius, and by early 1944 the possibility of invasion was regarded as negligible.

Despite the Governor's dire warnings throughout 1942 and 1943 as to the island's unpreparedness, as the Japanese threat receded so his calls became easier to ignore. The proposed air defence of the island provides an example. The anti-aircraft cover planned in September 1942 was: Grand Port 12 heavy anti-aircraft (HAA) guns; Plaisance aerodrome four HAA, four light anti-aircraft (LAA); Tombeau Bay flying-boat base four HAA, four LAA; Port Louis eight HAA, eight LAA.[16] In June 1943 the total allocation of HAA and LAA guns was dropped from 44 to 28.[17] In December 1943 the Commander-in-Chief Eastern Fleet ordered the cessation of the air defence scheme for Mauritius.[18] The moment of danger had passed. However, it takes an imperial power to *think* imperially and Britain, though threatened on all sides and short of men, money and materials, still managed to conceive of the need for such precautions and to turn conception into action; Mauritius got its anti-aircraft guns, even if not to the measure initially proposed.

Though the War Office and Admiralty took comfort from estimates that minimized the likelihood of attack on islands like Mauritius, in early 1942 there was no room for a false sense of security among the military authorities responsible for the region's defence. German and Japanese submarine activity in the ocean had yet to reach its peak. The importance of Mauritius as an intelligence-gathering base was factored into defence calculations. As a strategically placed naval and air base – as well as an island with a civilian population to defend – action was required to protect Mauritius. This process gathered pace after the region was transferred from India Command (a historical legacy) to EAC in September 1942.

EAC was more able to conceive of the Indian Ocean islands as part of a strategic whole, not as distant outposts. After losses in the Far East had crippled British power east of India, an upgrade in the island's defences was ordered.[19] The transfer of commands was important for Mauritius as it had not been well served by anomalies in the command structure. Too often the island and its dependencies seemed to fall between eastern and western stools; was it to be the responsibility of India, Ceylon, South Africa or East Africa? Even after transfer, it found itself shifted again to the new Islands Area Command, an EAC subsidiary under Major General G. R. Smallwood with headquarters at Diego Suarez. This was 'a new appellation covering Mauritius and the Seychelles as well as Madagascar', though Mauritius was soon returned to EAC.[20]

The Eastern Fleet did what it could to provide for naval defence. Searched channels were in operation in Mauritian ports, checking for enemy mines and guiding in friendly ships.[21] A minewatching organization was established.[22] Booms were sent to Mauritius to protect the ports.[23] Mines were laid around the coast; in April 1942 HMS *Manchester City* arrived from the Cape on mine-laying duties at Grand Port, as later did HMS *Brittany*.[24] Work was undertaken to install a fresh water supply and a pier at Grand Port, and to build permanent accommodation for Controlled Mining Personnel (tasks undertaken by the Mauritius Civil Labour Battalion).

Lieutenant General Sir William Platt, Commander-in-Chief EAC, visited his new command in January 1943 to inspect its defences, accompanied by Air Vice Marshall H. E. P. Wigglesworth, Air Officer Commanding East Africa.[25] Many changes resulted, chief among them the 1943 update of the Mauritius Defence Scheme, the takeover of all Mauritian armed forces by the imperial government and the arrival of a battalion of imperial troops to beef up the defences. Platt's view was that local troops were 'not sufficient to defend more than selected points of particular importance'.[26] At least one brigade group was needed to defend the island properly. The island was divided into two defence areas, the first covering the Grand Port-Plaisance area (the main port and the RNAS) and the second covering the Port Louis–Tombeau Bay area (the second port and the flying-boat base). There were important inland sites to be defended; an armaments depot in the Midlands, a torpedo depot at Floreal, an explosives store at Rose Belle and the Admiralty Wireless Telegraphy (W/T) station.[27]

Locally raised troops could not be expected to do all of this alone in the event of enemy attack. Late in 1943 the island was divided into seven defence areas, each the responsibility of a Mauritius Regiment unit, with a mobile reserve based at Abercromby Barracks, Vacoas (Vacoas was, and still is, 'the garrison town of Mauritius and rather like Aldershot without the Odeon').[28] Platt's visit led to the transfer of the 1st Battalion The Mauritius Regiment to Madagascar as part of the Diego Suarez garrison, to be replaced by a battalion of more experienced KAR troops.

Another result of Lieutenant General Platt and Air Vice Marshal Wigglesworth's visit was the total reorganization of the various military units of Mauritius. Platt recommended that the MTF and the Home Guard be taken over by the War Office with retrospective effect from 1 July 1942 (including financial responsibility). This meant that the MTF – now renamed the Mauritius Regiment (MR) – became liable for service overseas as it was now an imperial unit. A separate Mauritius Artillery and Mauritius Pioneer Corps was maintained, and a Mauritius Labour Corps formed for the Navy's and RAF's internal defence works.[29] The Mauritius Coastal Regiment of the Mauritius Artillery had been formed in December 1942.[30] The Home Guard was disbanded and reformed as the Mauritius Defence Force (MDF), with a strength of 1500.[31] A general stepping up of Home Guard strengths had been encouraged by the Colonial Office in a circular to all Governors. Given the situation that had pertained in Malaya before its conquest by the Japanese, and the people's apparent indifference at the prospect of the Japanese replacing the British, it was considered a good idea to associate the people of the colonies more actively with their own defence.[32]

The Colonial Office approved Platt's proposals for the restructuring of the island's defence forces and their transfer to imperial command.[33] The Governor (who had attended the same school, Marlborough) wholeheartedly supported the reorganization, particularly as there had been confusion for too long as to the control of the MTF. Mackenzie Kennedy had been struck by anomalies in the command of the forces based on Mauritius, involving both civil and military authorities.[34] From now on the War Office, through its regional representative the Commander-in-Chief EAC, would assume unhindered control.

Local defence initiatives

Upon his arrival as Governor in July 1942 Sir Donald Mackenzie Kennedy (former Governor of Nyasaland) determined to prepare the island for invasion (Sir Bede Clifford had left to become Governor of Trinidad in April). He wanted to work up the Civil Defence Service to the highest possible state of readiness, deeming this necessary given the island's isolation, the lack of rapid sea communications and the 'temper and habits of its people' which made it almost impossible to build an effective organization quickly.[35] The Governor attacked those on the island who complained that it was all too much 'fuss and bother ... too much khaki and guns'. In a speech at the Plaza Theatre in Rose Hill he said that the high state of military preparedness would be maintained 'until it is certain that the Japanese are in full retreat'.[36] Mauritius became an island in uniform. There were over a dozen different war-related organizations vying for both male and female volunteers: the Civil Labour Corps, Pioneer Corps, RAF, Royal Engineers, RASC, Mauritius Regiment, Mauritius Artillery, Coastal Defence Squadron, Auxiliary Police, Mauritius Signals, Mauritius Air Force, ARP, Free French Forces, Czech Army, Jewish Brigade (both recruiting among the 1700 Jewish detainees), Women's Volunteer Corps, Malaria Field Unit, Red Cross (by August 1942 there were 25 Red Cross detachments and 50 First Aid posts)[37], Child Welfare Society and the Nutrition Demonstration Unit. The Phoenix Military Camp was opened for the first time since 1918, St Joseph's College in Curepipe became a Military Hospital under the East African Army Medical Corps (EAAMC), a camp was built at Plaisance for the Mauritius Labour Corps, a Recruitment and Training Base for the RPC was opened outside Port Louis, new MTF camps were built (including that at Cannoniers Point) and tented Home Guard bases sprung up, such as that at Grand Bay. The high visibility of the military was reinforced by frequent parades and public events.

War led to an extension of the colonial state's knowledge of its people and to a greater interference in their lives. To aid the efficient employment of Mauritian labour, the National Service Office was created in June 1942, followed by a Manpower Board. In December 1943 the 'Review of Manpower' estimated that 64 000 men of between 16 and 50 years of age were employed as agricultural field labourers. Government departments employed 6350, the MDF and Civil Defence Service 2500, and docks and sugar factories a further 8200. Commerce employed 21 840 and the defence works undertaken by the Mauritius Labour Corps employed over 7000.

Mauritius was walking a manpower tightrope. The Review of Manpower estimated Army requirements for 1944 to be 2744. If the East African Army Service Corps (EAASC) was to reopen recruitment for shoemakers, tailors, clerks and printers (Mauritius had agreed to supply these special categories to EAC), an additional 1800 men would be required. The Governor noted the disturbing fact that over 80 per cent of the eligible men were found to be medically unfit for military enlistment.[38] The war might lead to further demands on Mauritian labour as Ceylon needed workers and was considering a request to Mauritius.[39]

Civil defence measures were surprisingly widespread, mirroring those in Britain. Given the colony's exposed position, Mauritius had more to worry about than many other colonies. ARP measures were in place across the island, with sirens installed at police stations and shelters marked in towns. 'The island's bridges were cited as points of refuge in case of air raids and access steps were constructed on the banks of streams. The letters ARP were painted on signs with red arrows'.[40] Street lamps were shaded and ARP patrols ensured observance of the blackout, particularly on the coast.[41] Air-raid information was distributed in the form of a pamphlet issued by the ARP Constable and the Commissioner of Police[42] (ARP handbooks first arrived in December 1939).[43] There were invasion scares on numerous occasions and some of the island's wealthier families constructed trenches and air-raid shelters in their gardens.[44] In March 1943 the Governor presented the Council of Government with plans for the evacuation of Port Louis in the event of invasion. The Labour Department had prepared a scheme for the evacuation of Port Louis involving transport, feeding and evacuation centres, and the construction of camps for 15 000 evacuees.[45]

A Military Ambulance Service was started in July 1941, when 14 cars were converted into mobile medical units. An armoured train was built for troop movements and the fire-fighting services were amalgamated under Government control from September 1943:[46]

> When war broke out it soon became evident that the unconnected [fire] services were not in a position to render efficient assistance in the event of an attack. Consequently, the Controller of the Passive Air Defence Service was empowered to co-ordinate the activities of all the Brigades to ensure adequate protection to the whole island.[47]

In November 1941 a Compulsory Service order gave the Governor the power of conscription for defence purposes. As a direct reaction to the entry of Japan into the war the following month, Home Guard and Coastal Defence forces were created.[48] The latter chartered 30-foot power-engined vessels and its 'duties [were] to patrol the entrances through the reefs and [to] give alarm by rocket or other means' if enemy vessels were sighted. The new naval force was to patrol and mount guard on the breaks in the island's natural front line of defence, its encircling coral reef.

Thus the island prepared to meet an invader. Further measures were taken. The police were mobilized as a paramilitary force for emergency defence duties in October 1941.[49] The entry of Japan into the war led to a strengthening of the police force, and the Commissioner of Police became the Officer Commanding Field Force. The police force doubled in size as a result of the war. An Auxiliary Police force was created in April 1942 for defence purposes, like the manning of coastal look-out posts. The police were armed and given military training. The Governor wanted legislation to make the police liable for military duty. The Colonial Office reacted cautiously to such legislation and its likely effects, and decreed that it could only apply to new recruits and to existing policemen who submitted voluntarily.[50] The Colonial Office had to temper the autocratic tendencies of Governors in a time of war, as it had done in previous conflicts.[51]

Mauritius was put to other military uses. Early in the war the Mauritian Electricity Department organized a school to train wireless operators for the RAF, recruited from March 1941 by newspaper advertisement. The Army established a Signals Training Centre and Reginald Sheldon was sent from Kenya to oversee it.[52] The colony's Observatory was requisitioned by the RAF for military meteorological work after the East and Central Africa Meteorological Service was extended to include Mauritius. At the Plaisance aerodrome 'forecasting for aviation was principally carried out', and A. Walter visited the lesser dependencies in order to link the islands to the network of meteorological wireless reporting stations that spanned the Indian Ocean.[53]

To support the RAF a Mauritius Volunteer Air Force (Marine Crafts Section) was created to service flying boats in Mauritian territorial waters. In February 1945 the Mauritius Women's Volunteer Corps was founded for service with the ATS and sent to Egypt via South Africa in April 1945.[54] Aware of South African racial sensitivities, Colonel C. M. Ross of the General Staff asked the Quartermaster General South Africa if 200 coloured members of the Mauritian Women's Volunteer Corps en route to the Middle East could be accommodated in South Africa, as no direct passage was possible and no suitable accommodation was available on the East African mainland.[55] The Quartermaster General replied that this could not be arranged due to a shortage of shipping, and suggested an alternative route via India![56] The women finally left Mauritius aboard the *Franconia,* to work as clerks, telephonists and nurses.

The Mauritius Civil Labour Corps

Throughout the colonial empire – despite Whitehall embarrassment – conscription for war-related work on the home front was common. Conscription was introduced by ordinance in Northern Rhodesia

Southern Rhodesia, and Kenya; for the tin mines of the Jos plateau in Nigeria and the construction and maintenance of the infrastructure that saw West Africa become a strategic highway supplying the fighting in the Middle East; and for the plantations of Tanganyika producing vital crops like pyrethrum and sisal.

In 1942 Mauritius followed these colonies when the Government was empowered to conscript civilian labour. The Mauritius Civil Labour Corps was created to provide labour for defensive works required by the RAF and Royal Navy. Behind the formation of the Corps was also the need to regulate the labour supply to ensure that military, subsistence and export agricultural requirements were met. In preparing legislation for the creation of the Civil Labour Corps the Governor examined legislation promulgated elsewhere in the empire, like the Northern Rhodesian Emergency Powers (African Labour Corps) Regulations of 1942. He proposed a Civil Labour Corps formed on a compulsory basis (without prejudice to volunteers) under Edward Twining as Controller.[57] All departments were to indent for labour on this organization.

Sensitive as ever to issues of colonial conscription, especially on an island with a history of slavery and indentured labour and with the 1937 riots fresh in the memory, the Colonial Office found the Governor's proposals 'not acceptable in their present form'. Compulsion was only to be used if directly related to *essential* war work and not if results were obtainable without compulsion. 'Forced labour' was not countenanced by the Colonial Office.[58] The labour troubles of 1937 had led to the creation of a Labour Department to try and address grievances and neutralize popular support for the newly formed Mauritius Labour Party (MLP).[59] The creation of Labour Departments was encouraged by the Colonial Office in the 1930s, and receipt of aid under the 1940 Colonial Development and Welfare Act (CDWA) was made contingent upon adequate labour legislation.[60]

Despite metropolitan sensitivities, the Governor insisted on the need for conscription for civil and military purposes (the Aborigines Protection Society objected to the Corps).[61] In May 1942 he telegraphed the Colonial Office stating that 12 000 skilled and unskilled labourers were wanted by the OCT for War Office, Admiralty and Air Ministry defence works.[62] The OCT also wanted conscription into the Royal Artillery for the defence of Mauritius and its dependencies. A call for volunteers could not be made 'without seriously interfering with the production of sugar, the cultivation of food and the general economic life of the Colony'.[63] The Governor therefore announced regulations under the Emergency Powers (Colonial Defence) Orders-in-Council, 1939–40.

The need for adequate labour supplies for domestic food production, sugar production and the military elicited a great deal of bureaucratic planning. In 1943 a Manpower Board was established when the Labour Corps was created by Statute (and its membership placed under quasi-military discipline).[64] Recruitment for the Pioneer Corps had to be suspended.[65] Edward Twining reviewed the island's labour situation with Colonial Office officials on a visit to London in August 1943.[66] Twining reported that demand for defence works on the island was at its peak – over 8000 were employed by the Civil Labour Corps. Recruitment for the Corps on a voluntary basis without any disciplinary sanctions had been tried and had failed. Absenteeism and 'industrial inefficiency' were prevalent in the Mauritian labour force. Before the war, men had not been accustomed to working more than four days a week. These were the reasons Twining gave for conscription. To mobilize Mauritian manpower, an Occupational Register (of all men between 16 and 50 years of age) was compiled and the National Service Office created in June 1942. Its task was to meet the demand for labour for defence and other purposes without unduly disturbing estate labour and military enlistment.[67]

The Mauritius Territorial Force and the imperial garrison

The Mauritius Garrison was established in 1810. It was supplemented in 1935 by the creation of the MTF. However, in 1942 it was considered – given the Japanese threat – that the imperial garrison needed strengthening. The garrison's primary role had been to man the island's artillery defences, but with invasion likely infantry was needed. Though by mid-1943 the MR consisted of two infantry battalions, it was considered too untested to be fit for the task of defending the island against the Japanese. The Governor called the 1500 men of the MDF a 'comic force', and MR officer Alfred North-Coombes considered them 'toy soldiers' and a 'waste of money'.[68] Whitehall's confidence in locally raised forces was also low (see the episode involving HMS *Liverpool* in Chapter 1).[69]

The Mauritius Garrison was commanded by the Officer Commanding Troops. Major A. Smith gave way in 1943 to Colonel H. G. Veasey (formerly Commanding Officer of the 2nd Battalion The Northern Rhodesia Regiment). Then from Kenya came Colonel Ronald Yeldham.[70] The war years 'were years of revival for the Mauritius

Garrison. In early 1944, for example, it had about 80 officers, and some 20 Queen Alexandra's Imperial Military Nursing Service (QAIMNS) sisters for military hospitals'.[71] To illustrate the wartime expansion, the RASC establishment increased from five to ninety men.[72]

The Governor believed that the MTF could not be counted upon to defend the island in the event of a Japanese attack, partly because of pro-Vichy and anti-British sentiment among its white members. In the Governor's eyes, the loyalty and morale of the MTF, and therefore its efficiency, were doubtful. This was one of the factors leading to the swap of the 1st Battalion The Mauritius Regiment with a battalion of the KAR. However, other factors were present. The Governor was almost certainly keen to get 'his' soldiers overseas in pursuit of glory for the colony, and the Commander of the 1st Battalion The Mauritius Regiment, Lieutenant Colonel Yates, was itching to take his Battalion to a more active theatre.

In May 1942 the Colonial Secretary Sydney Moody told Whitehall of reports from the OCT that the majority of white conscripts at Fort George were openly pro-Vichy and anti-British, and undesirable as soldiers.[73] Though Moody considered fears of mutiny exaggerated, the situation was serious. At the time there were 611 local troops (this was before the expansion of the MTF in 1943). Of these, 291 were volunteers, the other 320 conscripts – and the 123 whites among them were mostly pro-Vichy. At Fort George, where white troops were stationed in the Artillery, there were 111 imperial and 72 local troops. Of these local troops, 31 were conscripts and pro-Vichy. This also applied to white conscripts in Diego Garcia and Rodrigues. Unofficial members of the Council of Government considered the defence of the island to be an imperial responsibility and objected to local lives being jeopardized by military service.

The issue appeared again in 1945, when the OCT decided that the Coastal Regiment was no longer needed.[74] It consisted of 255 whites and 530 non-whites. The Government wanted 162 of the whites transferred to East Africa on the unit's disbandment. The Governor received a deputation of leading Franco-Mauritians attempting to prevent this. They said that morale among the whites at Fort George was poor because of lower pay than British troops, and a feeling that whites had born the brunt of conscription in Mauritius. The Colonial Office was unimpressed by these reasons and the general attitude of which they were a manifestation. E. E. Sabben-Clare minuted that the white community 'do not appear in a good light'.[75] It was pointed out that overseas service would secure Mauritian servicemen the same rate of pay as British troops and that virtually all of the Mauritians serving overseas were non-white. The Colonial Office also recalled that resentment of the fact that whites were not being sent overseas was one of the main causes of the 1944 Madagascar mutiny of the 1st Battalion The Mauritius Regiment (see Chapter 5).

In July 1942 the Colonial Office passed on this information to the War Office, especially the recommendation that imperial troops were needed to 'stiffen morale'.[76] The uniqueness of the colony with regard to the Franco-Mauritians was highlighted. T. I. K. Lloyd of the Colonial Office wrote that 'there is little doubt that the political attitudes of the Franco-Mauritians has impeded the growth of an active loyalty to this country among the people as a whole'. Recruitment for the Pioneers had been successful because of the high pay in comparison with local rates, but on the question of combat service, 'the picture is hardly reassuring'. Out of a population of 400 000, only 300 volunteers had come forward for combat service and many of them were openly pro-Vichy. The Governor rued the fact that not enough effort had been made in the past to Anglicize the island. Instead, the island suffered under the 'entrenched and infective' position of the French elite.

Some Franco-Mauritian conscripts refused to swear an oath of allegiance to the Crown when joining the British Army. The OCT said that such men would be charged with treason.[77] However, Whitehall considered it improper to insist on oath-taking in the first place, given that British conscripts were not so obliged.[78] In backing the OCT's position, 'the Mauritius Government has got itself into an awkward predicament'.[79] The Colonial Office thought it 'unfortunate that the Officer Commanding Troops should have threatened these men with consequences which cannot be brought about'.[80]

To provide a more realistic level of protection against invasion, Lieutenant General Platt ordered a KAR battalion to Mauritius. Its arrival in late 1943 was hardly welcomed, especially as the ship from which it disembarked was immediately loaded with the 1st Battalion MR. Many MR soldiers were unwilling to leave their home island and strongly resented being relieved by African troops. The barefoot African soldiers marched from the wharf with their red fezzes and puttees, stopping first at Bell Village, the Pioneer Corps base, then moving on to the Vacoas barracks. Recalled today by all elderly Mauritians, the African soldiers are universally referred to as 'KAR' (few knowing the expansion of the acronym) or as 'Zulus', reflecting a common feeling in Mauritius that Africans were racially inferior.

The KAR was housed in permanent barracks in Curepipe. The 30 or so officers lived well and were entertained by the local white community. Given the style in which affluent whites lived, some officers could be forgiven for thinking that the war had not yet arrived in Mauritius. There were dinners, bathing and cocktail parties, tennis and sundowners, dances, stag hunting and the club life common to elite colonial society. As army doctor Rex Salisbury Woods put it:

> At Diego Suarez we heard of Mauritius as a remote haven for brigadiers from Nairobi who periodically dropped in on us when returning from inspecting this strategic outpost bringing back rare nostalgic merchandize such as golf balls, watches, fountain pens, lipstick, and silk stockings.[81]

Edward Mayne, a KAR signals officer, recalled the friendliness of the inhabitants, though 'one discordant note occurred when the RAF bought up the entire stock of golf balls in Mauritius and exported them to Kenya!'.[82]

But it was not all fun and games, though one can understand the feelings of servicemen in war zones when regarding those posted to regions beyond the fighting line. Lieutenant J. F. C. Harrison was dismayed to discover that his troops were to have a role in civil policing when Mauritius experienced serious labour unrest and disturbances in 1943–44. The riots were partially motivated by declining dietary standards caused by the war and the runaway inflation that devalued wages. Harrison's 'company was sent to a village to quell what was designated a riot. When we arrived, in full battle order and with fixed bayonets, we found a small crowd of miserable-looking Tamils who shook their fists at us and threw a few stones'.[83] Two weeks later, KAR troops were marched around the whole island in full battle kit to 'show the flag'.

Even with the departure of the 1st Battalion MR to Madagascar in December 1943, the 2nd Battalion remained on the island as a reserve but also fulfilling its traditional role as an infantry shield in case of invasion. It undertook a considerable amount of patrolling around the coast. North-Coombes records how his company would send out two patrols a night from Cannoniers Point to go to the look-out post at Mount Choisy, then on to Cap Malheureux before returning to camp.[84] Training exercises were mounted in which various stages of invasion alarm would be rehearsed – for example an 'alarm purple practice' in 'Port Louis saw "C" Company in Marching Order moving to their defence stations'.[85] There were a few invasion scares, as when the Coastal Defence Squadron accidentally gave an 'alarm red' signal which brought troops of the MTF out from Abercromby Barracks to Mont Choisy on the coast.[86]

Fortifications

The longest established feature of home defence in Mauritius was its coastal fortifications. Over the centuries Mauritius had been fortified by the Dutch, French and British, and the fortifications were considerably enhanced during the war. It had always been a strategic base liable to naval attack, and in 1810 the British had considered it sufficiently defended to require an invasion force of 10 000 troops.

During the Second World War particular attention was paid to the gun battery protecting Grand Port, the main naval port. No. 1 Coast Battery manned the guns on Ile de la Passe defending the main channel into Grand Port. The Dutch had first fortified this point in 1752. Twelve-pounder and 90-mm guns were mounted and accommodation for over a hundred men constructed. No. 2 Coast Battery manned 6-inch guns with a range of 5000 yards and searchlights with a range of two miles on Ile aux Aigrettes. The other east-coast batteries were at Pionte a Diable and Pointe aux Feuilles. The latter base housed fuel reserves, searchlights and guns. A tug boat would drag a floating target before the east-coast batteries for target practice.[87] The Pointe aux Feuilles site comprised observation posts, a buried magazine, semi-buried barracks, offices and a generator complex.[88] The fuel reserves and large jetty were situated at nearby Bois des Amourettes where the Royal Navy oil tanks still stand.

Fort George protected Port Louis with a four-gun battery supported by coast artillery searchlights and fighting lights. High above the city on Signal Mountain a range-finder battery and radar unit aided the accuracy of the guns and the detection of approaching vessels. The guns had a range of 24 000 yards. In the early days of the war Fort George had two 6-inch guns manned by 150 Franco-Mauritians from 'A' Company of the MTF, and four 6-pounders directed at the port and manned by about a hundred British soldiers of the Royal Artillery.[89] When Lieutenant General Platt visited the island in January 1943, he is reported to have said that Fort George's gunnery was the best in EAC, and the Fort won the Command gunnery competition.[90] Before being allowed into Port Louis harbour, ships had to identify themselves and the Examination Battery of the Port War Signal Station had to grant permission.[91] Coastal artillery duties in support of the Royal Artillery garrison troops were the main task assigned to 'A' Company (the white company) of the MTF. There was also a look-out post on Lion Mountain 'to keep watch on aerial manoeuvres, and a group of Franco-Mauritians trained in semaphore and Morse code telegraphy were installed at Queens Point'.[92] The forces defending Mauritius took part in regular training exercises. Operation 'Sugarcane' 'simulated the disembarkation with a regiment acting as invaders and another defending the territory'.[93] In May 1944 Mauritius Coastal Regiment 'limpet exercises' (featuring reports of enemy submarines, seaplanes and bombing) caused seven deaths.

Another important MTF role was to garrison the Mauritian dependencies. The Governor told London that Mauritius would pay for the defence of its mini-empire in the Indian Ocean. On 20 April 1941 the first MTF contingent was sent to Diego Garcia.[94] As the last chapter showed, Diego Garcia was an important naval base and cable station. Rodrigues had a large population and was a link in the imperial cable communications chain. A company and a half of the MTF garrisoned the island from 21 December 1940.[95] A 6-inch gun battery was mounted on the hill at Creve Coeur, manned by Mauritian, then Rodriguan, gunners.[96] In 1943 a 55-mm anti-submarine gun was mounted on Point Venus to protect the cable and wireless station. There were 180 officers and men; 215 Rodriguans were employed on the island by the military, 350 left as Pioneers and some served on Diego Garcia. In line with general defence reductions following the decline of Japanese offensive power, in December 1943 Lieutenant Colonel Rogers of the Rhodesia Rifles visited Rodrigues to review its Defence Scheme. As a result of his recommendations, the Rodrigues company of the 2nd Battalion MR was reduced from six to three light machine-gun platoons.[97]

The Special Operations Executive and the scorched earth policy

The SOE was established on the orders of Winston Churchill to promote subversive warfare in enemy-occupied territory.[98] Given the Nazi conquest of most of Europe, it was intended to keep the fires of resistance smouldering in occupied territories by organizing acts of sabotage and gathering intelligence. SOE activities were extended to non-European theatres.[99] In Africa it countered enemy subterfuge, smuggling, and efforts to disrupt British commercial and industrial centres such as the goldfields of the Rand. British intelligence was involved in monitoring and countering the work of enemy spy networks, like that active in Portuguese East Africa.

Mauritius became the first colony to have an SOE organization, intended to harry the enemy should the island be conquered. This is an aspect of SOE history that has been overlooked by those who have acted so successfully as the guardians of the organization's historical record.[100] The link between Mauritius and the SOE was initiated by Governor Sir Bede Clifford. His support for the SOE's African organization won him its high praise. The SOE had to struggle against opposition in Whitehall and inter-service jealousies on the part of the secret services and the military. It was noted at the Colonial Office – with a distinct air of disapproval – that the SOE was becoming 'quite as independent as the RAF' after its foundation in the First World War. There was only limited liaison between the SOE and the War Office, the latter department being 'always keen to pick a quarrel' with intelligence forces.[101]

When Donald Mackenzie Kennedy arrived as Governor in July 1942 he was accompanied by Captain Michael Adams of the Ministry of Economic Warfare, the Whitehall department supervising the SOE. The new Governor had already worked with the SOE whilst Governor of Nyasaland. The operation and support of a covert military organization on colonial soil was a new departure for the Colonial Office. An official considered that it might be successful in Mauritius, 'but I doubt whether it could be done effectively by Africans and I would not want to encourage African colonies to make similar arrangements'.[102]

Captain Michael Adams was SOE agent D.Z.11, an Oxford-educated lawyer, who had previously served the SOE in Rome, Greece, Crete, Egypt and South Africa. There, in January 1942 he joined the SOE's Todd Mission, which had Madagascar as its principal target. In June 1942 he took over the SOE station in Mauritius. In his own words:

> Principal targets: penetration of unoccupied Madagascan territory from East coast; penetration of Reunion; establishment and training of post-occupation sabotage and clandestine W/T organization in Mauritius, against Japanese invasion.[103]

After leaving Mauritius he worked for the SOE in Portuguese East Africa establishing a chain of W/T stations along the coast, 'for passing reports of enemy submarines etc directly to the Navy'.[104]

The Mauritian SOE team was established as a self-contained unit under the overall control of the SOE's Todd mission in East and Southern Africa. If the island was invaded, it was to destroy civil and military supplies and installations such as the Admiralty areas and the furnaces and boilers vital to the sugar industry.[105] Provision was also made for the covert maintenance of contact with outside British authorities. It was to collect intelligence and 'maintain contact and sources of information if the Japanese occupied' the island. A network of prostitutes in Port Louis was organized to garner information about enemy movements and intentions from 'off duty' Japanese soldiers.[106] Arrangements were made with Post Office staff to keep the SOE informed of the movement of Japanese warships should the port fall to the enemy. The director – who the SOE was reluctant to name even to the Colonial Office – was Philip Raffray, owner of 'a vast estate' that fringed the coast and could be used for the secret disembarkation and concealment of SOE reinforcements. When in June 1942 the SOE finally revealed his identity to the Colonial Office, it insisted upon absolute secrecy.[107] The Colonial Office's first impression was that Raffray was 'such a staunch supporter of our cause [that he] would be one of the first to be put under surveillance'.[108] The SOE team consisted of a Director, Deputy Director, a W/T section, an intelligence section, a political section and 'toys experts' (weapons and explosives experts).

The Ministry of Economic Warfare was pleased with this pioneering arrangement. It was considered 'especially encouraging to the head of our East African Mission [who] has in mind initiating similar schemes in other British territories in his charter area'.[109] Enthusiasm was dampened somewhat by the Colonial Office's warning that if SOE operations and plans for post-occupational 'guerrilla activities' in the East African colonies were to be undertaken, they would have to be pursued in consultation with EAC. The Commander-in-Chief EAC, Lieutenant General Platt, was not an admirer of the SOE.[110]

Like all colonies, Mauritius had a Defence Scheme that included a scorched earth policy to be pursued in the event of invasion. Installations to be 'denied' to the enemy included the wireless transmitters, Admiralty oil fuel tanks, dock facilities, quays, wharfage, rum warehouses and the island's tugs.[111] The RNAS at Plaisance was to be destroyed, as were all reserves of coal. The SOE intended to destroy all power stations as Mauritius was likely to be of considerable use to Japan as a naval base.[112] The Governor pointed out that it was difficult to destroy things without adequate explosives, estimating that one shipyard would take 500 men four hours with heavy hammers and fire to destroy.[113]

There was resistance from the Council of Government to one pre-invasion precaution, the policy of distributing food supplies throughout the island in order to prevent large stocks falling to the Japanese in one fell swoop. The Government viewed this as yet another example of the Franco-Mauritian community's inability to see beyond its selfish interests. It noted with exasperation that 'unofficial members seem more afraid of a free for all among the Indian population, if foodstuffs were distributed, than of the Japanese themselves ... Obvious[ly] their desire is to remain neutral'.[114] The Governor reported that the unofficial members of the Council were:

> emphatically and unanimously opposed to the destruction or indiscriminate distribution among the population of foodstuffs and refuse to be persuaded ... in support of that policy. They are concerned that owing to the timorous character of the people, any threat of violence from the enemy would induce them to surrender every pound of rice distributed to them and that if rice were destroyed by us, they would not believe this but would mob-raid the houses of the upper-classes in search for hidden food and do violence to the occupants.[115]

The unofficial members believed that the distribution of foodstuffs would lead to riots.[116] The episode demonstrates the power of local bodies to thwart British policy and the need for accommodation between British officials and representatives of local elites if maximum support for the war effort was to be secured (in the light of the hunger marches later in the war and the widespread belief that the Government was concealing vast stocks of food, the attitude of the Council of Government seems understandable).

Much of the rice supply had already been distributed, though the bulk remained in the fire-proof granary where it would take days to destroy, even by the simple expedient of dumping it into the sea. Stores distributed over the island were kept under the supervision of police and the Home Guard.[117] The Secretary of State said that there was no intention to destroy the food, but that it must be distributed.[118] The Ministry of Economic Warfare and the Ministry of Food were consulted and replied that there was no wish to press for destruction given the attitude of the people, but that as much food should be distributed as possible.[119]

Although invasion never came, it will be seen from the evidence presented in this chapter that there were surprisingly thorough local and imperial precautions taken to provide for the island's defence, as an exposed imperial outpost needing the extension of a protective wing of empire, and as a military base capable of aiding offensive action. With the passing of the Japanese threat, the guard could be relaxed, for British supremacy in the Indian Ocean was not to be overturned. In November 1943 the SOE told the Colonial Office that it wanted to close down its Mauritius operation, as 'the moment of danger for Mauritius has passed'. The organization was costing the SOE £6700 per annum.[120] Little more than a seaborne raid was considered likely, and so the SOE's Mauritian outfit was liquidated in December 1943. In 1944 the Admiralty approved a decrease in the Controlled Minefield (Mining Station) at Grand Port to a care and maintenance basis, and downgraded work on military infrastructure throughout its Indian Ocean bases.

Likewise, the home defence formations were terminated as the threat of invasion receded, as happened in Britain where the Home Guard stood down in September 1944. The Mauritius Coastal Defence Squadron stood down in November 1944. In the same month it was decided that there was no reason for retaining the MDF. The Governor believed that the force would be little use in a civil emergency and that there was negligible social benefit in men serving in the formation.[121] The Colonial Office consulted the War Office and the MDF was disbanded on the final day of 1944. In November 1946 the Women's Volunteer Corps was dissolved. In one particular sphere, however, Mauritians were to continue to perform a military role. Mauritians became the mainstay of the Royal Pioneer Corps supporting British land forces in the Middle East where they were to remain until 1956. The following chapter chronicles their participation in the region, dating from 1940.

4
Colonial Military Labour in Europe and the Middle East

The most valuable military contribution of the colonial empire to the war effort of 1939–45 was its provision of the military labour force upon which imperial troops fighting in the Middle East and Southern Europe depended.[1] In North and East Africa, the British had by early 1941 extinguished the imperial ambitions and the core of the military forces of Italy through spectacular victories in Libya, Abyssinia and Somaliland. Yet these bold successes were overshadowed by the arrival of General Rommel in February 1941 to command the Afrika Korps, and his successful attacks prolonged the desert war for many months.[2]

The British inability to hold the spoils of their early victories was largely due to the distractions of the Greece campaign that led to the break up of the hitherto victorious Eighth Army. The stage was set for the titanic desert struggle that see-sawed across Egypt, Libya and Tunisia, and that eventually – after many thrusts counter thrusts, and false dawns – went decisively the British way after the second battle of El Alamein in October 1942. After the Anglo-American landings in Morocco in 1943 the Axis powers were removed from Africa and the Allied focus shifted to the Mediterranean and the invasion of Southern Europe. The British army that fought these battles was a truly imperial army, comprised of Indian, New Zealand, Australian, British and South African infantry and armoured divisions. What is seldom realized is that a host of colonies provided the logistical support that sustained them. These were the men of the RPC and other service branches such as the RASC. Major histories of the war in the region fail to acknowledge Pioneer labour and the role of colonial troops in providing it.[3]

Egypt, particularly the Suez Canal Zone, was the British empire's main military base and the 'largest military complex of its kind'.[4] MEC, with its headquarters in Cairo, covered a vast area bristling with various threats to British territories and vital British strategic interests – to British East Africa, Egypt, the Suez Canal, the oil of Arabia and the Gulf, the Eastern Mediterranean and to the Balkans. 'Set up in 1939, Wavell's MEC encompassed nine countries and parts of two continents, an area 1700 miles by 2000 miles'.[5] The whole of North Africa and East Africa (where Italy threatened with massive armies) came under MEC. In the Middle East, MEC had to contend with the Vichy position in Syria, German influence in Turkey and Iraq, Mussolini's war against Greece and Germany's attacks on Greece and Crete. MEC:

> formed the connecting cog round which revolved the great wheels of the allied coalition. It joined Britain to India and the Far East; British and American factories (through Persia) with soldiers of the Red Army; Africa and Asia. It was Russia's southern flank; it was the moral and physical prop that kept wobbling Turkey out of the Axis ... And above all, in Iraq and Persia, it contained the oilfields without which the British armed forces would be paralysed.[6]

MEC and its subsidiary Central Mediterranean Forces (CMF) required a vast military labour pool in order to operate. This was provided by prisoners-of-war (POW), civilian labourers (many were Libyans) and by a massive colonial army recruited into the RPC and other British Army service branches. The tasks were legion; transporting and unloading supplies for forward fighting formations; dock work; building and repairing military infrastructure on a fluid battle front (bridges, docks, airstrips, tank traps, railways, roads); camouflaging vehicles and supply dumps; building dummy tanks; movement deception measures; guarding supply dumps from a sometimes acquisitive local population; building up those supply dumps; guarding prisoners; forming fire-fighting and military salvage units; providing garrison troops in base areas; and providing a range of craftsmen, from drivers to carpenters and metal workers.[7] Mauritian Pioneer Corps troops served in Egypt, Libya, Tunisia, Palestine, Malta, Sicily and Italy, and formed part of the Order of Battle of the Eighth Army from its creation.

In 1942 Iran and Iraq were transferred to MEC from India Command given the prospect of German invasion through the Caucasus (the overland Russian threat to India had traditionally kept Persia, Iraq and the Arabian Gulf in India's sphere). Iraq had been invaded by British empire forces in April 1941 to counter rising German influence and to protect the British air base at Habbaniya. In 1942 Persia was invaded by Britain and Russia, and the Shah sent into exile (spending months in Mauritius). A Persia and Iraq Command (PAIFORCE) was formed in August 1942 with Tenth Army at its core, as German victories against Russia made it likely that the Caucasus would be crossed and the oilfields of Iraq and Persia destroyed or seized by the enemy (in 1940 Persia's oil output was 8.4 million tons and 'vital to Britain's war effort').[8] The region was also an important conduit for Lend-Lease to Russia (23.8 per cent of aid delivered to Russia went through the Persian Gulf).[9] EAC was formed towards the end of 1941 as the threat of Japan loomed, removing the burden from MEC.

As for the armies under these commands (that the colonial Pioneers supported), Eighth Army was formed in September 1941 with the Western Desert Force at its core. After victory in Africa, Eighth Army took part in the invasion of Southern Europe and the Pioneers followed its advance. Ninth and Tenth Armies were formed within MEC to counter the threat of German advances across the Caucasus, but 'never numbered more than a few divisions, never saw combat as a formed body [because the Germans did not advance], and were used instead to reinforce the Eighth Army'.[10]

Without Pioneers, fighting could not have taken place, let alone been sustained. The 21st Army Group that was responsible for the empire's D-Day contribution (British and Canadian armies) serves as an example. In August 1944, two months after the Normandy landings, 56 per cent of the troops were fighting men and the other 44 per cent belonged to the 'services' – the units that supported the fighting troops.[11] Of the 660 000 personnel involved, only 14 per cent were infantry soldiers; 10 per cent alone were from the RPC. In planning for D-Day it was estimated that for every division (approximately 16 000 men) ashore, there would be another 25 000 men in the theatre as corps, army, headquarters and lines of communications troops.[12]

Logistics – the movement and supply of army units across battle zones – has been a neglected subject of study in the history of war, and the Pioneer Corps role in logistics has received scant attention.[13] Unlike the British, having no base in north Africa and no chance of finding useful material in the barren desert, all Axis supplies had to be shipped from Italy across the Mediterranean, a sea in which British naval forces increasingly had the upper hand. In the desert war, all commanders were hampered by the issue of supply. Able to make dashes across the uninhabited sea of desert, their effectiveness turned upon the ability of supplies of food, fuel, water and ammunition to reach them. As the distance between fighting troops and their bases increased, supply lines tautened and supply dumps in the open desert needed to be established and guarded to sustain the fighting. There was no railway beyond Mersa Matruh in Egypt and only one road, running alongside the coast. Therefore ports like Tobruk, Benghazi and Tripoli were great prizes, for they enabled seaborne supplies to reach the occupier. As for the rest of it, as Correlli Barnett writes, 'victory depended on the three-tonner' – the three-hundredweight army lorry.[14]

Pioneers were the essential labour force of the British Army, mentioned as early as 1346 in the Muster of Pay Rolls of the British Garrison at Calais.[15] A Labour Corps was formally raised for the First World War in 1917 when a Labour Directorate was formed 'to co-ordinate the demand for labour and apportioning the available labour as the tactical situation demanded'.[16] Infantry battalions were converted to form the British part of the new Corps,[17] and foreign and imperial manpower was depended upon – a Fijian Labour Detachment was sent to France,[18] as was a Chinese Labour Corps,[19] an Egyptian Labour Corps and a South African Native Labour Contingent.[20] The Mauritius Labour Battalion of 1700 served in Mesopotamia. Of the 791 men of the Seychelles Labour Battalion, 341 died, mostly of disease.[21] By 1918 there were 80 000 British Pioneers and a staggering 1.5 million foreign nationals. The Pioneer Corps badge was created in 1917 – 'a rifle, a shovel and a pick "piled" on them a laurel wreath, all ensigned with a crown. Beneath, the motto *Labor Omnia Vincit* (Work Conquers All)'.[22] An unofficial motto reflecting the Corps' vital role was 'No Labour, No Battle'.[23] The Corps was disbanded in 1919 as 'no nation could afford in peacetime the luxury of a regular Corps of unskilled labour in its Order of Battle'.[24]

The Second World War made huge manpower demands and was the most elaborate logistical deployment in British military history. Not surprisingly it led to the re-creation of the labour corps. In October 1939 Army Order 200 created the Auxiliary Military Pioneer Corps (AMPC), initially formed as a combatant corps.[25] In August 1940 a Directorate of Labour was formed under the Quartermaster General's Department to allocate civilian and military labour for the Army, and the AMPC became the RPC.[26] The 'Auxiliary' in the title was dropped – it was disliked for being non-martial, especially after Pioneers had fought alongside the infantry at Dunkirk.[27] Furthermore, the task of the Pioneers in aiding British fighting formations to engage the enemy after the fall of France was about to become crucial, and it was the colonial empire that was to take the leading role:

> After Dunkirk, the Middle East became the most important base outside of the UK. A Directorate of Labour was formed at GHQ (General Headquarters) Middle East in May 1940. At that time three Pioneer Companies had been formed – two Palestinian and one Cypriot, and the Army was employing about 10 000 civilians ... The Greece and Crete campaigns of April and May 1941 proved extremely costly to the Corps, some 80 per cent (about 50 officers and 4500 men) fell into enemy hands or were listed as missing ... The greater part of the Pioneer Corps in the Middle East had been lost, and we had to begin all over again.[28]

This was where the empire entered the manpower equation. At the outbreak of war the Colonial Office did not envisage large-scale colonial recruitment. On 25 March 1940 the War Cabinet decided that colonial manpower was to be oriented towards agricultural and mineral production at home, and the provision of *local* defence formations (like the MTF) so as to release British troops for service elsewhere.[29] A constraint on raising colonial units in 1939 was the fact that military equipment was in short supply, and this situation was likely to prevail for at least two years. The KAR and Royal West African Frontier Force (RWAFF) were to be maintained as an African Division for possible service in the Middle East and North Africa (there was also the Sudan Defence Force, Somali Camel Corps, Northern Rhodesia Regiment and Rhodesia Rifles).[30] Pioneer labour was envisaged as a task that colonial manpower might be directed towards, though this possibility was to remain in abeyance for the time being.

However, events hijacked this timetable. The fall of France, the belligerence of Italy and British losses in Greece and Crete meant that new sources of Pioneer labour would have to be identified. The Commander-in-Chief MEC urgently appealed for 130 000 military labourers and it was to the colonies that the appeal was directed. By October 1942, MEC was supported by 36 000 men recruited from the High Commission Territories (HCT), 18 400 from West Africa, 30 000 from East Africa, 5600 from Cyprus, 4500 from Palestine and at least 5000 from Mauritius, Rodrigues, and the Seychelles.[31] A total of 40 Indian companies (15 000 men) were raised for service in the Middle East. The Arab Native Labour Corps reached a total strength of 30 000 civilians, and 75 Companies of Italian POWs were employed. Mauritians were the first to arrive in the Middle East as the new colonial 'rear echelon' army was built to provide essential support for military operations in the Middle East, Mediterranean and Southern

Europe.[32] By the end of the war, 166 782 British, 277 809 non-Europeans, and 1 074 932 civilian labourers had served in the Pioneer Corps.[33] The original plan was for HCT Pioneers to support the Ninth Army in Palestine and Syria, whilst those from India, East Africa and the Indian Ocean would work in the Nile Delta and Western Desert in support of the Eighth Army.[34] The 43 Pioneer companies that served with the Eighth Army were divided into labour groups: 62 Group at Tobruk, 59 Group at Fort Capuzzo, 44 Group at Bardira, 55 Group at Sollum, 58 Group at Mischiefa and 73 Group at Mersa Matruh.[35] (One Group comprised six or more Pioneer Corps companies, each company about 350 men strong.)

Recruitment in Mauritius

Recruitment began in the summer of 1940.[36] The first units to be formed were two Pioneer companies and a company for the Royal Engineers, to be known as 741 Artisan Works Company (building tradesmen).[37] Most Mauritians served in Pioneer companies, though there was also a Motor Transport Company and a company of RAOC stevedores. Recruitment for the RPC was voluntary and was to remain a major source of employment for Mauritians until the mid-1950s. This voluntarism contrasts with the conscription needed to find men for the MTF. Mauritians knew that combat was not the purpose of the RPC, whereas the MTF might see service against the Japanese.

Recruitment into the Pioneer Corps 'solved the unemployment problem of dockside labourers'.[38] This was also the case in the Seychelles; in 1945 the Governor, visiting the Seychelles companies in the Middle East and Italy (about 1300 men) asked that the companies not be demobilized hastily, as he was concerned about employment for them upon their return.[39] Mauritian recruits were trained at the Recruiting Centre and Training Camp at Bell Village. The Mauritius Pioneer Training Centre was part of HQ Mauritius Garrison, with a training establishment of three officers and 45 other ranks.[40]

Bell Village, south of Port Louis, had its roots as an experiment in housing for poor labourers. According to the Colonial Office's Labour Adviser it was on a malarious site, was crowded and poorly constructed. However, at the time of his visit in 1943, it was 'serving a useful purpose by providing temporary quarters for troops awaiting shipping' to the Middle East.[41] Understandably, this new concentration of well-paid soldiers attracted entrepreneurial spirits. Shops and eateries flourished around the training camp, encouraged by soldiers' pay and the money of relatives who had moved to be near them. Monaf Fakira recalls an illiterate man who made a business selling Chinese indelible ink for soldiers to write their name, number and company on their kit bags. Others plied their trade as cobblers. There was a surplus of Army food which found its way out of the camp to the eager and often hungry civilian population.[42]

Recruitment was conducted by Army officers and official agents using radio and press propaganda and public meetings in bars and on the sugar estates. An article in the Indo-Mauritian newspaper *Advance,* entitled 'Our War Effort', reported that thousands had offered themselves for the Pioneer Corps, with the 'supply always far in excess of demand'. Over a thousand had already gone, a third batch of Pioneers and Artisans had just enrolled and 200 more drivers were needed. 'Throughout the country there is great enthusiasm to join'.[43] Unlike colonial Africa, Mauritius did not have a network of chiefs or a district administration that could facilitate recruitment. However, it was a compact and densely populated country where rumour and information spread rapidly. Literacy rates were high. Civilian and military authorities broadcast their message using newspapers, the wireless, public meetings and pamphlets. One such recruitment pamphlet claimed that 'le Corps Royal des Pionniers de L'Armée Britannique vous offre Camaraderie, Aventure, Voyage et un travail dont vous serez fier. [The Royal Pioneer Corps of the British Army offers you friendship, adventure, travel and a job of which you are proud]'.[44]

The attractions of adventure overseas and the prestige of a military calling were equalled by the relatively high rates of pay on offer. Flora Moody, wife of the Colonial Secretary, recorded the desire of some members of her domestic staff to join the Army in 1941. Though 'Alice's boy' would 'not know one end of a gun from another, the pick and shovel are to be his weapons'.[45] He was under age, but Captain Ray explained that the age issue was overlooked 'if they're up to weight and standard'. 'We've got to get 1000 by the end of September, so we can't afford to be too particular' (it was common for physical standards to be lowered as further drafts of Pioneers were sought).[46] Mrs Moody asked the captain, 'Why did you turn down my gardener if you're so hard up? He was wild to go – it's his only chance of earning a decent living'. She was told that the man in question was underweight. 'Poor Pashad, he thought his and his families fortunes were about to be made'. Captain Ray suggested she 'tell him to try again in October when another draft would be made – I guess we won't be quite so particular'. Mrs Moody said that she would tell him to put weights in his pockets, and Ray replied, 'Yes, they all know that trick, but unfortunately, so do I!'. After this exchange, she asked Pashad, '"Do you really want to go?" His two eyes nearly focused on me in his eagerness.'

Colonial troops had their physical fitness and general health greatly improved by service in the Army:

> When we left Mauritius rank and file were of a very poor physical standard, many with bad teeth and quite a number suffering from endemic VD [venereal disease], malaria, and dysentery which had not been detected at the time of their medical examination. From their arrival in Egypt up to the present they have improved in health and general physical fitness to an extent hardly believed possible. Over this period they have been gradually weaned from their native diet of rice and lentils etc. to the ordinary British soldiers' diet. This, I am assured, has contributed largely to the excellent physique now pertaining among them ... Their health on the whole has been exceptionally good ... Their officers consider that they are capable of standing up to a Southern European winter.[47]

The families of prospective servicemen had motives for welcoming military employment. Wives of soldiers were entitled to comparatively generous allowances. On overseas service soldiers received the same rate of pay as British troops, so they could easily increase allotments to families.[48] The Director of Labour, Edward Twining, believed that many had married just to receive the married allowance. 'Women used to getting Rs. 10 [75 pence] to 30 per month [£2.25], can with a soldier get Rs. 50 [£3.75] to 80 [£6]'.[49]

As an old Mauritian recalled:

> [Some] 'Madames Pioneres' were married within a few days of the departure of their 'symbolic' husbands to war. The reason – to benefit from the generous allowances paid to wives of soldiers. The author even mentions the possibly apocryphal story of one Pioneer who after vainly trying to find a suitable wife, ended up marrying his grandmother! 'Madames Pioneres' were above all known for their purchasing power. As soon as they received their allowances, they would buy whatever they fancied from the market, to an extent that it became a common joke at the bazaar, if a customer

complained about the prices, the stallholder would reply, 'Too expensive for you Madam? Then leave it here, someone will be able to afford it. Soon "Madame Pionere" will buy it without complaining'.[50]

The first contingent of Mauritians left for the Middle East on board the *Tin-How* on 19 August 1940; the second on board the *Talamba* on 16 January 1941 (thousands lined the streets to the harbour as the Police Band paraded the men to the ship).[51] The British Resident in Cairo, Sir Miles Lampson, personally welcomed it.[52] 1502 Company left for Suez on board the *Carnarvon Castle*. By the end of 1941 eight Mauritian companies were in the Middle East and more were to follow in 1942.

Mauritian recruits were imperial soldiers under War Office command, destined for the Middle East as part of the RPC, RASC, or Royal Engineers. RPC companies often served under other British units, for example an Airfield Construction Group was a Royal Engineers unit, but might have Pioneer companies attached to it. One of the first calls upon Mauritian manpower was for expert stevedores and dockers, tradesmen and craftsmen ('artisans' in Army parlance) and RASC drivers. Tradesmen were needed throughout the Army, as were office, mess and telephone orderlies, cooks, drivers, postal workers, stone masons and storekeepers.[53]

The first unit to be raised in Mauritius was known as 741 Artisan Works Company, a Royal Engineers unit.[54] Among other tasks, 741 Company built dummy tanks, a hospital near Port Tewfik, repaired a Royal Navy torpedo boat at Mersa Matruh, built exercise targets for tanks, worked on a hospital and water pipe to El Alamein and a road from Kattara to Cairo. In Agouza the company built a landmine factory, in Jisr el Majami it constructed fortifications to protect the Iraqi oil pipeline, in North Africa repaired the runway at El Adem, and added two wings to a hospital in Tobruk.[55] In November 1943, 1501 and 1502 Companies were converted into Royal Engineers Works Companies. In 1944 there were six Mauritian companies in Italy (the rest were in the Middle East and Malta) working as General Headquarters and line of communications troops.[56] Mauritians were to serve in most of the various service branches of the British Army. The Assistant Deputy Adjutant General wrote from Cape Town in April 1941 that Mauritius had 1000 more Pioneers ready for the Middle East, as well as 250 for the Royal Engineers, 250 for the RAOC, and 100 for the RASC.[57] Mauritians, because of their high educational standards, 'are frequently skilled craftsmen and in natural aptitude are normally best suited to serve in Artisan Works Companies of the Royal Engineers'.[58]

The British authorities in Mauritius had reasons other than support for the imperial war effort and employment opportunities in mind when backing recruitment. It was hoped that service in the British Army would lead to a degree of Anglicization of the Mauritians involved. Ever since the island was conquered in 1810 British officials had recommended Anglicization of the population. However, progress was imperceptible, and even in the 1950s officials were bemoaning the cussed 'Frenchness' of the island. In 1941 Edward Twining wrote that Army service:

> will take an appreciable number of young men into a robustly British environment and should get them away from their slave complex and from the French language and cultural associations which tend to maintain this distressing psychological outlook. We will have our problems when they return no doubt, but that is another story.[59]

Twining was later to write of the non-white Mauritians:

> Since the collapse of France there has been a tendency to look towards us again for leadership and sympathetic understanding. There are several thousand of them now serving in the British Army in the Middle East, where they are not only becoming Anglicized in their outlook but are finding that they like it. There is an opportunity now and after the war that may not be repeated for a long time, to give them a British outlook and to make them feel the benefits of being British subjects ... We must go forward with the idea of making Mauritius a British Colony, with a British outlook, whose people can enjoy the privileges of British Citizenship, where British modern Colonial standards are operative and where British Justice is administered.[60]

In April 1942 the Colonial Secretary, Sydney Moody, reported that service in the Middle East war theatre was 'automatically and quickly bringing the Troops over to British habits, language, and methods'.[61]

The Mauritian Pioneers were officered by British Army officers and 'by businessmen of the islands and by British in Mauritius'. The racial hierarchy prevalent in the colonial world was imported into the

Army.[62] As in the MTF, officers were almost exclusively white.[63] It was useful if officers spoke French, which of course most British officers did not. In May 1941 a selection for Mauritian RPC companies was made among officers of a West African draft based purely on their knowledge of French. For a few weeks in South Africa the 'officers and [Non Commissioned Officers] NCOs had daily lessons in French and general preparation for their prospective work in Mauritius'.[64] Language also hampered non-white Mauritians who wanted to become officers, as their English was rarely good enough.

White Franco-Mauritians seem to have endured racial discrimination due to British ignorance of the peoples of their colonies. As an officer in the Coldstream Guards reported in 1944:

> Each Company still has one or two white Mauritian officers, the remainder being from the United Kingdom. With one exception, no Mauritian officer has risen above the rank of Captain, and circumstantial evidence would seem to bear out remarks expressed by them that only officers of English stock are considered for higher appointments. A case in point was the appointment of a Mauritian officer bearing the name of Brown to a majority. This it is alleged was only affected because the promotion board thought that he was English, though his attitude of mind and spoken word have a gallic [sic] flavouring. I regret that I have to share the feeling of these Mauritian officers and sympathize with it, especially as I have met some of the senior officers appointed from the UK, one of whom was very surprised to find that Mauritians were not 'black men'. To support this I may add that in January 1942 General Legentilhomme's Chief of Staff assured me that one of the best young Mauritian officers had transferred to the Fighting French forces for this very reason. On the whole, though getting on well with their English brother officers, the latter (especially the more senior ones) do tend to treat them with that characteristic air of English superiority to all Colonials.[65]

At Bell Village the recruits received basic training before boarding ship for the Middle East, often calling at Rodrigues and the Seychelles to collect other Indian Ocean Pioneers on the way. The 'finishing school'[66] for the Pioneer Corps was a huge camp in the desert through which all colonial Pioneers passed upon arrival in the Middle East. This was the massive Pioneer Base Camp at Quassassin (near Tel-el-Kebir, site of the famous British-Egyptian battle of 1882) where acclimatization and further training occurred prior to deployment. In May 1941, Lieutenant Colonel H. G. L. Prynne (Director of Pioneers and Labour Middle East) had surveyed three square miles of desert four miles north of Quassassin, after being ordered to establish a Pioneer Corps Depot to accommodate 1600 Pioneers 'to receive, clothe, equip, and arm Native Pioneer Companies' as they arrived in the Middle East.[67] In the event, the camp was to take up to 26 000 men.[68]

The Western Desert, Tobruk and Alamein

As dock workers, artisans, drivers, gunners, clerks, stretcher bearers, hospital orderlies, fitters, steel benders, sheet metal workers, general mechanics, telegraph engineers etc., Pioneers performed essential though unglamorous tasks in base areas and behind front line troops, often in the face of grave danger. They built and stocked Field Supply Depots as troops advanced in the Western Desert, and operated the crucial North African ports enabling supplies to reach the infantry and armour. In the final analysis Pioneers were armed soldiers trained to fight as well as to labour. As the Army advanced in the North Africa campaign, 'Pioneers moved with it and their work in the rear areas was taken over as quickly as possible by native civilian labour recruited on the spot by Officers of the Labour Pool ... by the end of the campaign in North Africa, 16 000 civilians had been recruited'.[69]

The name Tobruk is familiar to all who served in the desert, and left an indelible imprint on the memory of many colonial Pioneers.[70] One of the few blots on the colonial war record was the breakdown of East African units during the retreat from Tobruk in the summer of 1942.

> The strain of combat proved too great, and a number of AAPC [Auxiliary African Pioneer Corps] companies disintegrated during the British retreat from Libya ... 1821 [East African] company mutinied during the retreat from Tobruk ... Discipline broke down in units caught in the British mass withdrawal.[71]

The East Africans were withdrawn from front-line duties and switched to base-area garrison duties and construction work. Other Pioneer Corps troops replaced the East Africans provisioning and working with the front-line forces, particularly those from the HCT. When Tobruk fell to the Germans in 1942, 1823 (East Africa) Company was captured. According to Parsons, the Italians murdered 202 of the men, 71 escaping to British lines and 49 surviving to become POWs.[72]

Many Mauritians worked at Tobruk, with considerable loss of life and the capture of a whole company. In April 1941:

> 800 Mauritians (1501 and 1502 Companies) embarked from Egypt on the day that German reconnaissance vehicles reached the perimeters of Tobruk, their destination. As they sailed into Tobruk harbour on board the *Bomora* [or *Balmoral*], they saw smoke from air raid damage to the beleaguered city. There the merchantman was spotted by nine German and Italian attack aircraft, as they were about half an hour away from the port.[73]

'Calmly taking aim, the bombers flew low over the vessel and dropped bombs, one of which landed, fair and square, shattering the decks and causing heavy casualties'.[74] Twenty-six Mauritian soldiers died and 48 were wounded. 'Once berthed the Mauritians were informed that as rear-echelon troops they should not have come. They turned around and went back to Egypt'.[75]

Worse was to come when Tobruk fell in what Churchill considered one of the bleakest hours of the war. On 20 June 1942 more than 300 Mauritians in Tobruk, working the harbour under heavy attack, became POWs when the port surrendered to the Germans.[76] Most of the men came from 1503 (Mauritius) Company that had formed part of the port's garrison since its capture.[77] The other companies of 66 Group 'had been evacuated from Tobruk to Sollum. 1503 Mauritius Company, skilled in dock operations, was the sole remaining Pioneer unit in Tobruk on 21 June when the fortress surrendered'.[78] In total, more than 30 000 empire soldiers were captured.[79] On that day the 'defence was disintegrating in scenes of apocalyptic confusion and doom'.[80]

One historian claims that Mauritian POWs 'were forced to unload munitions ships at Mersa Matruh, Tobruk and Benghazi whilst prisoners of the Axis forces. During Allied air raids they were denied access to shelters'.[81] It would appear that Mauritian POWs were singled out – along with Free French servicemen – for worse treatment by their captors than any other imperial nationality captured at Tobruk. A South African officer wrote:

> Homs (Tripolitania). 400 Natives. One month no attention. Hygiene nil. Severe dysentery. Average daily sick 50. Men in moribund state. Sent three ambulance loads to hospital ... Working party on roads. Six days of eight hours. Ration, 400 grammes bread, rice, and greens. No meat.[82]

The officer recorded that at Benghazi 'conditions were appalling, the hygienic standards very bad, the men infected with lice, suffering from scabies, and without bandages or dressings':

> [South African] natives, Free French, Mauritians and Indians singled out for bad treatment … with rifle butts, whips and sticks by Italian officers and men. Several shot. Men who tried to escape manacled together or hands and feet. Free French and Mauritian Natives singled out for more severe treatment.[83]

After the fall of Tobruk, imperial forces withdrew to Mersa Matruh, which Rommel soon took, forcing the British to fall back on El Alamein. During this retreat, the 'Indians and Mauritians were as reliable and efficient as they had been from the outset'.[84] The official historian of the RPC reserves high praise for the Indian Ocean Pioneers:

> The Mauritians and Seychellois, better educated than the Africans, proved adaptable to all conditions. Their standard of discipline was high and they could always be trusted to continue working unflinchingly in the most dangerous situations. They quickly mastered any new technique they were called upon to perform and were highly proficient at dock operations.[85]

On 13 August 1942 General Bernard Montgomery took command of the Eighth Army, and the subsequent second battle of Alamein – though not as clear cut a turning point as the Montgomery myth would have it – saw the British Army's fortunes in the Western Desert alter decisively. Mauritian Pioneers played their part. Prior to the battle of Alamein, 1507 (Mauritius) Company and 1509 (Seychelles) Company:

> had been constructing dummy Grant and Sherman tanks which, on 20th October, they sited in locations occupied by the Queen's Bays, 10th and 11th Hussars, and the Yorkshire Dragoons, who vacated the area as soon as the dummy tanks were placed in position leaving the Pioneers to create the illusion that the armoured units were still there by lighting fires and doing maintenance work on the dummies. The Headquarters of 1509 Company (Major W. F. Abercrombie) had meanwhile taken up the location in the desert of Headquarters 1st Armoured Division to hide from the enemy the

fact that the division had moved. These deceptive measures, it was later learned, were highly successful.[86]

By the end of 1942 the Eighth Army had advanced 1200 miles since Alamein. Tripoli was taken on 25 January 1943, and Indian Ocean Pioneers helped make the port operational:

> The port was severely damaged, the entry completely blocked by sunken ships, and the approaches heavily mined. At Buerat a Mauritius and Seychelles Company did a particularly fine job of work on petrol ships from which drums of petrol had to be lifted out of the hold by hand (the hold being heavy with petrol fumes), thrown overboard, and then swum ashore in rough, cold seas.[87]

The surviving war diaries of the Mauritian companies give a taste of the diverse tasks they performed, the way in which they were shunted around an ever-changing war theatre and the constant danger that threatened them.[88] 1501 (Mauritius) Company was formed in late 1940. It docked at Durban en route to Suez where it arrived on 17 February 1941. It then departed for Mena where the company trained throughout March. Its first operational experience was on the ill-fated trip to Tobruk in April 1941, diverted to the beleaguered port en route to Sollum (1502 suffered 34 casualties in the bombing). Despite this, five days after the tragedy the company 'disembarked at Mersa Matruh [the railway terminus in Egypt] and commenced unloading trains and stacking Royal Engineers stores'.[89] In June the company experienced the intermittent bombing of the area. In July 1942 it moved to defence works on the Cairo–Alexandria road, in August it worked on quarrying and September saw it unloading ammunition and petrol supplies. In November 1942 it was working on an RAOC dump at El Imayid, and then at the Mersa Matruh and Tobruk docks. In December 1942 the Tobruk docks were bombed again and the company lost six other ranks killed, one missing and sixteen injured. It then moved to Ras-el-Ali for road maintenance work where a mine killed another soldier and wounded four others. Later in January the company moved to Misurata for work at a Field Maintenance Centre (FMC), and in February returned to Tripoli. 1505 (Mauritius) Company was also at Tripoli working with a Harbour Reconstruction Unit.

On 7 March 1942, 1502 (Mauritius) Company had four soldiers killed and seventeen wounded during German bombing of Tobruk. The company also served at Benghazi and Sidi Barrani, with a return to Tobruk in November 1942. At Benghazi, men were working on a lighter unloading petrol when it burst into flames, killing three and severely burning three others. In March 1942, 1508 (Mauritius) Company endured 'air raids most days', and on 7 March five men were killed and five wounded by 'air machine-gunning'.[90] In May the company moved to Sollum with 5th Indian Division, and worked at Sollum, Halfaya Station, Halfaya Pass and Capuzzo. On 17 May 1942 it moved to Tobruk – 'constant air and artillery activity during month. Today tank battle proceeding all day in vicinity of Knightsbridge'.[91] On 14 June, with the tank battle having recently 'flared up again' (and Tobruk about to fall to the Germans), the company was evacuated by road to Capuzzo. Two days later it was moved to Mersa Matruh to unload petrol under 73 Group, and then 'hitch-hiked last three days to Bahig' as Eighth Army retreated.[92]

The 1504 (Seychelles) Company was transferred to Tobruk in early 1942. It suffered a 'fair amount of bombing' during February, and in March it was remarked that there was 'trouble in the Company. Men reluctant to work on petrol ships. Several placed under arrest ... Some REs also refused to work on ship in harbour in daylight'.[93] Such unwillingness was not surprising given the extreme danger involved in the work, unloading highly flammable material at a port receiving the ardent attention of enemy bombers. The company was evacuated from Tobruk on 16 June 1942, and in July found itself at Il Garawi constructing roads and piers, and dismantling the Felucca bridge.

Central Mediterranean Forces

After British victory at Alamein, Axis forces were pushed back into Tunisia where they were finally extinguished by the joint British-American landings of Operation 'Torch'. Attention now turned to invading Italy after first taking Sicily. For this task the CMF was formed (under MEC) from an amalgamation of the British First Army and the Eighth Army, under General Alexander. Many Mauritians worked on the British island of Malta, stockpiling supplies for the invasion of Sicily and Italy, and constructing aerodromes.[94] In February 1943, 1507 (Rodrigues) Company went to Malta, where it built pens for aircraft out of petrol tins and stone.[95] In March 1943 1502 (Rodrigues) Company moved to Tripoli, then to Malta for works on the Luca aerodrome; 1501 and 1505 Companies soon joined them in Malta. In March 1943, 1501 Company was working with the RAOC making gun pits. Mauritian companies took part in the invasions of Sicily launched by the Eighth Army and the American Fifth Army. On 3 August 1943, 1501 Company landed at Syracuse in Sicily, moving on to Palagonia.

The initial invasion of Italy required the movement of 160 000 fighting troops, 14 000 vehicles, 600 tanks and 1800 guns. In this 'the skill of the Mauritian Pioneers as stevedores came as a surprise'.[96] Throughout 1944 the CMF labour establishment consisted of six Mauritian, one Rodriguan, one Seychelles, 12 Basutoland, 11 Bechuanaland and nine Swaziland companies. When the Eighth Army invaded Italy on 3 September 1943, 800 Mauritians 'hit the beach alongside the infantry' and immediately 'began stockpiling supplies'.[97] On 9 September a further 400 Mauritians, along with 400 Seychellois, landed with the infantry of the US Fifth Army at Salerno in the face of fierce opposition. They spent the following three weeks unloading landing ships under German shellfire. 1508 (Mauritian) Company, along with 1941 (Basutoland) Company, 1991 (Swaziland) Company and nine British Pioneer companies supported a simultaneous British commando landing north of Salerno.[98] Three Mauritian companies were mentioned in despatches for bravery under fire, especially during the battle for Cassino when they 'performed outstandingly'.[99] They spent the remainder of the war supporting the advance in Italy. This was a new kind of work for the Pioneers, who found themselves working more closely than ever before with fighting units and often having manually to deliver supplies and help in casualty clearance.

The War Diary of 1505 (Mauritius) Company illustrates the movement and variety of tasks performed by Pioneers during the Italian campaign.[100] It arrived in September 1943 and in January 1944 left Nola to porter for 167 Brigade and 169 Brigade of the 56th Division. On 17 January Lieutenant Dutton and 26 other ranks crossed the River Garigliano with an advance force. The rest of the company was carrying ammunition down the river bank and was heavily shelled. The whole company crossed the river on 19 January, portering for Battalion headquarters to the forward line, coming under heavy mortar and shell fire. On 27 January the company left the forward area for a rest, returning to porterage and stretcher bearing three days later. For stretcher bearing there was an officer and 90 other ranks at relay stations on the side of the mountain. The rest carried ammunition to the front.

In March 1944 the company was portering and stretcher bearing for 88th US Division on Mont Damiano. A normal load was 40lbs for a three- to four-mile carry. In May 1944 it was at Cassino. Half the company then moved to Senigallia, and the rest worked on the air evacuation of casualties from Falconara airfield.

In Italy on New Year's Day 1944, 1507 (Rodrigues) Company was engaged on road work for the 46th Division:

> Men stunned by wind and cold and few could be wakened for breakfast. Many bivvys had collapsed and the men had dispersed to caves and buildings – anywhere to get away from the storm. Most tents blown to shreds. Impossible to get water heated but by 1100 hrs the men had had a mug of tea. Request for rum issue failed. A hot meal and wine at night helped to improve morale. ... The Company has been employed throughout the month on road maintenance and track laying, and handling stores. The men are making a reputation as road experts. After the blizzard on 1 January the weather was fine and calm, though very cold. The men stood this well, especially as jerkins were issued to all men. Hygiene difficult owing to cold weather and lack of bathing facilities.[101]

In September 1943, 1508 Company landed at Salerno, where it unloaded landing ships. Seventy other ranks portered in support of 7th Oxfordshire and Buckinghamshire Regiment in the front line.[102] A further 75 were on ordnance and 150 on ships. In October the company worked the docks at Castellamare and then at Naples. On 22 October it was portering for the Guards Brigade, moving with them and suffering casualties. In February 1944 it 'moved to a sight on right bank of River Garigliano for work with 56th Division. 100 men on stretcher bearing. Relay posts established on Mont Damiano. 140 on porterage for Queen's Regiment'.[103] Later the company worked with 141 Field Ambulance and portered for the 2nd Battalion Royal Scots Fusiliers. It moved around a great deal and its work also included rubble clearance (September), railhead and aerodrome work (December) and roads and bridging (February 1945).

Welfare

The British Army successfully provided for the welfare of the thousands of imperial soldiers who volunteered for the Pioneer Corps.[104] The military authorities were kept up to the mark by colonial governments anxious to secure the interests of their men – for their own sake and for the benefit of postwar society. The handling of colonial troops had come to reflect the liberal imperialism of the age, as well as the mechanization of military transport that greatly reduced the need for human porterage, and the combating of tropical diseases. 'British officials worked hard to avoid repeating the abominable suffering of the Carrier Corps'.[105] Colonial governments were determined to limit effects of the war that were considered corrosive to colonial society. They did not want disaffected ex-servicemen returning to their colonies and politicizing the masses. So pressure was kept on the military authorities. This made the task of British commanders even more difficult. Their fighting formations were made up largely of Dominions troops under generals who were subject to political pressure from their home governments; likewise, the variegated colonial troops of the Pioneer Corps were represented at MEC HQ by representatives of the colonial governments always quick to protest if it was felt that their troops were not getting a square deal. Responding to this pressure, the Adjutant General's branch set up an organization responsible for welfare, known as 'A' branch.[106] A7b was responsible for troops from Mauritius, the Seychelles, Rodrigues, the West Indies and Ceylon. These measures were successful and soldiers' complaints tended to be about minor racial niggles and the more common, universal soldierly grievances – rations, pay and poor communications with relatives back at home. The pay issue was resolved when full British rates were granted from April 1943.[107]

The Government of Mauritius hoped that the Army would significantly Anglicize the coloured Mauritians. As well as a potential threat to colonial stability, Army service was seen as offering opportunities for entrenching British rule. It was suggested that English language learning facilities be provided alongside a welfare officer to tour among the troops in the Middle East.[108] The War Office advised against this as the Mauritians were scattered throughout the theatre. However, a Welfare Officer, Lieutenant Paul Hein, was appointed.[109] His main job was to liaise between welfare organizations in Mauritius and the dispersed troops in the Middle East and Southern Europe.[110] He was 'responsible for distributing monies collected on their behalf in Mauritius. He visits the companies at intervals from his base in Cairo. The men appear happy and contented though mail facilities with Mauritius (which is one of their main grievances) are poor'.[111] All companies made provision for the recreation of their men, and 'set up a full range of social and sports activities, with libraries, and arranged for radio broadcasts in French and local dialects on Middle East Land Forces (MELF) Radio Network [this latter in the postwar period]'.[112]

An older historiography suggested that Army service politicized men, who then returned to their home colonies and contributed to the coming of independence. However, the men were successfully screened from politicization. Mundane matters were more likely to be the source of postwar gripes as opposed to the perceived injustices of the colonial system. As one Mauritian ex-servicemen exclaimed passionately, neatly illustrating this, 'I can't get bacon and eggs, and they ask me to fight for freedom and democracy!'.[113] Mauritians served alongside South African and Australian troops and noted the friendliness of the latter and the racial intolerance of the former, but this did not mean that they were inspired to try to reform the colonial world after the war.[114]

Pioneers in the postwar world

By the end of the war over 10 000 Mauritians had been recruited.[115] However, the work of the Mauritian Pioneers did not end with the war, and they were to be the mainstay of the newly designated MELF right up until the Suez Crisis in 1956. The island continued to send thousands of men to join the British Army, in a period when African and Indian Ocean colonies were looked to for more troops to support the overstretched Regular Army after the loss of the Indian Army. These Pioneers served in Palestine, Egypt and Libya. Though not a British colony the desert campaigns had led to British bases in Cyrenaica and Tripolitania (a 'veiled protectorate').[116] 'In return for aid, the new State [of Libya] allowed Britain and the US to maintain military Bases'.[117] Thousands of Mauritians continued to make the journey to Quassassin, the base for all non-British Pioneers attached to MELF. They provided guard companies, special works companies and fire-fighting sections.[118] Though the war had ended, it remained a dangerous occupation. For example, on 3 December 1951 eight Mauritian Pioneers and two British soldiers were killed when a bomb was thrown into their vehicle near Port Tewfik.[119]

In Palestine the Indian Ocean Pioneers, in addition to their normal tasks, performed guard and escort duties to protect British troops at a time of rising tension and terrorist attacks in the British Mandate. This necessitated an increase in the British garrison, but British troops themselves were targets for the terrorists. The Pioneer Corps was divested of its British personnel who were replaced by Mauritians and other Indian Ocean islanders. The number of British Pioneers at the Haifa Base Depot and Workshops was gradually reduced, and the last British company was disbanded in March 1948. Their place was taken

by 14 Pioneer companies from the Indian Ocean who were thereafter
in constant demand, not only in their primary role as military labour
but as static security guards and convoy escorts. An early task was
packing military stores to be despatched to the main British Middle
East Base in Egypt prior to Britain's departure from Palestine.[120]

But the British were on the retreat in Egypt as well. All stocks were
withdrawn to the Suez Canal Zone, the naval base at Alexandria was
abandoned, as was the GHQ complex in Cairo. The 1936 treaty
between the Egyptian and British governments was coming to an end
and was unlikely to be renewed. The British would no longer remain
in Egypt through *force majeur*. In the Canal Zone 'a whole complex of
Depots and Storehouses containing millions of pounds worth of materials were stockpiled, for the maintenance of which a great deal of
labour was required'.[121] Stocks of military stores and equipment had to
be returned to the UK.[122] In the early postwar period the labour force
included 87 000 German POWs organized into working companies
under the command of two Pioneer Groups. However, once the POW
labour had been released, more Pioneers were needed. The Foreign
Office ruled out the employment of aliens, so the Colonial Office
narrowed the field of recruitment to the West Indies, Mauritius and
the Seychelles.[123]

Egypt and the Middle East were of vital importance in the Cold War,
carrying Britain's strategic air offensive potential against the Soviet
Union.[124] In 1951 there were three Pioneer Groups in Egypt, totalling
sixteen Mauritian and three Rodrigues companies in Egypt; 211
Mauritian Group in Cyrenaica had headquarters at Derna, Benghazi,
and Tobruk. Cohen claims that in 1950 there was in the Middle East a
Land Striking Force of 7000, an RAF presence of 10 000, 13 000
personnel in headquarters and the Canal Base, and 8000 Mauritians
'guarding the base'.[125]

More colonial Pioneers were urgently needed from 1951 when the
Anglo-Egyptian treaty – on which Britain's presence in the Canal Zone
rested – was abrogated by the Egyptian Government. Thereafter 40 000
Egyptian workers left British employ, creating an acute labour
shortage. Recruits were found in Cyprus and permission was granted
to recruit 1000 more Mauritians.[126] Another source was the 'East
African Pioneer Corps especially formed to meet the abrogation emergency'.[127] 20 000 East Africans were taken on. However, the shortage
ended in 1954 when Britain agreed to give up the Suez Canal Zone and
Egyptians again made themselves available. This meant that there was
no longer any need for colonial Pioneers. 'HQ 214 Group [was]

disbanded in February 1956, together with its last three Companies, 2057 Seychelles, 2063 Mauritius, and 2216 East African'.[128] Even after the Suez crisis, Britain sought to maintain a base for MELF, turning to the Mackinnon Road project in Kenya on which Indian Ocean Pioneers were employed.

Mauritians as military labourers and infantry soldiers

The Mauritian record of military service in the Pioneer Corps is a proud one, lasting for 16 years. Mauritians, Rodriguans and Seychellois were regarded as excellent Pioneers. Their high standards of education and trade skills marked them out from the African crowd. They were sometimes viewed as being less physically impressive than Africans, and in contemporary British military eyes Mauritians were never likely to become one of the 'martial races' of the empire, especially given their French orientation.

An overall assessment of Mauritians as Pioneers was provided by a Coldstream Guards major who had had occasion to view them throughout the war:

> The opinion expressed to me by the then Director of Pioneers and Labour, GHQ, Middle East at the end of 1941 was that he considered Mauritians amongst the best that he had, and this opinion was confirmed when I passed through Cairo in May 1943. From my own observations, the Mauritians have a smart turnout and are well disciplined (pace some other British units), and in recent engagements as in the past, when their work took them just behind the front line, they stood up well to heavy shell fire and completed their assignments. Their relations with British troops has been most cordial as I myself can bear out when my own Regiment had Mauritians working alongside it for some weeks. The relations of the Mauritians with the local inhabitants both in Malta and Italy has been of the most cordial; their departure from Malta being marked by harrowing scenes of dismay on the part of the local female population. In conclusion, I would say that the Mauritian has conducted himself well and been a credit to his country.

The official British view – shared by military officers, Government of Mauritius officials and civil servants in Whitehall – was that Mauritians made excellent Pioneer soldiers but poor fighting soldiers. Of course, such assured judgements quickly became circular and self-supporting, and before anything was known about it a stereotype had been created and enshrined, slipping easily into the intricate matrix of British racial categorization. It did not take much for a new stereotype to be cemented – the East African collapse during the retreat from Tobruk marked their card – and East Africans 'acquired a reputation with senior British officers for being prone to "blow ups"'.[129] The Swazi Pioneers, despite strong evidence to the contrary, were viewed as being unusually backward and savage – even for Africans – and not to be allowed in European areas.[130]

It is clear that Mauritians made excellent Pioneer soldiers; but as the next chapter will demonstrate, the notion that they made poor fighting soldiers is unfair and founded largely upon the misread evidence of an incident – the Madagascar mutiny – that was more deeply rooted in complex racial tensions and bad man-management than has hitherto been appreciated.

5
The Mauritius Regiment and the Madagascar Mutiny

On 17 December 1943 the 1st Battalion The Mauritius Regiment boarded the troopship *Burma* and embarked for the grand harbour of Diego Suarez in Madagascar. It was a new Regiment of the British Army that had only had its colours granted in principle by King George V in October 1943.[1] During the three-day crossing from Mauritius conditions onboard ship were cramped, the food was unpleasant and many of the men were sea sick. Arriving in Madagascar, the Battalion was made to parade in full kit in the afternoon sun before beginning a route march to their camp at Orangea, about 12 miles inland. This was in spite of the provision of motorized transport and was indicative of the attitude of the Commanding Officer (CO), Lieutenant Colonel Yates, who was determined to seize the moment and show off his troops and himself. In the course of the march, order disintegrated, men began to fall out and the Battalion arrived at Orangea in straggling batches. At the camp, by accident or design, a grass hut was set alight. Others followed through deliberate ignition. Men left the camp against orders. The following day hundreds of men failed to appear on parade for physical training. African soldiers of the KAR were ordered to round up the mutinous Mauritians and hundreds were charged with indiscipline. Some ringleaders were sentenced to death. The Regiment survived for eight months before its disbandment in August 1944. These events constituted the mutiny of the Mauritius Regiment.

An older historiography construed 'imperial defence' as a rather exclusive branch of imperial history in which Britain and the Dominions argued at Imperial Conferences about contributions to empire-wide defence provisions. Britain was always pressing for a New Zealand cruiser here or an Australian battleship there, and ultimately for a centrally directed Imperial Navy funded by all of the empire's taxpayers. Working against this centripetal force, the Dominions – especially Canada – emphasized their own national and regional defence preoccupations. Though some progress was made and an Imperial War Cabinet formed in 1917, a fully integrated imperial defence system was not to be. Whilst Dominions politicians were aware of their ultimate dependence on the Royal Navy for their security, it was too late for the imperial federationists dream of a truly centralized imperial defence system to become a reality.

Today, however, the subject of imperial defence demands a much wider construction, one that it does not always receive. For whilst the Dominions were moving towards legal independence within the British Commonwealth (symbolized by the 1931 Statute of Westminster) and away from formal military integration with Britain, the colonial empire was becoming increasingly enmeshed within Britain's imperial defence system. Whilst in 1939 the Dominions supported the imperial war effort with a surprising readiness and depth, just as they had in 1914–18, the colonial empire also provided massive support and contributed large sums to Britain for the purchase of military hardware. This colonial empire contribution tends to be overlooked. The participation of hundreds of thousands of colonial troops is all the more remarkable due to the fact that the colonies, unlike the Dominions, were in no way autonomous. The colonies were at war because Britain was at war, and had not an ounce of choice in the matter.[2] The colonial empire's role in imperial defence mushroomed during the Second World War, as too did its economic significance for Britain in the age of the 'second colonial occupation'.

The British empire did not maintain a large colonial army as a permanent supplement to the regular Army, though the idea had received some consideration.[3] This was in contrast to the French, for whom the thought of an empire at arms ready to come to the aid of the mother country sustained an unrealistic belief in the capacity of the colonies to rescue France should the Germans choose to make war again. However, in the British empire there *were* permanent (i.e. maintained in peacetime) military formations that were designated Imperial troops and, like the Indian Army, liable for overseas service. In this category were units like the RWAFF and the KAR.[4] In addition there were locally raised units that were not Imperial, but recruited specifically to fulfil a military or paramilitary role in their home colonies and immediate areas, such as the Somali Camel Corps, Arab Legion, Transjordan Frontier Force and MTF.

British imperial defence policy must be understood against a backdrop of interwar financial stringency and the continuing belief – justified by the First World War – that the Royal Navy was the ultimate guarantor of colonial security. However, by the outbreak of war in 1939 there had been a noticeable increase in the strength of British colonial forces in the colonies, particularly as the revolution in air power increased the chances of a future war hitting the home fronts and weakening the naval shield. Shuckburgh claims that there were 43 000 military personnel in the colonies in 1939.[5] In that year the RWAFF stood at 4400, the KAR at 2900, the Somali Camel Corps at 600 and the Northern Rhodesia Regiment at 430.[6] The MTF comprised 200 locally recruited soldiers. By the end of the war, over 500 000 men from the colonies (i.e. excluding the Dominions and Indian Army) were in British uniform.

The fact that hundreds of thousands of raw recruits were drafted into previously selective units – or into newly created units such as the AAPC – and successfully employed overseas as soldiers is the most remarkable feat of the British empire in the Second World War. The further fact that these soldiers were effective in their various roles, with no higher incidence of mutiny or inefficiency than regular British Army units, is to the great credit of the soldiers themselves and the authorities that recruited them. New military formations had no peacetime military tradition to draw upon and no time in which to build up the unique regimental loyalties that are the bedrock of the British Army. Unlike existing formations – the Gurkhas, KAR and Indian Army – in which the welfare of the soldier and his family was well catered for according to long-established principles, the raw colonial recruit of the Second World War faced many uncertainties relating to his own terms of service and the care of his family. He also faced, for the first time, the bewilderment of unsolicited overseas travel during a world war.

The word mutiny is commonly used with a degree of elasticity; for example, the Indian Mutiny of 1857–8 covers what was, in its entirety, a full-scale war. The dictionary defines mutiny as an 'open revolt against authority', and the Madagascar mutiny of the 1st Battalion The Mauritius Regiment in December 1943 was certainly that. Mutinies were not new and by no means exclusively confined to colonial troops. One historian has filled an entire book with examples of mutinies in the British armed forces.[7] British and French units famously mutinied in the closing stages of the First World War, and British sailors mutinied at Invergordon in 1931. The West Indies Regiment mutinied at Taranto in Italy in 1917, there was a military mutiny in the Sudan in 1924, and KAR troops of the 25th East African Brigade mutinied after the battle of Gondar in the East African campaign.[8] In May 1942, 15 soldiers of the Ceylon Defence Force, 'prompted by pro-Japanese and anti-European beliefs, mutinied by trying to take over their gun battery on the Cocos-Keeling Islands'.[9] The Madagascar mutiny, from inception to suppression, witnessed no violence. As the Mauritian ex-servicemen who were there insist, it was purely passive. Maxime Labour, President of the Mauritius Branch of the British Commonwealth Ex-Services League, gives it a pithy description: 'It was an absence of discipline'.[10] Another 'mutineer' writes that the men 'had never been initiated into the King's Regulations, and had no understanding of the sense of the word mutiny. They believed they could behave like strikers'.[11] This chapter sets out to account for the mutiny of the Battalion and in so doing cast light on the considerable military preparations made in the most unlikely places on behalf of the empire. New evidence enables the construction of a comprehensive anatomy of the rise and fall of one of the British empire's least known and least celebrated regiments.

The Mauritius Territorial Force and the Mauritius Regiment

Local military initiatives were undertaken to supplement imperial garrisons and anticipate the shrinkage likely in a time of war when imperial troops would be needed more urgently elsewhere. At the outbreak of war the imperial garrison of Mauritius counted only 200 imperial troops, its lowest level ever. It was supported by the 200 men of the MTF, created in 1935 to support the imperial garrison. 'A' Company was recruited exclusively from the island's white Franco-Mauritian community and supported the Royal Artillery troops stationed mainly at Fort George. 'B' Company was non-white and trained as an infantry unit to defend points of strategic importance. In its tasks the MTF was supported in the Second World War by the local defence formations described in Chapter 3. The MTF officially became the MR on 24 April 1943 and control passed to the Army Council.[12] It thereby ceased to be a locally recruited force for service only on Mauritian soil and became an imperial unit that could be sent anywhere in the world.

With the coming of war, the MTF was greatly enlarged through voluntary enlistment and conscription into the two existing companies and through the creation of new companies. By 1942 there were nearly a thousand men in the MTF – four infantry companies performing garrison and coastal defence duties on Mauritius, Rodrigues and Diego Garcia. The 1943 overhaul of military units in Mauritius led to further expansion and the division of the unit into two battalions (the Regiment's strength was to rise towards 2000).[13] Captain Alfred North-Coombes raised 'C' Company early in the war when he 'personally examined 635 applicants before recruiting 125 of them'.[14] After returning to Mauritius in September 1943 from a stint on Rodrigues with 'C' Company, he was given command of the newly created 'D' Company 2MR, to be stationed at Cannoniers Point.

The 1st Battalion The Mauritius Regiment was posted to Madagascar in late 1943 in a swap that brought a battalion of the KAR to Mauritius. The island's armed forces had a regional role to play under the new EAC subsidiary Islands Area Command. After the departure of the 1st Battalion MR, the 2nd Battalion acted as a training and reinforcement unit and maintained the Regiment's original infantry role, ready to defend coastal positions and inland points of strategic importance, and performing 'garrison duties at places like Tombeau Bay [and] Plaisance aerodrome'.[15] Evidence would suggest that the dispatch of the 1st Battalion to Madagascar was partly motivated by the need to give the Regiment more experience. By moving from a peaceful garrison island that was home to all the men and their families to a recently conquered enemy territory, they would be seasoned in a different environment and learn to serve away from home. Then, perhaps, if the war so dictated, the Regiment could be employed elsewhere – for example in the Far Eastern campaign against the Japanese. This is where most of the men – few of whom had ever been overseas – thought that they were going. EAC 'therefore ordered that they should be sent to north Madagascar for battle training and toughening up',[16] before being sent to Burma. They were 'smartly turned out but had little field experience', and it was this that they were to gain on Madagascar.[17]

Before the Madagascar mutiny, the CO of the 2nd Battalion looked forward to the enhancement of his battalion's reputation as the MR became a first line infantry regiment. Major B. J. Landrock (seconded from the East Lancashire Regiment):

> appears to think he has achieved much in East Africa [on a visit to EAC headquarters]. The 2nd MR ... will come into its own when 1MR leaves and become a first line battalion ... So, the programme would be to push us up to full strength, then move us out to East Africa to team as part of a Brigade, then go in the first line, and

meanwhile the Mauritian Garrison would consist of inferior African troops.

The headquarters of the MR were the Abercromby Barracks in Vacoas, and much of the unit's basic training was carried out at the nearby Gymkhana Club. The organization of the island's defences is explained by Pierre Tonta, a member of the MR and, after its disbandment, the Pioneer Corps:

> Two platoons of white Mauritians trained to assist the Royal Artillery. Also two platoons of coloureds were formed in 1935–36, trained in infantry for defence purposes in case of attack on strategic points like petrol tanks, wireless, customs, Line Barracks etc. The two platoons of coloureds in late 1942 became part of the 1st Battalion The Mauritius Regiment, composed of four infantry companies of four platoons each, and a headquarters unit composed of a signals platoon, an anti-aircraft unit, one mortar, one carrier, one transport, and one platoon of non-combatants – clerks, cooks, waiters, orderlies, and personal servants. There was compulsory recruitment. The Regiment received intensive training in 'jungle warfare' to fight the Japanese in Burma.[18]

This is an important point; the MR was a *fighting* unit. Its training, particularly after the entry of Japan into the war, was in preparation for combat. Former members of the Regiment are at pains to make this point, tired of the common view that they were 'only parade-ground soldiers' who wanted to stay at home.[19] Roger Requin was a sniper sergeant and recounts an intensive training: 'grenades, route march with full marching order, bayonet fighting, free-for-all manoeuvres, mock battles, disarming techniques, compass-marching, sniper shooting, and camouflage'.[20] Ramsing Kusrutsing was trained as a Harley Davidson dispatch rider and also received Bren gun (a heavy Czech machine gun, sometimes vehicle mounted, used throughout the British Army) training. These men were not being trained for purely 'rear echelon' tasks.

The move that brought the KAR to Mauritius and sent the MR overseas was engineered by the Commander-in-Chief EAC, Lieutenant General Sir William Platt, and the Governor of Mauritius, Sir Donald Mackenzie Kennedy, for several reasons (see Chapter 3). As the latter wrote, 'the Commander-in-Chief proposes with my full approval to transfer 1st Battalion to Madagascar or East Africa and to replace it by a KAR Battalion ... I feel that the experience gained will be of immense value to the Colony after the war'.[21] Both men also doubted the ability of the inexperienced MTF to defend the island in the face of a Japanese attack, and questioned the loyalty of some of the members of the Force suspected of harbouring Vichy sympathies that impaired fighting efficiency. So the Commander-in-Chief decided that imperial troops were needed 'to strengthen the defence of this part of East Africa Command'.[22]

Political opposition to overseas military service

The Governor foresaw no political or military difficulties arising from the overseas service of the MR, provision for which was made through the promulgation of the Mauritius Regiment Ordinance removing the previous home-service-only liability of the force.[23] In drawing up this legislation precedents were sought elsewhere in the empire.[24] Conscription was a thorny problem that compounded the defence policy controversy. The War Office was keen for conscription in order to obtain Europeans for 'certain purposes overseas', and the Governor wanted it for the MTF and the Civil Labour Corps.[25] In some respects conscription was favoured by would-be volunteers because leaving a job to join the forces was worse in terms of re-employment than if one was conscripted. The war's multiple demands on the colony's manpower resources raised some awkward questions. For example, did the Governor have the power to legislate for conscription? The Colonial Office in London looked to an earlier precedent in St Helena, and thought that it was not possible for a Governor to conscript men for British Army service, though he could conscript for the dependency's *own* locally raised forces (like the MTF). However, in that case, servicemen would have to *volunteer* for service overseas.[26] The 1943 Ordinance was to remove this obstacle. In 1941 the Colonial Office's view was that as volunteers (for the Pioneer Corps) were coming forward 'in adequate numbers', it was pointless to press the issue of conscription.[27] But this was one of many issues in which the cavalier and *fait accompli* style of Governor Sir Bede Clifford reddened faces back in Whitehall. On this issue, A. B. Acheson minuted: 'Without waiting for authority he is apparently going ahead and introducing conscription – which is [the word 'typical' is crossed out] not uncharacteristic of Sir Bede Clifford'.[28]

The issue of military service in the MTF/MR was first politicized in 1941 and flared up again in 1943 when it became known that troops were to be sent overseas. Concerns were expressed by non-white members of the Council of Government who claimed that troops being sent overseas were 'exclusively' from the non-white community (the whites-only 'A' Company would remain a coastal artillery unit). They told the Governor 'of the psychological reaction the decision of the Military [to send the 1st Battalion overseas] has had on the public mind'.[29] Recruitment for the Pioneer Corps had not required conscription, but enlistment in the MR was unpopular, and the authorities blamed this on the fact that the MR was more likely to see fighting action, and on the ambivalent Franco-Mauritian attitude to the Allied cause that led to an unenthusiastic response. The Governor tried to assuage fears that only coloured troops were being sent overseas, and denied that the troops themselves felt disgruntled.[30] He explained that the aim of sending MR troops overseas was to provide them with further training, so that the MR 'if called on, [can] play a full part in the military operations of the Empire'.[31] He continued:

> Personnel of these units, with very few exceptions, are most anxious to exchange the hum drum garrison life for more active participation in the war … It would be a thousand pities if [their high morale] were undermined by the local influence which I fear is being brought to bear upon some of the men … To those that feel there is inequality of sacrifice some percentages will be of interest.

He then furnished figures relating to the composition of the 1st Battalion that was to be sent overseas:

> Officers: British 0.3 per cent; white Mauritian 2.5; coloured 0.4.
> Other Ranks: Coloured 72 per cent; Hindu 16.3; Tamil 1.1; Mahomedan 7.4.[32]

The Governor concluded by trying to enlist the support of the coloured members of the Council of Government who had raised the issue (Edgar Laurent and Raoul Rivet):

> I am grateful to you both for addressing me on this matter and I know that I am writing to two friends who see through and beyond the bitterness and acrimony, due largely to misunderstanding, which hamper so much our progress towards the larger, fuller life which we hope to secure for all Mauritians.

However, neither mathematics nor sophistry were likely to stymie the feeling that the non-white population was getting a raw deal, or the simple apprehension with which service overseas was viewed.

In the month of Japan's entry into the war the Government was accused in the Council of Government of importing racial discrimination into the military forces. Dr Maurice Cure, founding father of the MLP though little more than an 'agitator' in the view of the Government, claimed that segregated recruitment into the MTF harmed race relations and hindered the island's war effort.[33] In a telegram to the Labour MP Arthur Creech Jones he requested intervention to resolve the matter for the sake of the colony's war effort. On 23 December 1941 the Council of Government debated 'the Motion of the Honourable Junior Member for Port Louis (Rivet) on Military Service'.[34] Rivet's (a Creole representative) motion was supported by Laurent, representative of the Indians. 'The foregoing complaints [for example, that the white company was stationed in a more temperate part of the island than the non-white company] prove conclusively that in regard to military service a colour bar has been *officially* established in Mauritius'.[35] Their complaints were taken up by local newspapers. Governor Sir Bede Clifford acknowledged that 'leading members of the coloured community endorse the grievances voiced by representatives at the Council of Government'.[36] He countered by reporting that there was 'a long waiting list of coloured volunteers for service and 400 Creole intellectuals had sent in their names since the debate took place'.[37] Clifford claimed that 'the matter is political rather than military or social', and his failure to recognize the depth or pedigree of disquiet among the MTF/MR other ranks was one of the 'time bomb' causes of the mutiny and illustrative of the fact – freely admitted by the Government – that it was out of touch with ordinary Mauritians.[38]

The Government claimed that segregation had been the recruiting principle of the MTF since its formation in 1935. Reporting to the Colonial Secretary Lord Moyne, the Governor said that an unsuccessful attempt had been made by the OCT to form a mixed company.[39] The Secretary of State needed to know, for he was being hounded in the House of Commons by Creech Jones (who through the Fabian Colonial Bureau was intimate with Mauritian affairs and Mauritian political figures – see Chapter 7). On 3 June 1942 the parliamentary Under Secretary of State for the Colonies, Harold Macmillan, responded to Creech Jones with the ammunition provided by the Governor.[40] The Governor denied the charge of encouraging racial division, claiming that the races divided themselves, and that, certainly in a time of war, it would not be sensible to conduct 'social experiments' in military units. Advancing his claim that this was a political rather than a genuine social issue, the Governor said that there was a waiting list to join the MTF. The Government also confirmed that both of the companies constituting the MTF received the same rates of pay.[41]

In his correspondence with the Colonial Office the Governor was less diplomatic than in writing to members of the Council of Government. From Government House Clifford penned a lengthy refutation of the charges made in the Council of Government.[42] The 'attempt to pin the blame on the Government is only an average example of the blind unreasoning prejudice against the Government and the Military Authorities in Mauritius'.[43] He pointed to 'the intrusion once more of the colour question ... Both [Laurent and Rivet] are being prodded by a bunch of mothers, wives, aunts, and sisters who do not object to their offspring and relations drawing good pay so long as they remain at home'.[44] He claimed that in forthcoming Port Louis municipal elections Laurent and Rivet were threatened with the loss of their seats. 'Our friend Millien [editor of *L'Ouvre*] is at (or near) the bottom of the agitation and Rivet told me the other day that [he] will stick at nothing in his efforts to embarrass Government and his political opponents'. However, the Governor assured the Colonial Office that there was nothing to worry about: 'this sort of thing is a feature of one's daily life'.[45] But this was a serious miscalculation, as the current of racial tension contributed to the unhealthy state of unit morale that was to see the 1st Battalion mutiny on Madagascar in December 1943.

It is clear that whilst some volunteered for the MR and some could be described as willing conscripts, others were opposed to military service and resented conscription, adding another layer to the geology that formed the bedrock of the mutiny. Suchita Ramdin remembers her brothers rubbing petrol in their eyes so that recruiters would think that the family was diseased.[46] Maxime Labour, like other young men, was conscripted straight from college to study Morse code and sema-phore for the Mauritius Signals unit.[47] Ramsing Kusrutsing wanted to join the Auxiliary Police. 'I applied and on the selection day about 125 men were selected and were at once transferred to the military'.[48] The Colonial Office was naturally concerned by such practices and the political and media attention they attracted. Throughout the empire it was sensitive to the issue of unfree labour, particularly during a war of 'freedom' versus 'tyranny'. The subject was raised in the House of Lords in May 1942.[49]

Racial tension, morale and leadership

The Government of Mauritius was acutely aware of the strong unofficial colour bar that permeated Mauritian society.[50] Franco-Mauritians were an insular social, economic and political elite. The Creoles resented the colour consciousness of the whites. On the bottom rung of the ladder were the Indians, mainly classified as 'labourers and peasants'. Racial discrimination was an issue from the date of the foundation of the MTF exacerbated by wartime expansion. Many MR troops were poorly educated Creoles who spoke very little English. 'The NCOs were a higher class of Creoles who resented the attitudes of the English officers towards them and their men'.[51] Given the numerical dominance of Creoles over Indians in the Army, the latter community could experience difficulties. One ex-servicemen recalled:

> All my best friends were Creoles and avoided Indian companionship. I tried to conceal my Indian identity, feeling ashamed of my origin ... This stupid attitude took greater hold of me when I joined the Army where anti-Indian feeling was particularly violent and Creoles enjoyed some power.[52]

The exasperating and intractable racial problems of Mauritius are powerfully summarized in a private letter written by Edward Twining, an official with firsthand experience given his role as Director of Labour:

> At any rate I pity him [the Governor] as it is one of the most difficult Governorships in the Empire. The French, Coloured, Hindo, Mahomaden, and Chinese communities all hate each other. The French try to keep control of all their ill-gotten gains through the exploitation of slave labour. They have deteriorated physically, morally, and mentally. They hate us and are pro-Vichy. The coloured people are accomplished, clever, inconsequential, degenerate, the descendants of ex-slaves. They despise us ... The Indians are a miserable lot, weak, lazy, *Indian*. They distrust us. The Chinese are just parasites ... The English – well they are beyond description and deserve all they get. 'Divide et Impera' is an easy doctrine but until Sir Bede Clifford came this place seems to have been grossly

misruled for hundreds of years.[53]

Twining thought that British officials were viewed 'with contempt ... The metropolitan "fonctionnaire" is traditionally unpopular in French colonies. Here, added to this is the fact that he is from a different race, and gets more pay than locally recruited officials'.[54]

The language barrier was a part of the Mauritius Regiment's malaise. The higher ranking officers were British. Few spoke French and none spoke the patois Creole that was the island's lingua franca. Translators were therefore used, for example when Major Landrock spoke through John Leclezio to inform the 2nd Battalion of the 1st Battalion's mutiny. The not inconsiderable achievements of the British in forming military units along British lines but with non-European peoples has rested on the closeness of British officers and their men. The ideal officer would know of their culture, take an interest in their and their families welfare, and learn their language. The KAR and Gurkhas are good examples. In the MR, there had been neither the time nor the desire to forge such bonds, and it showed.

Carried into the Army was a non-white resentment against the status of the white Mauritians whose social and economic dominance was translated wholesale into the structure of Army rank. This, according to Ramgoolam, 'ran counter to the Allied cause'.[55] Roger Requin says that there were:

just a few officers – you can name them – who to me were very bright people. We were at school at the same time, we know their calibre. Now when you join the Army, they came and gave you orders – that's the problem ... The first frustration that the Mauritians had at the time was the question why should the white people become officers and non-whites not ... when some were more or less idiots.[56] The treatment was not what as youngsters we could expect from Active Military Service. It was not at all conducive to contentment and patriotism. On my enrolment, I was posted to a platoon in 'C' Company where the Company Commander as well as the platoon officers all came from the MTF 'A' Company [all white]. The Franco-Mauritian officers were treated like their British counterparts, whereas 'Other Ranks' were put on the same footing as the East African troops; for example, food ration just like the KAR, and they were paid much less than the British soldiers got. In other words, though we were British subjects, we were not treated as such in the Army. A good number were better in intelligence, knowledge, and leadership than their officers. Such treatment was a proof of blatant injustice and was deeply resented throughout the other ranks.[57]

In his study of the KAR Timothy Parsons writes that 'military organizations are by nature hierarchical and authoritarian, but in colonial armies these divisions were defined almost exclusively by race'.[58] This was the way of the British Army at the time. Inequality was reflected in conditions of service that all could see. 'Officers had British pay, and we had Mauritian pay – African pay – [we were] treated as Africans'.[59] This point is often emphasized by Mauritian ex-servicemen – they strongly resented being classified alongside Africans, who they considered to be less civilized. Hence their great resentment at watching an African battalion march on to their island from the ship that was about to take them to an unknown land.

The views of non-white Mauritians were well known in Whitehall, where local political leaders were able to maintain a voice by bypassing the Governor and plugging into the British network of colonial critics and watchdogs. S. B. Emile, Chairman of the Mauritius Stevedoring Company, was one of a number of educated Mauritians in contact with the Fabian Colonial Bureau, and through it able to access a surprising number of British politicians interested in colonial reform and able to exert parliamentary pressure. In 1943 Emile wrote to the Permanent Under Secretary of State for the Colonies, Sir Cosmo Parkinson, complaining that in the war, all of the well paid, important new civil and military posts were going to the Franco-Mauritians, whilst for war labour it was the non-white population that was called upon.[60]

The racial gulf imported into the Army was also reflected in the widespread feeling among the white community that, firstly, it was dangerous to give the non-white population military instruction, and that secondly, they would never make good fighting soldiers anyway. North-Coombes recalled:

Goldschmidt – when the MTF was first formed – telling the NCOs and officers of 'A' Company (the White Company) that 'B' Company (the Black Company) was no good only a political necessity; that they would only be used in the rear as Pioneers if it came to a showdown, and that the defence of the island would fall mostly on white shoulders … Mauritians of all classes are not fighting men.

After speaking to two Franco-Mauritian officers North-Coombes wrote (rather as South African whites were to write of their misgivings about having blacks trained and armed in their midst) of:

> the danger it is to have these [non-white] fellows taught the use of weapons and the menace to the white community – still the back-bone of the Colony. He [Raffray] said Andre [Nairac] said he would take up the matter with the Governor. I quite agree with him. To my mind our men would be more useful to the war effort if they were Pioneers or members of a Labour Corps rather than soldiers which they can never become. They have reached that state of civilization when the native mind is distorted and dangerous. Higher officers do not discuss these matters with Mauritian officers who, like myself, although very junior in rank, at least understand the local native mind and mentality. The English officers and officials think the world of these men but they only see the externals not the real inside workings of their minds. It is a thousand pities for the island.[61]

Evidence suggests that the Mauritius Regiment suffered from danger-ously low morale. Regular entries in North-Coombes' diary refer to this problem and to a lack of respect among the officers of the 2nd Battalion for its CO, Major B. J. Landrock. Morale was acknowledged as a problem by the OCT, Colonel Ronald Yeldham. In an interview he said that he was sent to Mauritius to train troops:[62]

> Training [is] difficult when you know you're not going off to do some fighting. Difficult job for officers to keep up morale ... When you're remote from the battlefield one of the problems is main-taining morale ... if you know you're going to the front line, it's okay.[63]

Indiscipline was a sign of low morale and did not auger well for the overseas service of the 1st Battalion. There were numerous cases of soldiers refusing to obey orders, like that of a sergeant and men refusing to empty latrine buckets, complaining that they had 'not enlisted for this type of work'.[64] A constant problem was men leaving barracks without permission at the weekends – 'breaking out of barracks was very common as was malingering', recalls a former soldier.[65] 'As the CO does little to punish those AWOL (absent without leave), many take leave.'

The fact is that some of the soldiers had joined the MTF when overseas service was not an expectation, and – war or no war – they did not want to leave home. Others were simply not fit enough for the exacting standards demanded when the exigencies of war turned the small, amateurish MTF into a Regiment under the authority of the War Office that could expect service overseas as frontline soldiers. As Sir (then Major) Guy Sauzier claims, the MTF 'at its formation was designed only for service on Mauritius itself, and the medical examination was relatively superficial.'[66]

North-Coombes thought that 'morale has sunk to zero'.[67] Self-mutilation was a crystal clear index of low morale and reluctance to leave Mauritius. There were disturbing rumours:

> now circulating of several men of 1MR maiming themselves so as not to leave the colony on Active Service. One man smashed his right thumb to pulp by hitting it with a heavy hammer, another broke his leg (tibia) on purpose, many are inducing 'alesees de fixation' by injecting themselves with turpentine, mostly in the chest. And so more men with barely any training are being taken from 2MR to replace them.[68]

Self-mutilation did not stop when the soldiers reached Madagascar. The medical officer overseeing the 1st Battalion on Madagascar, Rex Salisbury Woods, recalls that there were:

> among coloured Mauritian troops a few undisciplined men of low morale who burnt their bandas and would run any risk to avoid being sent to Burma and battle. Some paid Chinese to lash-whip their knees to produce 'water-on-the-knee'. Others risked blindness by inducing acute gonococcal ophthalmea with pus from a friend; or amputation by pushing nails, purposely fouled with faeces, into the knee joint to provoke an infective arthritis. This sort of thing, when not spotted, notoriously inspired others, as it did when a veritable epidemic of 'low backache' followed the success of a few men in being excused duties, and the resulting sick wastage began to assume such proportions that all fresh cases had to be referred by the RMOs [Regimental Medical Officers] to me as Surgeon Specialist. Practically, none, I found, were genuine [Woods would recommend acupuncture, the threat of which worked a miraculous cure].[69]

Men of the 1st Battalion viewed their impending departure with gloom. A fellow officer told North-Coombes 'that the feeling of the men in 1MR was such that if they knew the time of departure of their transport it would be necessary to look for them 'avec des bougies'.[70] When news of the Madagascar mutiny filtered back to Mauritius there were clear signs that the men of the 2MR did not want to follow their 1MR comrades overseas. Sergeant Felix told North-Coombes that 'the men's morale is such that they have been heard to say "if the [authorities] want to make us cross the sea we'll set fire to this Camp before we go"'.[71] As North-Coombes wrote, 'a strong undercurrent of passive resistance, if not blatantly apparent, is nevertheless clearly perceptible'.[72]

It is difficult to escape the conclusion that the MR was poorly officered, at company and platoon level and at the higher level, where British officers – few of whom wanted to be in Mauritius in the first place – had little appreciation of Mauritian problems. At the lower level, some of the Franco-Mauritians were poor officers, and the fact that communalism was a part of Mauritian life made for natural resentment and a coldness in inter-racial and inter-rank relations. This is not to say that *all* officers were bad.[73] There were signs of strained relations between British and Franco-Mauritian officers, and disquiet on the part of British other ranks who resented having 'part-timers' placed above them.

It seems clear (and the view is universal among MR ex-servicemen) that the 1st Battalion's ambitious CO, Lieutenant Colonel Yates, must shoulder much of the blame for the state of the battalion that led to its mutiny. At all levels there was bad man-management. The Colonial Secretary's wife wrote that Colonel Ronald Yeldham, the OCT and therefore the senior soldier on Mauritius, felt ashamed of 'the lack of hardship in his war service ... [He] regrets the name he would like to have made'.[74] Likewise, Yates perhaps felt that the war was passing him by. So when his opportunity came, he was determined to grasp it. Mauritian ex-servicemen claim that Yates was keen to be promoted to the rank of full colonel, but could not do this on Mauritius as he would then be equal in rank to the OCT. Yates was 'a Regular Army officer who was, I suspect, anxious to fashion his battalion into a first-class fighting force'.[75] The Regiment had a reputation for being amateurish and only good as 'parade ground' soldiers, and with Yates' arrival in 1942 'the troops began to lose their amateurism and be better trained'.[76] Yates has been described as 'a tyrant in colonel's uniform'.[77]

In June 1944 Yates visited the Colonial Office. Naturally he had his own opinion as to where the blame for the mutiny that had blighted his career lay:

The only six good officers were white non-Mauritians. A high percentage of Other Ranks were conscripts and only among Creoles was there any genuine enthusiasm to serve ... [the] rest thought most they should be asked to do was a little quiet training in Mauritius.

He highlighted the fact that no white troops were ordered overseas, leading to resentment, particularly among families back at home. NCOs were considered 'all right on parade, but had no influence when off it'. In Yates' view Mauritians would never make good infantry soldiers. Ex-servicemen draw attention to the fact that during the mutiny the officers of the battalion, as well as the men, were 'nowhere – even our own officers were out of control'.[78]

It would appear that British NCOs were also to blame, though the salty language and unbending discipline of the Regimental Sergeant Major (RSM) are recognized as backbones of the British Army. Many ex-servicemen recall an RSM named Clark whose attitude was not appreciated by Mauritian soldiers. 'I'll break all the fucking bones in your fucking body', was how one soldier recalled him. He was also remembered as particularly harsh on the march from Diego Suarez to Orangea when exhausted soldiers fell out of marching order, even kicking soldiers who had fallen to the ground.[79]

Fear of the Japanese and dislike of Africans

Rumour was endemic on the small island and played a part in 'putting the wind up' those soldiers who did not particularly want to serve overseas anyway. One problem was the reputation of the Japanese as ferocious soldiers (a psychological obstacle encountered by British soldiers of Burma Corps), and the currency of the belief that the Mauritians were destined for Burma and the war against Japan. Some believed that Mauritians were to be sent as cannon fodder and that the East Africans who had preceded them had been wiped out.[80] George Andre Decotter, a Pioneer Corps officer and later Reabsorption Officer, recalls:

I think that the men were reluctant – absolutely reluctant – to go to Burma. That was one of the reasons why they threw everything over the wall. Because they simply did not want to go to Burma. The official reason for our going to Madagascar given by Yates himself – I have seen it by his own hand in a minute in a file to the OCT – was they are going to Madagascar to be trained in 'ideal circumstances'.[81]

Clearly there were problems of leadership and morale in the MR. An unwillingness to leave the island was compounded by anger when it was learned that African soldiers were to replace them and be left to protect their families. The animosity between the Mauritians and the KAR seems to have returned when, on Madagascar, the KAR took great delight in goading the disgraced Mauritians whom they were guarding or whom they passed as they performed humiliating repair tasks on the roads around Diego Suarez following the mutiny.

The 17th Battalion KAR (mainly recruited from Nyasaland), commanded by Colonel E. F. Whitehead, was ordered to Mauritius in November 1943. Major Guy Sauzier recalls that 'rumours were circulating in Mauritius that the regiment was about to leave, and would be replaced by members of the King's African Rifles. The regiment took this badly – unhappy that African troops would be charged with the protection of their families'.[82]

Lieutenant J. F. C. Harrison recalls his Battalion's arrival and the departure of the 1st Battalion The Mauritius Regiment:

> Our reception was something less than enthusiastic. The big, fierce-looking askaris struck terror into the hearts of the islanders, who feared for their goods and women ... When the KAR arrived there was a great fear that the askaris, who looked like savages to them, would molest the Mauritian womenfolk and rumours soon spread. Hence the reluctance of the Mauritius Regiment to embark.[83]

'Most were Creoles, small men, and they clearly did not want to go', and Harrison recalls the 'KAR lining the streets, seeing them off almost at bayonet point'.[84]

> Our first surprise was the emotional nature of their embarkation. As the Mauritius Regiment marched down the quay ... amidst much waving and shouting, I could not make out whether the crowds were protesting or encouraging their embarkation. There were tearful scenes as women, children, parents, and friends tried to kiss, embrace and hold on to the marching soldiers, some of whom seem to me to be reluctant to let go.[85]

On board the ship, the 'British officers were to travel in cabins, whilst the Mauritians and their men would go in the hold – this fact also created resentment'.[86]

Criticism of the MR-KAR swap was not confined to the coloured members of the Council of Government. Alfred North-Coombes, reflecting no doubt the view of other MR officers, wrote: 'We hear rumours that a KAR Battalion is to fill the place of the 1MR. An awful waste ... Replace one battalion by another – wasteful of time, ships, money etc. The KAR's influence on the local population could be disastrous'.[87]

The Government of Mauritius had not learned the lesson of the hostile reception given to African troops in 1899, though there are signs that it learned the lesson of 1943. Writing to the new Commander-in-Chief EAC in April 1945, the Governor requested to be kept informed about the tribal composition of KAR battalions destined for Mauritius, as some might not be suitable. For example, 'the Awemba from Northern Rhodesia which have furnished excellent fighting soldiers in two world wars but which might well be troublesome in this island of curious peoples'.[88]

Mutiny: the official version

The official reasons given for the mutiny were recorded by the Governor of Mauritius, the Commander-in-Chief EAC and the colonel who had had the misfortune of commanding the Battalion. Lieutenant Colonel Rolleston wrote to Lord Mancroft from Downing Street, sending pre-mutiny correspondence showing that the Governor of Mauritius had considered moving a contingent of white troops overseas to decrease political criticism, before the 1st Battalion went to Madagascar 'and behaved so badly there'.[89] The Commander-in-Chief EAC, Lieutenant General Sir William Platt, reported the mutiny to the War Office three days after the event. '[I] regret to report that 1st Mauritius Regiment on arrival at Diego Suarez from Mauritius burnt some of their huts in protest against the standards of accommodation and next day carried out a sit down strike'. The 'mass refusal to do PT' (physical training) was cited as the central act that turned insubordination and indiscipline into mutiny.[90] 'Officially the men were said to be "browned off" ... and angered about their removal from Mauritius'.[91] The Battalion was disarmed, and 343 (500 according to some figures) were arrested for being out of bounds of camp.[92] The Colonial Office was told, and duly informed the Governor of Mauritius on Christmas Day 1943. Speculating about causes, the Governor

referred to the 'over-long delay' in announcing the Battalion's departure, the politicized colour question, and the fact that there were 'more
than likely subversive elements within the Battalion'. On the grounds
of this speculation, the Governor confidently offered his remedy:

> A healthy purge and some hard living for the next few months,
> coupled with firm but sympathetic handling, should do a great deal
> for the coloured Mauritian soldier who, in common with the rest of
> his countrymen suffers from extravagant complexes and a funda-
> mental lack of discipline ... In no, repeat no, circumstances should
> the battalion or any portion of it return to Mauritius until this
> disgrace has been lived down. [93]

Days later Lieutenant General Platt forwarded to Mauritius and
Whitehall the report of the General Officer Commanding (GOC)
Islands Area, Major General G. R. Smallwood. The men of the 1st
Battalion had endured a 12-mile march to their camp at Orangea after
landing. Upon arrival, 'discipline had virtually collapsed'. The accommodation provided was partly of old French brick barracks and partly
good standard *bandas* (grass huts) and the Mauritians 'took exception'
to the latter. The following day the men refused to stay in limits and
'were addressed by agitators'.[94] Of 19 interviewed, 14 said they did not
want to leave Mauritius. Many of the men had signed up not knowing
that they would be required to go overseas. The GOC reported that all
identified ringleaders had been court-martialled, and over 500
offenders put on minor charges.

Back in Mauritius, officers of the 2nd Battalion did not know of the
mutiny until a month later. North-Coombes recorded in his diary on
27 January 1944:

> News leaked out that the 1st MR had mutinied at Madagascar. It
> appears that the battalion marched from the harbour, and about
> half the men fell out on the roadside. When they reached their
> camp ten to twelve miles away the same evening they set fire to
> some of their huts. These were straw huts. Only 117 men were not
> involved [out of 1000] – the baggage party which had been delayed
> at the port. Yates is supposed to have been sacked – it being usual
> to sack at once the CO, the adjutant, and the RSM in cases like this.

Soon after the officers of 2MR received an account – 'the Official
Version' – from the CO, Major Landrock:

The boat was crowded and accommodation poor but there was no sign of any trouble brewing. Reached Diego Suarez on 20 December. They were marched to this camp 12 miles away. Half way up the route men began to fall out. By the time they reached the camp a large number had fallen out and discipline had fallen to zero. The men were quartered in old French barracks and in *bandas* i.e. huts of straw, in which even British NCOs live. That night the men set fire to some of the *bandas*. The CO tried to stop them and to obtain a hearing by the men, but they would not listen to him. Bounds were set, but the men broke bounds. More huts were set on fire, and as the position became uncontrollable two Battalions of KAR and one armoured Battalion were ordered to disarm them. The next morning a PT parade was ordered. There were 400 absentees. They are still disarmed and are now building roads. Of 1000 men, 300 are awaiting trial by the new CO. Colonel Yates is on his way to England, but he has been found not responsible. There has been a reshuffling of the officers. Ten to 15 men have been court martialled and sentences of three to fifteen years imprisonment passed. There has been no sentences to penal servitude. Fourteen out of sixteen of the most culpable men gave as the chief reason for the mutiny that they did not want to leave Mauritius ... The Battalion will no longer be a first line Battalion. But in order that the 700 odd men who took no part in the mutiny be given a fair chance to make good, officers here are asked not to discuss the matter, the facts now stated being given to enable them to refute any exaggerated rumours likely to go around.[95]

The official views expressed thus far all contain elements of the truth. But contemporary British officials did not know all of the contributory facts, and were not inclined to seek for answers where answers might have been found. The 'time bomb' reasons can be found in racial tension, poor officer-men relations, low morale caused partly by conscription and an unwillingness to serve overseas and the unpopular decision to replace the 1st Battalion with African troops. It only needed a spark for the mutiny to occur, and this was provided upon arrival in Madagascar by an arduous route march to accommodation considered inadequate.

Mutiny: eye witness accounts

Major Guy Sauzier had been sent ahead on 12 October 1943 with an

Advance Party to prepare for the arrival on Madagascar of the 1st Battalion The Mauritius Regiment:

> The men were already tired and demoralized on their arrival at Diego Suarez. Sauzier had organized a military band to meet them, but this had no effect. On the march to Orangea, the temperature was overpowering and some men began to leave the ranks and lie down at the roadside, without even having obtained permission of the officer in charge, already a grave indiscipline. Sauzier decided to collect some lorries to pick up the men who had fallen out of the ranks. [At the camp] the men were served with a hot meal. As Sauzier was warning the men to take care not to set fire to the huts, one went up in flames, and he exhorted the men to put it out. One of the men said, 'Let it burn'. This was the first act of insubordination. Several huts then went up in flames, and it became obvious that they were criminal acts of arson. As they struggled, largely in vain, to put out the flames, snakes emerged from the huts and added to the general fear. A few men left the camp and took refuge in a small village on a beach close by. Those left at the camp struggled to regain order ... The next day Sauzier and other officers went to round up the men, with little success. One soldier, elbow propped against the counter of a little ship, told Sauzier, 'Sir, everything you are telling me is going in one ear and out the other'. The next evening further fires were lit and more men left the camp. A military operation was launched to round up the men and submit them to military justice ... and a detachment of KAR encircled the men using bayonets, under orders from Mauritian officers. The men attempted to run away, and then surrendered.[96]

In May 1943 Geoffrey Elcoat was a captain in the 2/3 Battalion KAR, based at Sakaramy near Diego Suarez. 'We were part of the garrison of Fortress Diego, charged with the defence of the large naval base of Diego Suarez'.[97] With the threat of Japanese and German submarine attacks in the Mozambique Channel receding, the frontline forces were moved on:

> 22 (East African) Brigade was in the process of moving back to East Africa, the South African Brigade had gone home, and the British troops involved had moved East. Friendly French forces were now in control of the south of Madagascar. The Royal Mauritian Regiment, with some British officers, was sent to Madagascar in

December 1943 to complete some arduous training and to replace 22 Brigade in their defence of Diego Suarez. There was, we were told, much resistance in Mauritius to the departure overseas of the Regiment, with rioting and civilians lying down in front of transport to prevent the operation.[98]

Elcoat describes the 'strange event [that] took place just before Christmas 1943'.[99] The 5th Battalion KAR was withdrawn and replaced by the 1st Battalion The Royal Mauritius Regiment (additions made by Elcoat in a letter to the author are in parentheses):

> The Mauritians, with white officers but with other ranks of all colours, were obviously in a mutinous mood. [On arrival they were made to parade for an hour in full kit, and then march for three hours to their new camp ... Common enough practice for well-trained, fit troops, accustomed to the good old British Army practice of waiting patiently for something to happen, but too much for this very raw battalion.] There had apparently been political agitation in Mauritius against the battalion being posted overseas and they clearly thought their grass bandas to be unworthy of them. [Malcolm Page states that the camp was infested with snakes, scorpions and other vermin, but the same quarters where I spent several not unpleasant months with my battalion were standard KAR camps ... The camp was close to pleasant palm-shaded beaches on the sea shore.] After a few days they imprisoned their officers in Battalion HQ, seized all the arms and ammunition and took up a battalion defensive position under their self-appointed leaders.
>
> [One witness claims that in Diego Suarez harbour a cruiser had its guns trained on Orangea camp.] Immediately Fortress HQ formed a composite battalion (2/3 KAR, 6 KAR, and 2 Northern Rhodesia Regiment) of all the British ranks, and all the African ranks of the rank of sergeant and above. All ranks were armed with rifle and bayonet [and our normal *panga* – machete] and British ranks with 50 rounds of ammunition, only to be used if the Mauritians opened fire. [We went by transport to the base of the Orangea peninsula. We were ordered to advance in silence, with strict orders not to open fire unless we were fired on first. Our askari, who had scant respect for the Mauritians whom they had already seen, were spoiling for a fight. The Mauritians themselves were obviously apprehensive and trigger happy, and we were fully aware of the danger in which the arrested officers found themselves.] A full

battalion attack went in in eerie silence and the mutiny was quelled. [As we advanced in open order through the palm groves, the silence was deafening. We steadily overran the Mauritians who showed little resistance. In one of the groves, a Mauritian Colour Sergeant aimed a pistol at my head at an alarmingly close range. I was accompanied by my dear old friend Sergeant Muindi Kitolo who rushed at the Colour Sergeant, pushed him against a tree, and butt stroked the back of the tree against which he was standing. This shook him so much that resistance quickly came to an end. There were no casualties as far as I know, the officers were released and we all went back to the camp to enjoy the Christmas festivities.] Several of the ring-leaders were sentenced to death, although these sentences were all commuted, and most Mauritians ended up working on the appalling roads in the district, where they were always treated with derision by passing askari.[100]

Major Tom Higginson was serving with 19th Battalion KAR in December 1943 in the Diego Suarez area (he was transferred to the MR after the mutiny): His men were:

Training especially in jungle fighting in preparation for Burma, presumably our next theatre of operations. In the eastern forests we made acquaintance with the Madagascan creepy-crawlies – much larger than elsewhere – including the huge local cockroach which was some three inches or more in length which used to devour the sweat-soaked linings of our slouch hats hung up in the banda to dry. Eventually we received notice of our posting back to East Africa and, with some regret, vacated our comfortable banda camp at Orangea for occupation by the Mauritius Regiment, which were taking over our garrison duties. Having embarked we were astonished to see, from the decks of our troopship, our vacated camp go up in flames, with running commentary from the *watu* – '*Sasa* A Company, *sasa* HQ Company' etc. The Mauritians had mutinied, and it was a question of disembarking and rounding them up with fixed bayonets.[101]

These testaments are corroborated by the recently released memoirs of John Basil Hobson, a lawyer responsible for court martials. He recalls:

The camp at Orangea was very suitable for the climate of Madagascar. The troops slept in bandas roofed with palm branches and open at the sides. The Mauritians who had, it was said, done their soldiering from their homes, didn't think the camp was good enough. They mutinied on the grounds that the march from Diego Suarez was too long and that the bandas were not good enough. They ran through the camp setting the roofs on fire. A couple of companies of, I think, 1 KAR had not yet embarked and were brought back to Orangea. They surrounded the camp and, when the Charge was blown, wearing only shorts and armed with their pangas, they went in. The defendants were senior NCOs. They included one, if not two, CSMs (Company Sergeant Majors). They had run about the camp urging the soldiers to set the huts on fire.[102]

Major General Rowley Mans, President of the KAR and East African Forces Dinner Club, recalls:

At the time of the mutiny I was stationed in Joffreville, about 15 miles north of Diego Suarez, commanding a company of 1/6 KAR training for Burma and about to return to Kenya in early 1944. Heard that the MR arriving to replace us in the garrison. Disembarked and that evening a number of officers and NCOs of the Battalion ordered to go to Diego and assist similar parties from the other Battalions to round up the Mauritians who had mutinied. Most of them had run off into the town and the surrounding countryside. They were easily rounded up and offered no resistance. Some said that they resented leaving Mauritius and being relieved there by a KAR Battalion.[103]

Pierre Tonta, one of the Mauritian soldiers, blames poor man- management and racial factors:

The soldiers were completely exhausted. It is unfortunate that the then officer commanding Lieutenant Colonel Yates through a lack of judgement or proper vision refused the transport facilities which were ready to carry the troops to Orangea. After some few miles of marching, some soldiers started to collapse, followed by some more, some British officers lost their temper and started beating the Mauritian soldiers ... The other officers lost control of their men and it was no more a route march but a sort of do it as you can. Arriving at Orangea, no food was available, the accommodation was straw huts, no sleeping facilities apart from one's groundsheet, one straw hut was set on fire followed by three or four.[104]

Michael Rose suggests that many of those arrested and charged as mutineers in fact had little knowledge of what was going on. CSM Augustin, identified as a 'ringleader', was apparently inspecting a *banda* trying to find out why it had caught fire, when a British soldier saw him and accused him of starting it. When his company, 'D' Company, was sent before adjudicating officers, the whole company was put under arrest because of Augustin's alleged crime.[105]

Roger Requin recalls that:

> Each night for consecutive nights there had been tents on fire, with flames illuminating the sky and creating a fairy-like atmosphere, described as 'feux de joie'. That Monday night was really a nightmare. All during the night, we heard the footstep of soldiers arriving at Orangea. Exhausted, they just threw their heavy body wherever they could, using their pack as a pillow. Discipline was a dead word; they were tired and hungry, it was no use reasoning with them. On Tuesday afternoon, orders were received that every soldier must fall in for physical training on Wednesday morning, but practically on that day no one turned up. They stayed in their tents, doing nothing but playing cards or dominoes. Some strolled to the sea side and spent the day there. For about three days running, they enjoyed such sweet idleness, doing no military work, refusing orders from anyone. These do-nothing days, baptized 'Vacances Payees', were not to last forever. On Friday, they noticed from the stone buildings that African troops were lurking around their encampment. They took it that these soldiers were being deployed as part of their training and thus they did not pay any heed to their movement and continued relaxing. All of a sudden, these African soldiers, fully armed, encircled all the premises, seized all the rifles, and drove all the troops to a plain nearby.[106]

After the mutiny

The Mauritius Regiment was disbanded in August 1944 after attempts to reform the 1st Battalion following its mutiny the previous December. It was broken up into an Artisan Works Company for the Middle East and two companies of garrison soldiers and clerks for EAC's headquarters in Kenya. However, it should be stressed that the Regiment was *not* disbanded immediately after the mutiny and was not disbanded *because* of the mutiny. Whilst the mutiny did a great deal of damage to the fledgling Regiment, it was not a fatal blow. A combination of factors caused the disbandment: its period of 'reformation' after the mutiny had not produced sufficiently encouraging results; its personnel could be better employed by the Army in other areas; and with the war going relatively well for the Allies, there was less need for an inexperienced infantry regiment.

Immediately after the mutiny the Commander-in-Chief EAC consulted his friend the Governor and his subordinate Islands Area Commander-in-Chief, Major General Smallwood. Platt decided that the 1st Battalion was to 'be reformed (in more senses than one, I hope!), and [the] Commanding Officer replaced'. The exchange of KAR and MR officers was considered, and some MR personnel were to be posted to the Pioneer Corps. The 2nd Battalion MR would be converted into a training centre and depot for all Mauritian units.[107]

The much-maligned Lieutenant Colonel Yates was replaced by Lieutenant Colonel Jackie Fisher of the Royal Inniskillen Fusiliers, who was to attempt the re-formation of the Battalion.[108] All ex-servicemen remember Fisher with warm regard, in contrast to their universal castigation of Yates. 'Colonel Fisher being a gentleman was liked by all the soldiers'.[109] Before Yates left, he had hundreds of the 'mutineers' marched before him, in batches of ten or twelve, to be put on a charge with no opportunity to protest. The men were sentenced to periods of around 28 days' detention (some recall the maximum 56-day sentence). Ex-servicemen remember the anger of Yates, who accused them of ruining his career.[110]

Those who had received the death penalty (four or five) had the sentence decreased by the Commander-in-Chief. Some of those identified as ringleaders were imprisoned in Beau Bassin in Mauritius from July 1944, with sentences ranging from seven to fifteen years.[111] After the war former soldiers petitioned for their release.[112] Ex-servicemen resent the episode to this day: 'My nights are still haunted by my "discharge with ignominy from the Army" and the twenty four months spent in hell [prison]. The whole is made worse by my total innocence and the fact that I had naively wanted to serve my country'.[113]

Former KAR officer Tom Higginson writes of their task of re-forming the Battalion under Colonel Fisher, offering the most succinct summary of the causes of the mutiny:

> From East Africa we returned to Madagascar, and commenced the hard slog of converting the mutineers into soldiers, in which we

flattered ourselves we were successful, even instilling into them a degree of *heshima*. Although the mutiny could not and cannot be condoned, there were reasons for it. These were raw, half-trained polyglot troops with little regimental tradition, homesick for their "Jolie petite ile" which they had never previously left. They had been translated, for purely political reasons, over a rough sea and decanted onto a large, strange, hot and apparently hostile land, there to be forced into a long, mid-day march under a scorching tropical sun to accommodation which by their standards was primitive. An example of bad man management.[114]

Guy Sauzier recalls that after the mutiny:

The General [Smallwood] instructed me to draw up a declaration, urging the men against further insubordination but exhorting them to forget the past and reform into the effective unit he had seen in Mauritius [Smallwood had visited Mauritius in the autumn of 1943 and been impressed by the Regiment's efficiency]. The Colonel [Yates] however, now instituted a reign of terror, seeming to believe that Mauritian officers had not done their duty.[115]

The mutiny occurred in December 1943, and disbandment did not come until eight months later. In that time, the Battalion was moved from Orangea to Sakaramy. New British officers were brought in, and the Mauritians continued their military training, and performed general works, particularly road repairs. Upon assuming command Colonel Fisher addressed the Battalion: 'I know quite well your past behaviour, but for me it's a challenge, thus I am trusting upon your good will and discipline. Without any doubt, I am confident that you will not let me down'.[116]

Some ex-servicemen feel that the morale of the Battalion was low, battered by the mutiny, the punishments meted out and the labouring tasks they were required to perform. There is also a strong memory of a sickness in the ranks caused by jiggers, that led to long queues outside the medical centre each day. Groogobin Pem claims that it was this illness alone that accounts for the Regiment's disbandment. One day Fisher paraded the whole 1st Battalion. After it had presented arms, he told the men that the Regiment was to be disbanded; 200 men had been found medically unfit for further service and reinforcements were not available.[117]

Major General Rowley Mans remembers that 'they used to march past our camp en route to the hills but on the return many fell out exhausted. They were obviously not up to the physical efforts demanded. Eventually Fisher reported to GOC that they could not reach the required standard'.[118] The Commander-in-Chief, Lieutenant General Platt, wrote that he 'consider[ed] quality of Mauritius personnel in unit does not justify retention as first line unit'.[119] He proposed to convert the Battalion into one Artisan Works Company, and two Independent Garrison Companies, 'with consequent saving of British manpower'. The former went to the Middle East, the latter to Kenya. Some were sent to the Military Records Office and Pay Branch in Nairobi, and Guy Sauzier took a contingent to Gilgil (EAC's Ammunition Depot in Kenya) 'where it remained in training, awaiting possible orders to go to the Far East'.[120]

The Governor of Mauritius agreed with the Lieutenant General Platt's prognosis. 'Despite efforts, General Platt and I reluctantly conclude that they are not up to scratch'. Mackenzie Kennedy wrote of the 'shocking' military efficiency of the unit, and that the mental attitude and mediocre medical condition of many was 'most disquieting'.[121] The Government of Mauritius clearly viewed the episode as one bringing disgrace to the colony and arranged some small restitution by sending Franco-Mauritians to EAC's Combined School of Infantry at Nakuru in Kenya. 'The white elements in the Mauritian communities were given a chance to retrieve the reputation lost by the 1st Battalion at Diego Suarez in December 1943'.[122] This was permitted by the Commander-in-Chief EAC, General Sir William Platt, as a favour and was undertaken for political reasons. The Governor asked Platt's replacement to continue this arrangement and to retain the first batch to have completed the training rather than returning them to 'ease and comfort in this indolent isle'.[123]

The maladroit handling of Mauritian troops by their officers did not end with the mutiny and is illustrated by the treatment of the 2MR after the 1st Battalion had mutinied. If ever there was a time to tread carefully, this was it. On 1 February 1944 the 2nd Battalion was 'paraded to be told about the 1st MR by Landrock'. In North-Coombes opinion, the 'CO performed very badly. Committed the stupid error of telling the men that "they should be ashamed for what had happened to the 1st MR". [This] particularly upset the more enlightened among the men.'[124]

Landrock also told the parade that 'a General would visit on Monday or Tuesday to see if they could be made into soldiers or if they should be disbanded' – another psychological mistake. I would not be surprised if many of them are absent without leave on Monday.

The general in question was Major General G. R. Smallwood, Commander-in-Chief Islands Area Command. In the interim, there was:

no training for four days in view of forthcoming General's visit. Men washing and cleaning, trimming lawns etc. Hats being exchanged, slouch hats issued on loan. There will be a Battalion march past tomorrow with the Police Band playing. When hats issued men said, 'Hats with which we are going to be sent overseas'. When they hear the band tomorrow they'll get the wind up properly. GOC coming from Madagascar. Complaints and low morale. This state of affairs is a very bad sign.

North-Coombes was dismissive of the '"window dressing" for the General's visit [which] belies the real state of affairs'. On 7 February 1944 Smallwood inspected the Battalion consisting of 'D' Company, part of 'A' Company, and one Platoon of 'C' Company. The following day the Battalion's CO held a conference to tell his company commanders what the General's visit had revealed about the Battalion's future in the light of the mutiny of the 1st Battalion:

The Battalion will cease to exist in a few days when it will become a Training Company of four Platoons with a fairly large HQ. Some will be transferred to the Artillery. The General says he has dealt with the 1st MR very gently this time but that he won't stand any more nonsense either there or here and men who do not comply with orders will be shot.[125]

So ended the short life of one of the British Army's least famous regiments.

6
The Secret War: Censorship, Radio Propaganda and Code-Breaking

Warfare is rarely confined to the sphere of combat alone. In the Second World War the role of military intelligence was pivotal and the employment of propaganda to undermine the loyalty of enemy subjects reached new heights of sophistication. It was a war of the airwaves in which propaganda was beamed across enemy frontiers, and the enemy's cable and wireless signals intercepted and decoded. The war also saw the extensive use of censorship to screen the correspondence of private individuals for disloyalty or the revelation of sensitive information, and to filter the accounts of the war received by the general public in the newspapers, at the cinema and over the airwaves.

As this study has demonstrated, aspects of the British war experience can be applied with equal measure in the colonies. Most people are aware of the development of code-breaking associated with the Government Code and Cypher School at Bletchley Park, particularly the cracking of the codes sent from the German army's Enigma machines, and the high-grade intelligence derived from the codes, widely known as Ultra.[1] Broken codes yielded readable information and played a major part in Allied victory, shortening the war by an estimated two years. Much intelligence derived from the interception of wireless signals, by stations of what was known as the 'Y' service. This undertook the monitoring of signals 'traffic patterns and networks; the decryption or cryptanalysis of encoded or enciphered signals; and the interpretation of decrypted signals'.[2] Some decryption could be done 'on site', but high-grade signals were broken at Bletchley Park or one of its major regional outposts, such as those in Cairo, Delhi and Colombo (which had moved from Singapore before its fall, and at the height of Japan's power retreated with the Eastern Fleet to

Kilindini on the East African coast). The British empire furnished
Bletchley Park with a worldwide network of 'Y' stations and other facilities for the interception and decryption of enemy military, naval,
diplomatic and commercial signals. Mauritius supported a Naval
Reporting Service, a 'Y' station intercepting and re-transmitting radio
signals from all of the Vichy French colonies in Africa and the East,
Siam, and Japanese radio signals to Europe. It also supported a Cable
and Wireless station used to read cable traffic passing through the
island.

The use of propaganda and broadcasting is another common theme
in the popular memory of the war, encompassing the work of the BBC,
Political Warfare Executive and Ministry of Information. 'Careless Talk
Costs Lives' and other famous posters are still remembered, as are the
broadcasts of Lord Haw Haw, the newsreel images of Pathe and
Gaumont news, and patriotic films like Olivier's *Henry V*.[3] Such propaganda tools were extended to the British empire where there was also
a population to be both disciplined and encouraged. In Mauritius, a
Ministry of Information mobile cinema unit toured the island and
there were nearly 50 permanent cinemas to be controlled. Radio was
an important source of official information. There was 'propaganda
designed to keep the morale high among the population. Colourful
posters presented the Allies in a favourable light. One showed an
English armoured ship escorting a convoy of merchant ships, with the
slogan, "Safely arrived thanks to the British Navy"'.[4]

Mauritius became the centre of covert SOE, Government and Free
French radio stations broadcasting to the enemy islands of Reunion
and Madagascar in an effort to win them over to the Allied cause (the
transmissions were picked up in other parts of the French empire, for
example Syria). Censorship was used to ensure that personal mail,
newspapers, radio broadcasts and the cinema did not disrupt the
island's war effort. Central to all of these 'secret war' activities was the
looming figure of Edward Twining, arguably the most important figure
in wartime Mauritius.

Intelligence

As Chapter 2 demonstrated, 'when in April 1942 Vice-Admiral
Nagumo burst into the Indian Ocean with his carriers, sinking
anything he found, Admiral Sir James Somerville had withdrawn his
scratch Eastern Fleet from Colombo to Kilindini in Kenya'.[5] Naturally
the Chief of Intelligence Staff of the Eastern Fleet moved as well, as did

the whole intelligence operation that had been located in Colombo and had alerted Somerville to Japanese intentions against Ceylon (Far East Combined Bureau had been established in Hong Kong in 1935). Indeed, the sinkings of HMS *Dorsetshire, Cornwall, Hermes* and HMAS *Vampire* could have been avoided if the intelligence provided had not been doubted at a crucial moment.[6] Until the Fleet's return to Ceylon in September 1943, when the intelligence headquarters moved to [the shore base] HMS *Anderson*, it was based at Kilindini, and the Kilindini Intelligence Sub-Centre established at HMS *Alidina*, a requisitioned Indian school, on 23 December 1941.[7] Conditions for the interception of Japanese signals were poor at Kilindini and so it can be surmised that forward intercept bases like Mauritius were doubly appreciated.

Though (reflecting their part in the war) the Americans came to lead in the field of Japanese signals interception, the British maintained an independent operation against Japanese codes, at Bletchley Park and in the East. Before the war, the British had been at the forefront of Japanese code-breaking, particularly in India (prewar intelligence gathering was divided. The Army was responsible for the Near East and South Russia, the Indian Army for India and Burma, and the Royal Navy for the Far East).[8] The Admiralty in particular insisted that Britain never become dependent upon American intelligence in this field, even when Britain's fortunes against Japan were at their lowest and the facilities for intercepting Japanese signals correspondingly weakened (mainly due to geography – Colombo was inferior to Singapore for interception purposes, East Africa was poorer still). This was not helped by the low priority that was sometimes given to intelligence operations in the region and the attitude to co-operation and information-sharing often evinced on the American side of the alliance.[9] This situation meant that Admiral Somerville was often starved of useful intelligence, and given this, it is no wonder that he valued so highly the information that he *did* receive. This included valuable intelligence from Mauritius.

The largest Bletchley Park outstation in the East was at Delhi, originating as an Indian Army organization. As Alan Stipp writes:

WEC [Wireless Experimental Centre] at Delhi was part of a comprehensive array of Allied sigint [signals intelligence] units, large and small, which co-operated to ensure good coverage and exchange of news when progress was made. Furthest back were the large units at Bletchley Park and Arlington Hall, Virginia [this was the US Army intelligence HQ. It's bitter rivals, the US Navy, were based in Washington] ... There was also a large naval sigint unit at [HMS]

Anderson, near Colombo and smaller ones at Kilindini and on Mauritius. They worked closely with US naval stations at Guam, Leyte, and elsewhere, and acted as longstops for signals, travelling 4000 miles or more, which through the vagaries of short-wave transmission, had evaded the main chain of interception stations. These, quite apart from the huge US network in the Pacific, ran in a great arc from Melbourne, Canberra, Brisbane, and Darwin, through Ceylon to Calcutta, and southern China.[10]

The empire's code-breaking operations in the East were centred upon Delhi, Colombo (moving from Singapore and to Kilindini then back to Colombo – though a small team did remain in Colombo throughout) and various Australian cities. They were supported by many smaller units throughout the region.

In addition to the Navy's signals interception station in Mauritius, a remarkable new organization was created, largely on the initiative of Edward Twining, the Chief Censor and Information Officer. This secret organization (codenamed 'Chesor') began life with only 16 staff but was to grow significantly, with the pre-existing Censorship Office as its general cover. Twining recruited additional staff locally and from overseas, employing code-breakers, wireless operators, 'lady readers' to work as clerical assistants, typists and translators, and the wives of British officials who enciphered messages before transmission to Britain. By 1943 over 300 people were employed, including 80 'intercept operators', making it, by all accounts, a very large operation; WEC at Delhi – the largest Bletchley outpost in the East – had only an estimated 1000 workers.[11] The maintenance of secrecy was a remarkable achievement, especially in an environment in which the Official Secrets Act had less purchase than among British people. Michael Smith writes that the size of Twining's organization attracted the criticism that 'they were a waste of public money and were engaged in everything from censoring letters to fixing the prices of cabbages'.[12] Little did the population know, and this remains the case to this day. In July 1943 the Wireless Interception Service was separated from the Censorship Department though kept under the control of Edward Twining.[13] The role of Mauritius was initially to intercept Vichy French signals, by virtue of the fact that cable communication between France and the neighbouring Vichy islands went via Mauritius (a link in the submarine telegraph cable network that had wired the Victorian world), and secondly to intercept Vichy wireless signals. The Vichy empire was used to gather intelligence about

France's enemies. Shortly before the British invasion of Madagascar high-power radio antennae were installed in Madagascar and the French Consulate in Portuguese East Africa.[14]

The 'Y' Service grew into a worldwide network of interception stations and listening posts, intercepting enemy wireless and radio communications and feeding them to Bletchley Park and regional command centres. The 'Y' Service specialized in intercepting and interpreting lower-grade enemy signals (those that did not need the code-breaking skills of the Bletchley cryptographers), 'mostly of a tactical nature, and in making sense of plain language transmissions ... In their ceaseless task of monitoring and interpreting enemy radio transmissions the members of that Service provided information of inestimable value to commanders in the field'.[15]

As all cable messages to and from Madagascar and Reunion went through the Mauritius cable office, 'it struck Twining that interesting information might be gathered from this source. Cable and Wireless were obliged by the British Government, under the Official Secrets Act, to permit official inspection of all traffic carried on its cables in all British territories.[16] The company, having a virtual monopoly of the world's cable system, was able to provide a wealth of information. 'Twining had operators trained in Morse code, and obtained a lot of information regarding cargoes from commercial cables, often learning of individual departures'.[17] Convoys sailing between Indo-China and France could be intercepted by the Royal Navy using this information, thus tightening the British blockade of Vichy France and her empire. A huge amount of intelligence flowed out of Madagascar by wireless transmissions from the Mauritian Percy Mayer and his wife in Tamatave. This information played a key part in the successful British invasion of the island in 1942.[18] Before the invasion the SOE hoped to create, through Mayer, a network of Mauritians in Madagascar to act as SOE agents.[19]

The official history of the Postal Telegraph and Wireless Department in London records that:

> In peacetime the communications between France and her Indian Ocean islands was by way of a regular shipping service and a cable owned by a private company running from Mauritius to Reunion to Madagascar. The Madagascar section was usually out of order, so a long-wave wireless link was substituted. In the first half of 1940 the link between Madagascar and Paris was broken [by the British, later relinked] and telegraph traffic was routed via Reunion and cable to

Mauritius, thence on the British cable system via Imperial [Cables]. [When France was overrun, wireless links from Madagascar to French stations in Paris and Bordeaux were broken and 200 to 300 telegraphs per day began to pour through the Mauritius Telegraph Office.] This traffic was collected and transmitted to London in weekly intelligence reports. In October 1940 Madagascar telegraph traffic via Mauritius virtually ceased. Attention [was then paid] to wireless messages from Madagascar to Reunion intercepted on a Cable and Wireless receiving set. The Chief Censor of Mauritius started to buy up what receiving sets he could and borrowed from the Postmaster General a number of Post Office operators. [In September 1940 Twining was in Cape Town, where he met 'all the Post Office officials from the Post Master General downwards'.][20] It soon became evident that a very much larger service was needed. Equipment was acquired or made, technical and intelligence staff were trained and in due course most of the stations operating in the French Empire were covered.[21]

Due to the interception service based on Mauritius, British knowledge of Vichy actions and intentions was comprehensive. Twining and his Censorship Department/Wireless Interception Service did even more to cover the wireless traffic of Britain's enemies:

British intelligence radio interception and military and naval signals intelligence maintained a base in Hong Kong, known as the Far East Combined Bureau, which moved to Singapore in 1939. In 1941 the Far East Combined Bureau requested the Chief Censor Mauritius to intercept and forward to Singapore Japanese diplomatic messages being transmitted to Germany and Siam. After Reunion and Madagascar had been taken by the British Empire forces, more attention was paid to Indo-China and Siam, and later the Japanese-controlled stations ... The Imperial Treasury took over the cost of the operation, and the Postal and Telegraph Censorship Department assumed responsibility at the beginning of July 1942. The service was transferred to the Foreign Office in April 1943.[22]

The intelligence organization on Mauritius was regarded as so important that special defensive measures for the island were considered.[23] The official Postal and Telegraph Censorship Department history wrote that 'in retrospect it seems remarkable that an organization which ultimately employed more than 300 persons could have been kept secret, but it is a fact that the only persons who knew what was happening were the Governor, Colonial Secretary, and Security Officer'.[24] Twining was asked to contribute to the writing of this official account because the initiation and development of 'Y' Services 'were built up entirely by your initiative'.[25]

The valuable Mauritian contribution in the intelligence field was achieved with traditional British make-do-and-mend parsimony. The service was dogged by lack of funds and had to beg, borrow and steal the necessary radio equipment before London came to appreciate its value. In 1941 the Commander-in-Chief Eastern Fleet reported to the Admiralty that the Chief Censor Mauritius had:

> informed London that because of exhaustion of funds [he was] unable to maintain a W/T watch on internal Madagascan stations as well as covering Far East stations. The military authorities value the information derived from the former and the Eastern Intelligence information derived from the latter. A request for £60 per month, to pay the salaries of twelve additional operators, was put forward ... The Staff Officer (Intelligence) Colombo, and the Captain on the Staff (Colombo), both informed London that the enemy shipping intelligence in eastern waters obtained through the organization at Mauritius is of the greatest value.[26]

This remarkable organization was initiated by a remarkable man. Edward Twining (1899–1967) rose in the Colonial Administrative Service to become Governor of Tanganyika and was elevated to the peerage as Lord Twining of Godalming and Tanganyika. Darrell Bates, in writing his biography in the early 1970s, sensitively omitted the material in Twining's papers that dealt with his secret intelligence work, as did the author of his *Dictionary of National Biography* entry. This was before accounts of the work of Bletchley Park began to be published from 1974.

Throughout his career Twining always sought, and was offered, unconventional jobs. 'He was a self-confident individualist who demanded recognition and worked best on ad hoc assignments carrying much personal responsibility'.[27] He arrived in Mauritius in 1938 as Deputy Director of the Labour Department (Director from 1939) created as a result of the 1937 riots, and rapidly gained a reputation as a man who could get things done. Twining was the pivot in the significant Mauritian contribution to the secret war of intelligence-gathering and propaganda, and was rewarded with a Commander of the Order of St Michael and St George (CMG) in 1943, invested by the Governor.[28] His wife, Helen ('May') Twining, was awarded the OBE for her wartime medical work on Mauritius.[29] In early 1944 Twining was appointed Administrator of St Lucia.

During the war, Twining was Director of Labour, Information Officer (responsible for internal propaganda), Chief Censor (responsible for censoring mail, radio, newspapers, and cinema), Free French Liaison Officer (responsible for smooth relations between the British authorities on Mauritius and the Free French who used the island as a base for operations against Vichy territories), Controller of the Civil Labour Corps, head of the Wireless Interception Service, and Chairman of the Development and Welfare Committee (early in the war he was 'made chairman of a committee of Heads of Departments, whose task was to draw up an overall development plan' for Mauritius in the postwar world, in response to the passage of the Colonial Development and Welfare Act of 1940).[30]

Governor Sir Bede Clifford, with whom Twining enjoyed excellent relations, knew of his background in intelligence (MI6) and 'a few days before war was declared he sent for Twining and put him in charge of censorship'.[31] He was to build up a large censorship, intelligence and anti-Vichy propaganda organization. This led to a prodigious amount of travelling during the war as the three passports he exhausted show.[32] Though unable to tell his family in his letters, he had an extremely important war job. He was prevented from joining the Army (he was on the Reserve of Officers List) and prevented from taking a job offered by EAC as a Lieutenant Colonel in the British Military Administration overseeing occupied enemy colonies. On both counts the Governor and the Secretary of State for the Colonies blocked his move, for he was too valuable where he was. His wartime travels took him all over the empire and beyond. Whilst happy in the knowledge that he was doing something important to help win the war, Twining was understandably riled by the view back at home that those lucky enough to be in Mauritius were having a topping war:

> I am very much amused at the general impression I gather from all our letters from home that we live a peaceful, comfortable life, remote from the war and its worries, untouched in fact by world events, on a romantic island populated by naked savages and that I romp round on luxurious pleasure trips … and at best dealing with labour matters. Actually we have, despite our remoteness, been very closely concerned with the war since 3 September 1939 (I since 21

August 1939). It is true that we have not yet been bombarded from the sea or air or invaded. That may be a treat to come. But from early morning till late at night we are at it and ninety per cent of the work is war work. What do we do? May [Twining's wife] is Assistant Island Director of the British Red Cross and Medical Officer of one detachment. She organizes, inspects, lectures, trains and heaven knows what not. The house is continually full of her cronies making bandages and other such things. She started, and runs, a naval canteen. She is secretary and Medical Officer of the Child Welfare Society and in her spare time does various other things. I have a busy Labour Department but with good luck and I hope wise policy we have so far avoided any labour troubles. I have a busy Poor Law Department with 17 000 paupers. We have recruited thousands of highly skilled artizans and pioneers for Egypt. I am Chief Censor which has its own peculiar problems.

I am Information Officer and as such am in charge of press censorship (17 daily scurrilous newspapers), cinemas (we have 49 on the island), and propaganda generally. I am in charge of broadcasting and our battery of transmitters broadcasts 14 hours of programmes a day and let me tell you some of our first class programmes are listened to as far away as Syria. We broadcast in four languages. I am Free French Liaison Officer, and I do a lot of other things that can only be told after the war but some are of very much wider importance than mere Mauritius.[33]

Twining's travels must have demanded a great deal of the man. In late 1941 he sailed on board HMS *Mauritius* to India, Malaya and Singapore, just before its surrender to the Japanese. During the war he visited or stopped over in Palestine, Greece, Egypt, Uganda, the Sudan, Mozambique, South Africa, Malaya, Ceylon, the Dutch East Indies, India, Burma, Thailand, Singapore, Iraq, Iran, Tanganyika, Madagascar, Nigeria and the Belgian Congo. He travelled by steamer, cruiser, battleship, flying boat, train and road. As he wrote to his wife from the Durban Club on 26 November 1941, 'sick to death of this continual travelling – 20 000 miles in eight weeks!!'.[34]

It is impossible to discover what he was doing on all of his travels, though some indicators are to be found in his letters and the War Diary of the Commander-in-Chief Eastern Fleet. He met senior military and civilian officials wherever he travelled, receiving red carpet treatment from Generals, Governors, High Commissioners, and Commanders-in-Chief, discussing intelligence matters and meeting other Chief Censors from around the empire. He was involved in monitoring the activities of enemy agents operating in Portuguese East Africa (the neo-Nazi South African organization, Ossewabrandwag, sent information to Germany via the German Consulate General who had escaped to Lourenco Marques).[35] MI6 was operating in Mozambique, interested particularly in stopping the German and Italian consuls from gaining knowledge of the passage of British convoys through the Mozambique Channel bound from Durban to the Red Sea or Persian Gulf. MI6 was also concerned to counter German efforts to infiltrate South Africa and compromise the Dominion's war effort. Malcolm Muggeridge, a wartime MI6 recruit, recalls how useful it was that Bletchley Park was able to supply British agents in Mozambique with the secret dispatches of the German and Italian consuls whose activities MI6 was attempting to thwart.[36]

In Cape Town in September 1940, Twining was recruiting for his Mauritian intelligence organization and holding talks with military officials and the High Commissioner and Governor-General.[37] He was in Ceylon from 9–18 October 1941, and the Commander-in-Chief Eastern Fleet reported that this visit was 'useful in establishing personal contact between Naval Authorities and the Censorship at Mauritius, through which a large amount of intelligence regarding movement of French shipping is gleaned'.[38] Twining was again in Colombo between 8 and 16 November 1941 (where he had a meeting with Duff Cooper). There was a 'thorough discussion regarding methods Mauritius used to intercept French shipping – limited by lack of equipment for the interception of high speed traffic. Also delays due to French censorship traffic, and the lack of deciphering tables for French marine ciphered messages'.[39] In November 1941 Twining went to Diego Suarez where he met all of the EAC top brass.[40]

Mauritius was able to forward a constant stream of intelligence that helped build a picture of the strengths and weaknesses of their enemies – militarily, economically and politically – and that was used to discern their intentions. In August 1940 Twining was able to report that commercial interests in Madagascar considered that the island's internal economic position would be desperate before the end of the year unless funds were advanced from France.[41] He informed the Commander-in-Chief in 1941 that henceforth all Allied shipping information to and from Lourenco Marques (Portuguese East Africa) would be referred to the enemy – the 'port is one of the most active enemy intelligence centres in the world'.[42] A radio message intercepted at Mauritius indicated attempts to obtain ships from Saigon to

Madagascar insured by a French company against war risks, suggesting another convoy for the Royal Navy to intercept.[43] 'Cables intercepted at Mauritius together with reports of sailings from Indo-China and French West Africa give a good record of the movements of French merchant shipping' – in fact, virtually complete coverage.[44] All messages from Madagascar and other parts of the French empire were read in Mauritius. During the British invasion of the island in May 1942, this intelligence provided an intriguing view of French minute-by-minute reactions.[45] After the invasion a new Censorship operation was set up on the island and the Mauritius Censorship department provided personnel.[46]

Since the 1920s the British had been breaking Japanese military, naval and commercial signals (signals sent by enemy ships were a valuable source of intelligence). Commercial signals intercepted on Mauritius provided a barometer measuring Japanese intentions even before war was declared. For example, on 17 November 1942 it was reported that the Japanese had asked for detailed information from the Italian consul in Lourenco Marques about Allied convoys between South Africa and Australia,[47] and on 8 March 1941 Twining intercepted a report that local insurance agents in Haipong had refused insurance against capture and sinking by an enemy, possibly indicating that war was imminent. It was later reported that the Tokyo Marine Insurance Company had instructed agents in Colombo to transfer funds out of Ceylon.[48] As Michael Smith writes, 'encoded and plain-text messages between Japanese companies and their offices abroad were intercepted at a number of interception sites around the world, including Edward Twining's Mauritius operation'.[49]

Twining's Censorship Department and Wireless Interception Service was staffed by a number of highly skilled imports, with local men and (mainly) women primarily in clerical positions. The organization was nicknamed 'Twining's twitties' or the 'Twining circus'. The Assistant Censor, appointed in January 1940, was Dr Reginald Vaughan, a British botanist long resident in Mauritius.[50] As a Japanese-speaker he was particularly useful as such linguists were in very short supply on the British side.[51] By the end of 1939 Twining had 16 people working for him. By August 1941 there were 'nearly 100 people under him in his Censorship organization not counting his Labour Department which does not see so much of him these days'.[52] By 1943 more than 300 people were employed. Those 'who couldn't get in or preferred to be more lady-like went and rolled bandages for the Red Cross under Mrs Twining'.[53] The outfit suffered a 'grievous loss' when seven

Examiners were lost aboard the torpedoed *Hoi How* in July 1943.[54]

Evelyn Du Buisson, May Twining's cousin, recalled that the censorship and intelligence services started from scratch with no expert knowledge:

> No one told us how to censor letters or how to deal with intercepted cablegrammes ... Our organization reported to the Ministry for Economic Warfare. Proper office accommodation was erected in Curepipe. There was a collected bevy of Mauritian young ladies of the best family to do typing, filing etc. This was much to the amazement as no Mauritian young lady had ever dreamed of entering an office of any kind before then. The establishment was christened by a visiting general from Diego Suarez, 'Twining's maison des pêches'. The Foreign Office thought it might also gain from Japanese messages sent *en clair*. There was use of the Japanese commercial language – 'Bomaji' – none of us knew Japanese. One learnt some from a dictionary. Eventually the Foreign Office sent out two experts ... Our little organization became much more important when Japan entered the war. The situation of Mauritius and reception conditions made the island peculiarly suited to intercepting wireless messages and the operators were able to pick up code messages in large numbers which were retransmitted to England.[55]

In 1942 the Mauritius 'Y' station had '75 operators and 24 sets and [was] handling some 1500 messages daily, of which half were from the Far East'.[56] In 1943 the station's tasks were 'the interception of a) all traffic between Japan and Europe, b) all traffic to and from Malaya and the Dutch East Indies, c) Indo-China/Siam traffic, and d) other Chinese stations including Shanghai, Tientsin and Skintaing. The next ambition was to deal with Japanese Morse code traffic'.[57] The entry of Japan into the war led to a great expansion. More specialist employees had to be recruited, and in April 1941 Twining travelled to South Africa to recruit extra staff.[58] C. A. L. Richards, formerly of the Colonial Administrative Service in Uganda where he had been a friend of Twining's, was on wartime secondment to the KAR when he was picked by Twining to help with his work on Mauritius. Pulled out of the KAR he was sent by flying boat to Mauritius at the end of April 1941 to supervise propaganda and news broadcasts to the enemy islands.[59] As his wife 'Babs' Richards recalls, 'Tony worked for Sir Edward Twining, breaking Japanese codes and supplying Bletchley Park with information. I worked in the Code Room along with other wives'.[60]

Other recruits were sent out from London by the Foreign Office and the Intelligence Services. Robert Milne Sellar:

> was in Mauritius during the war years, working in Curepipe with the Twining 'circus', a bright young Foreign Office recruit who had served at Bletchley Park with the code-breakers. His senior was C. W. Chilton. [He] returned to England for an academic career at Hull University, where he rose to be a reader in Classics ... With them in Mauritius was Arthur Pollard whose academic career led to a professorship, also at Hull.[61]

Arthur Stamberg was sent to Mauritius as an intelligence officer:

> My job was to set up an intelligence centre to find out everything we could about Madagascar. I found that Peter Twining had already started the ball rolling, listening in with a few ordinary commercial wireless sets, but now I had to enlarge this and create an organization capable of monitoring everything that was being sent out from Madagascar and Reunion ... Having acquired a much larger number of wireless sets we were able to find and train a sufficient number of operators who maintained a twenty four hour watch on everything that came out of Madagascar and Reunion. In order to evaluate all the mass of information thus obtained, we had to have an organized sorting office, a typing section, a cypher section, and a number of girls to do the filing. To obtain the necessary staff we had to rely on completely untrained volunteers and I had to interview a series of young Mauritian girls, few of whom had ever done a hand's turn of work in their lives. As often as not Papa came along to see whether I was a suitable employer! ...
>
> To run the cypher section I was lucky to have a team which consisted of the wives of Government officials. Although all these people were volunteers and completely untrained, I was amazed to see how quickly they adapted themselves and worked with such enthusiasm. We were very lucky to have an agent already in Madagascar; a young woman who worked fearlessly under the noses of the Vichy French police ... We were also working closely with the SOE cell who were arranging to put an agent into Reunion.
>
> On examining the intercepted signals we were surprised to note how lax the French were in matters of security. Many quite important messages to France were sent out 'en clair'. Whenever coded messages were intercepted we were still quite happy as Twining, by

some means known only to himself, had obtained or acquired a copy of the French *Code Nationale*, so we were able to decode the messages with ease. There were certain French individuals in Mauritius with whom we were supposed to work but unfortunately we could not rely on their discretion, so whenever some really important secret project was coming up we had to think of a red herring which we marked 'Top Secret' and confided to them. It was often interesting to hear rumours of this exciting leak from their close friends! We imagined that we would only be in Mauritius for a short time until we had gathered enough information for the Allies to launch the Madagascar campaign but, six weeks after our arrival, Japan came into the war and the whole theatre of activity shifted to the Indian Ocean and the Far East. We remained in Mauritius for three and a half years, with our organization being considerably enlarged.[62]

The island's intelligence role did not stop with Twining's organization. Mauritius had first been used as a military wireless base during the First World War when a station was built at Rose Belle, ensuring 'uninterrupted communication with other countries and ships within radius'.[63] The station was reopened in 1939, with a range of 800 miles by day and 1500 miles by night.[64] In September 1939 the British Admiralty had a worldwide network of 17 high-frequency radio stations which relayed W/T messages to British warships. By 1945 there were 65, and also scattered across the world were some 20 stations for intercepting enemy signals and 69 direction-finding stations.

The Royal Navy maintained a Transmitting Station on Mauritius run by the Naval Officer-in-Charge. The Commander-in-Chief Eastern Fleet was constantly fed information from this source. During the war the Admiralty began work on an enlarged wireless transmitting and receiving centre. Together with other bases in the region, the Admiralty was to spend a projected £855 000 on 'Plan R', the wireless and radar enmeshment of the Indian Ocean. In building the new W/T Station with its four 180-foot towers, Crown Lands were leased at Curepipe (the transmitting station), and use was made of War Office land at Vacoas for the receiving station.[65] The Army's Royal Corps of Signals maintained a Field Security Section in Mauritius (commanded by Major Humphrey Downes during the war). Anthony Clayton writes 'that in Mauritius their concern was link ups between Vichy French, Axis sympathizers in Mozambique, and Japanese submarines'.[66]

The Censorship Department and Information Office

The Censorship Department and Information Office also came under Edward Twining. War required the vetting of all incoming and outgoing mail, as well as the monitoring of the local press and radio stations. Orders in Council or Proclamations provided colonial governments with the emergency powers needed for the censorship of all incoming and outgoing mail, based on draft legislation circulated by the Colonial Office prior to the outbreak of war.

In Mauritius censorship was a more significant issue than in colonies where lower literacy rates prevailed. Mail exchanged with the thousands of Mauritians serving overseas in the Armed Forces was monitored, as was mail bound for family and friends in India and Europe. With the arrival of over 1500 European Jews in 1940, all anxious to receive news and speaking a range of languages, further efforts were demanded. A special section in the Censorship Department 'was developed for the Jewish detainees. All mail was tested, and much also for secret writing'.[67] The authorities were suspicious of the Jews because many were of German origin, and it was at one time thought that they were responsible for intelligence leaks leading to the sinking of ships in the region. Musical broadcasts on the wireless were banned for fear of secret messages being concealed in the music.

Local talent was collected to meet the censorship challenge. Evelyn Du Buisson was sent to the Censorship Department for Jewish detainees. Provided to aid them was 'the Syrian Jewish wife of the Director of Agriculture, and the Greek wife of another official. The detainees were to write in English, German, or French. In any other language, only one letter a month would be allowed. Someone knew Polish, the manager of the Bata Shoe Company knew Czech, etc'.[68] Twining's department was also responsible for the surveillance of individuals suspected of harbouring enemy sympathies. There was apparently a niece of Petain on the island,[69] and the manager of the St Brandon group of islands (dependencies of Mauritius), had 'espoused the Nazi cause'.[70]

As Information Officer, Twining was responsible for press censorship, surveying the output of 'the eighteen nasty, scurrilous little rags called newspapers'.[71] Paper shortages forced three of the island's leading newspapers to merge in April 1942, and eventually to appear together on a single sheet of paper, each retaining its own editorial column.[72] Twining also monitored the operations of the island's 49 cinemas, and on 17 July 1942 restrictions were placed on theatre and cinema opening times.[73] Books were also censored.

Mauritius supported a vigorous press, and by no means were all of the newspapers 'scurrilous rags'. One is struck by the excellent coverage that the papers gave to world events, and the shrewd eye that was kept on stories in the British press. Familiar British advertisements of the day were ubiquitous – 'Eno's for constipation', Van Houten Cocoa, Huntley and Palmer biscuits, Ovaltine and Bovril. A cursory survey suggests that, whilst being muted in direct criticism of Government, lively political debate was not entirely precluded by wartime censorship, and indirect criticism of Government was the order of the day. The Indian community sustained vigorous local political debates. Press analysis of, for example, the political changes gathering pace in India was mature. Parallels were not wasted on the politically active class of the population (for example extensive coverage was given to Harold Laski's criticisms of Churchill's India policy), and the Indo-Mauritian press campaigned on the issue of the franchise. As seems to have been the case elsewhere in the empire, local elites were loyal to the imperial connection but in opposition to the local colonial regime on some issues. The press did not miss opportunities to criticize the Governor and his officials. After publishing excerpts from a Fabian Colonial Bureau booklet entitled *Downing Street and the Colonies*, a commentator in *Le Cerneen-Le Mauricien-Advance* wrote: 'We dedicate them to those many officials who are still to learn that the Empire is being rebuilt and defended by citizens of all races'.[74]

Whatever their differences with local colonial authorities, newspaper editors were solidly behind the war effort. They encouraged public sacrifice and printed Government appeals when required to do so. One such article, aimed at scotching the rumour that the arrival of Jewish detainees would lead to cuts in rations, concluded that it is the 'patriotic duty of the public to rebuff all ignorant and ill-considered chatter'.

Elite loyalty was expressed in Radio Maurice broadcasts by leading Indo-Mauritians, even before the war. Seewoosagur Ramgoolam, later the first President of Mauritius, broadcast a speech entitled 'Our Duties to the Empire' in March 1939, in which he said:

> Speaking as a member of the Indian Community, I must say how the whole community is eager to serve the Empire at this time of crisis, and the telegram that was sent only yesterday to the Indian National Congress asking our countrymen there to support the

Empire is an eloquent testimony to our unflinching loyalty to the King-Emperor.[75]

Only officially approved broadcasts were permitted in Mauritius, and all wireless sets had to be registered with the Censorship Department. Twining enforced the registration of all privately owned radio sets and transmitters and had confiscated at least 18 illegal transmitters.[76]

'Public relations' were a new departure in Mauritius as in other colonies, as the war forced colonial governments to become more intimate with the people over whom they ruled:

> Public relations had begun in Mauritius as early as 1942 when an Education Officer was seconded for this purpose to the war-time Censorship and Information Department. Shortly after the conclusion of hostilities the decision was taken to retain the purely public relations aspects of the department and to separate them as speedily as possible from the propaganda activities of the Information Office [a Public Relations Branch was formed in 1947].[77]

Twining's Information Office was responsible for propaganda aimed at stimulating the war effort of the Mauritian people, taking over broadcasting and a local version of the Ministry of Information. One of its main tasks was to scotch the rumours. Lectures and speeches were used, for example, to explain the Government's food policy and the need to ration meat. It played a key role in the Government's 'Grow More Food' campaigns.[78] Pamphlets and maps about the course of the war were produced and distributed, and a Mobile Cinema Unit was given by the Ministry of Information in Britain.[79]

External radio propaganda and broadcasting

In the Second World War radio was used extensively for purposes of information, propaganda and intelligence in the colonies as elsewhere. The Governor of Mauritius announced the outbreak of war to his people in a wireless broadcast.[80] The island became the centre for covert and overt radio propaganda against the Vichy empire, an operation that witnessed collaboration between the British and the Free French. Before the war the island's only radio station was Radio Maurice. In 1941 Le Poste Radiophonique de l'ile Maurice was established, as was Radio Liberation. All three were taken over by the Mauritius Broadcasting Service when Government assumed control of all broadcasting.[81] (The Service was based in the former Training College at Curepipe.)[82] Soon 14 hours of programmes were being broadcast every day, in four languages. The SOE, as well as having a team in Mauritius in case of Japanese occupation (see Chapter 3), also 'dabbled in propaganda, by introducing a "Madagascar Libre" service from the Government radio station on Mauritius in January 1942'.[83] Raymond D'Unienville writes that:

> Government had been subsidising a private broadcasting station, Radio Maurice ... As soon as war broke out Government took it over and it became the Mauritius Broadcasting Service, operating from the attic of the Town Hall, Curepipe, until it moved to the Plaza Theatre in Rose Hill in 1944. Propaganda aimed at Madagascar was carried out by France D'Unienville. He created the Maison de France which broadcast Free French propaganda through the MBS regularly.[84]

The Vichy authorities in Madagascar and Reunion fought back in the propaganda war with the British and Free French. They maintained their own broadcasting station in St Denis, capital of Reunion, broadcasting anti-Allies propaganda.[85]

Care was needed to ensure that radio propaganda did not become counterproductive. After the entry of Japan into the war the Governor of Mauritius asked Whitehall if broadcasts should be provocative, or if it was considered that such broadcasts would lead to attacks on the island. Whitehall felt that broadcasts should not attack Petain or the French too much, but should take every opportunity to highlight the unpleasantness of the Japanese.[86] Sensitivity was also required in conducting relations between British and the Free French authorities in Mauritius. The Free French sent their own men to Mauritius to set up a secret radio station. The British insisted on retaining overall control of all broadcasting operations (the French broadcasting schedule was vetted by C. A. L. Richards on behalf of Twining), though sensibly allowed the French a wide margin of autonomy. An overriding concern was to conceal the origin of the broadcasts. One of the Free French co-ordinators, M. Barre, wrote to Twining:

> [I am] personally glad to notice that you consider how it is important, in the present conditions, to have a good stuff (sic) of French propaganda in order to convince the whole people of Madagascar that their main interest (and duty of course) is to join the Free

French ... You know how the French are difficult to manage from
the point of view of sentimentality and *amour-propre* and Mr
[France] D'Unienville is too well in course of that spirit for dealing
any matter without him. Moreover we must avoid any talking with
foreign or Mauritian accents ... I agree we should begin as soon as
possible the 'Malagache' emissions. As to my opinion it is useless to
have any talks in Hindoustani, that language not being used in
Madagascar ... Your Department is supporting the main part of the
propaganda financially, the Free French Forces budget dealing only
with the normal pay of my staff and our small sundry expenses.[87]

A balance was successfully achieved between British authority and
French autonomy:

It has always been agreed that the direction of the policy of the post
should remain under our [i.e. British] control; Mr D'Unienville has
abided loyally by this agreement. [While he] would never allow
British psychology to corrupt his French programmes, [he] has
always been prepared to consider and give effect to the British-
United Nations viewpoint.[88]

Barre outlined the structure of the organization. Max Moutia was
engaged as 'permanent speaker' for the Free French broadcasts to
Madagascar, as was a Malagache speaker. Moutia had been engaged as
a broadcaster by France D'Unienville for France Libre d'Outre-Mer. 'He
was a tenor in the Theatre de la Monnaie in Brussels, and had lost his
Mauritius accent. This was important to avoid the location of our
station'.[89] Lieutenant Montocchio assisted him (he had been considered a nuisance by the British in South Africa),[90] as did his wife 'for
every part of women voices and ladies talkings'. Barre wrote of the
need for new French records to play on air. [The following month,
Twining purchased 2000 records whilst in South Africa.][91]

Evelyn du Buisson remembers the station:

With Tony [C. A. L.] Richards he [Twining] started Radio France
Libre d'Outre-Mer. Right until the end of French resistance, the
islands didn't know where these broadcasts were coming from. To
sweeten the pill gramophone records were imported. Later on there
was a secret transmitter station. It was run by a disreputable lawyer.
He broadcast from a small hut, right in the middle of the sugar
cane, news and spicy scandals about Madagascar's notables.

Mauritian fathers became very upset about these broadcasts, and went in a group to protest to Twining. He declared complete ignorance of the matter.[92]

Lieutenant Loyseau was in charge of 'recruiting for the Free French Forces and for local propaganda among the French-born Mauritians'. France D'Unienville had joined the Free French Intelligence Service in London in June 1940. The Service was headed by Commandant Honore D'Estienne D'Ovres, executed by the Germans at Mont-Valerien on 29 August 1941. Before his death, D'Ovres gave D'Unienville the task of organizing a secret broadcasting service in Mauritius.[93] He was summoned to Carlton Terrace Gardens to discuss his task with General de Gaulle.[94]

As soon as I arrived in Mauritius I met the Governor, Sir Bede Clifford, and we agreed that the Free French would keep control of the broadcasts. One engineer was sent from South Africa and another by the Free French Services. The station was built in a cane field in the Highlands and started to broadcast on 23 April 1941. The great problem was to avoid the Mauritian accent of the speakers because it was very important that the geographical point of the station remained unknown. In fact, my other activities, like [the writing of] *La Maison de France* and *Dialogues d'un Temps Trouble*, were 'covers'.[95]

D'Unienville set up the Free French radio station (YP3) and made it 'a going, live concern'.[96] Writing to de Gaulle's official Franco-Mauritian representative, Hector Paturau, Twining attached a tribute from C. A. L. Richards stating that D'Unienville:

has tackled a difficult and onerous task. He had to build from nothing and the first few months were very disheartening owing to the repeated technical difficulties met with. Quite undaunted Mr D'Unienville by hard work, perseverance, intelligence and ability has played a leading part in making RADIO FRANCE LIBRE D'OUTRE MER one of the most efficient propaganda broadcasting stations in the Southern hemisphere.[97]

The propaganda efforts were considered a success:

[We] have always lacked knowledge as to immediate reaction of listeners in Madagascar. But reports suggest programmes have been consistently popular ... A radio could not receive a better tribute than the imposition of deliberate jamming, such as Governor General Annet ordered between September 1941 and January 1942.

The London *Daily Sketch* reported after the occupation of Diego Suarez:

We can now reveal that Radio Propaganda played a big part in the quick surrender of Madagascar. For weeks before the attack the British and South African Radios poured out, in French and also in Malagache, the facts about the Axis pressure, Japanese atrocities and Laval's prospective surrender of the Island. The result was that native troops deserted the French, the native population accepted the British as deliverers and the French defenders were too disheartened to carry on. This is believed to have been the most successful British Propaganda of the war.[98]

7
The Effects of War on the Home Front

As has been demonstrated, the colonial home front was deeply affected by the Second World War, and many of the widely remembered images of the British home front can be applied to the scattered dependencies in which Britain's 60 million colonial subjects lived.[1] A summary of the war's main impact on the home front is important for the balance of this study. The main areas are: wartime political developments; the economic effects of war; the food situation; development policy; the experience of the Franco-Mauritian community; and the story of the 1600 Central European Jews detained on Mauritius from 1940–1945.

The war was more than just a hiatus between the depression years and those of postwar nationalism and decolonization, as it is sometimes portrayed.[2] By the same token, it was much less than the seismic catalyst that caused colonies in the postwar years to burst at the seems with nationalist fervour, and colonial powers to turn heel and flee pell-mell at the sight. Some events that had significant postwar ramifications were caused or exacerbated by the war. Some were speeded up by wartime conditions; others happened during the war just because they happened then, for the period 1939–45 was a 'moment in time' in its own right and not exclusively 'the war'.

The war years did witness important alterations in the world's political, economic and military balance. Britain was momentarily defeated as a colonial power in the Far East, its economy was weakened to the extent that it became a debtor nation (owing even its colonies), and a new era of global politics shaped by two opposing superpowers came into being. One result was an unprecedented internationalization of colonial issues, with the rise of the 'anti-colonial' superpowers and the birth of the United Nations. War compounded a significant shift in the metropolitan view of empire, leading to the great postwar effort to develop imperial resources and uplift the colonial people, for the first time recognized as a metropolitan responsibility.[3] The war put new strains upon the metropolitan–colonial relationship through the demands of wartime mobilization and its attendant troubles, as did postwar attempts to use the empire as an economic crutch for the British national economy.

War and politics

Industrial and labour unrest in the late 1930s altered the political tempo in Mauritius, as it did elsewhere in the colonial empire. 'Strong parliamentary pressures in Britain and industrial troubles in Northern Rhodesia, the West Indies, and Mauritius', together with the interest of Secretaries of State like Ormsby-Gore and Malcolm Macdonald, meant that fundamental colonial policy was being reviewed at the highest level even before the war.[4] 'In Mauritius, as in the West Indies, strikes and riots finally led to government action', but it was arguably the war that led to real forward movement.[5]

The 1930s saw the establishment of the MLP and of the Government's Labour Department that it was hoped would negate the appeal of political movements by addressing the grievances of the workers. The MLP was primarily a party of Creole intellectuals, artisans and the urban working class that could be as hostile to the Indo-Mauritians as it was to the Franco-Mauritians. Government was hostile to the MLP and did all that it could to limit its appeal. However, for the first time the Indo-Mauritian population became effectively politicized, and this key occurrence was spurred by the war. The need felt by Government to exile its opponents (like the first two leaders of the MLP), or to detain them (like Ramnarain, a union leader, and Bissoondoyal, a religious-political leader) during the war period was a sign of the increasing success of political opposition in the colony.

During the war political pressure mounted on the imperial government regarding colonial issues.[6] The Fabian Colonial Bureau (founded in 1940 by Arthur Creech Jones – Colonial Secretary from 1946 – and Dr Rita Hinden) maintained links with a number of Mauritian politicians that enabled them to bypass local colonial authorities and access influential Labour Party politicians who would then raise questions or initiate debates in Parliament. Using this effective tool Mauritian politicians were able to mobilize powerful support in the metropole, often making local colonial authorities and the Colonial Office look clumsy. The publicity generated by metropolitan watchdogs was never favourable, and the island was seldom portrayed as anything other than 'a deplorable dependency'.[7]

These links gave Mauritian activists a hotline to the heart of empire, and provided ammunition for critics of colonial policy. As S. B. Emile, a Mauritian union leader, wrote to W. Paling MP, 'we rely on the valuable assistance of the Home Labour Party to promote the causes of labour here'.[8] Creech Jones had maintained an interest in Mauritian affairs since the late 1930s, and kept the Mauritian flag flying in Parliament.[9] Lord Faringdon, a 'patrician radical', regularly asked questions or initiated debates in the House of Lords on Mauritian issues.[10] The effectiveness of this pressure was compounded from 1943 when the riots, and the resultant Moody Report which upheld many of the labourers' grievances, was published. It was a field day for opponents of the colonial government, and 'the fact that the British Government decided to publish this report in the middle of war was a measure of the seriousness with which, at last, it was viewing the situation in Mauritius'.[11]

Low wages, wartime inflation and wartime food shortages led to riots on two sugar estates in September 1943. The underlying cause was the relationship between a wealthy class of planters and an underpaid work force. Because of the war, 'the prices of all commodities had doubled, but the wages of the labourers had increased to only ten or twenty per cent'.[12] The Report of the Moody Commission said that in 1943 labourers 'had marched to the capital and complained to the Department of Labour of low wages and the shortage of food'.[13] Prices had risen between 1939 and 1943 'by 100 per cent as regards foodstuffs and by 300 per cent as regards clothing'.[14] These conditions were ideal for agitators, some inspired by events in India, touring the estates making speeches against the Government and the planters.[15] The riots had an impact out of all proportion to their limited scale, leading to widespread condemnation of the Government of Mauritius in Parliament and the press. The Governor attributed the riots to poor employer handling of labourers, illegal strikes, subversives and the 'general malaise induced by the food situation'.[16]

Though only three people died in the riots, like the Hola camp massacre in Kenya or the Devlin Report on Nyasaland, metropolitan press attention in a liberal empire could be telling. Metropolitan and international scrutiny of colonial affairs meant that such relatively minor things as the 1943 riots could not be brushed under the carpet, even during a world war. An article in *The Economist* in late 1944 was damning:

Both the local government and the Colonial Office have been inexcusably dilatory in taking action on recommendations made to them, of which the most notable were made by the Colonial Office's own Labour Adviser, Major Orde Brown, who visited in 1941 ... Nothing can excuse the open victimization and slum life revealed in this report.[17]

Parliamentary attention increased. There was a House of Lords debate on Mauritius in late 1944.[18] Lord Faringdon tabled a motion on trade unionism and labour conditions. The Colonial Office duly went scurrying off to gather details to use as armour for the Secretary of State in the forthcoming debate. The Governor wrote of the 'unfortunate timing' of the debate, believing that a 'more liberal attitude' towards labour, 'after a period of bitterness and ill will', was in the offing.[19] Further questions about the situation in Mauritius were asked in the House of Commons in January 1945, by the Fabian Colonial Bureau in March 1945, and by the India Office in August 1945. Indo-Mauritians viewed 'the year 1943 as a milestone in the history of Mauritius. It saw the awakening of the Indo-Mauritians'.[20]

As the imperialization of opposition to colonial rule gained in strength, the Government of India came to have a bearing upon Mauritian political development. The course of India's own path to independence had an effect in Mauritius, and the Government of India kept a close eye on developments in parts of the empire where communities from the Indian diaspora had settled, exercising a novel form of sub-imperial influence. It feared nationalist politicians claiming that their kin were suffering under the imperial yoke in other parts of the empire. Each year the Government of India published a survey on Indians in all parts of the empire.[21] A deputation headed by Sir Maharaj Singh had visited Mauritius in 1925.[22] This was followed during the war by a significant report from an Indian Civil Servant, S. Ridley, acting as Agent General for Indians in South Africa. His report investigated the grievances of Indo-Mauritians, particularly in the light of the 1937 riots.[23] In visiting Mauritius in 1940 Ridley and the Government of India were told that his report must be kept confidential, and that discreet investigations should steer clear of the constitution, 'which is at the moment a very delicate affair'.[24] Indian newspapers also kept watch on events in Mauritius.[25]

An exasperated Government of Mauritius blamed its run of extremely bad luck in 1943 (the Madagascar mutiny occurred only three months after the riots) on its lack of contact with the Mauritian people and on agitators out to make political hay in the harsh sunshine of wartime conditions. As the Governor wrote, 'the fundamental weakness of this administration is the lack of sufficient personal contact between Government and the field labourer. Into this gap all kinds of undesirable elements intrude themselves'.[26] The situation was worsened by the war as the Council of Government was frozen and the administrative ranks depleted through military service.[27] A brief prepared in 1943 for the visit of Sir Cosmo Parkinson, Permanent Under Secretary of State for the Colonies, said that the Secretariat was understaffed, and highlighted the 'over-centralization' and 'excessive departmentalism' of the administration.[28] It concluded that the Government was 'largely out of touch with the people'. This led to change after the war with the implementation of a standard system of district administration based on Civil Commissioners and village councils, which was intended to 'provide that close and daily contact with Government which is still lacking'.[29] Mauritius was an anomaly in the colonial empire, neither directly or indirectly ruled by British colonial officials. Just as indirect rule was being phased out in British Africa, it was being introduced in Mauritius.

The Indian elite showed its two faces during the war. On the one hand there was vaunted loyalty to the empire, but on the other there was growing opposition to its local manifestation and a maturing capacity to mobilize the Indian masses for political purposes. This ranged from a stance of loyal opposition to that of outright hostility. The Indian elite backed the war effort wholeheartedly, symbolized by a book published by the Indian Cultural Association in 1940, forewarded by the Governor and including contributions from Edward Twining, the Mauritian poet Robert-Edward Hart and the former Colonial Secretary C. A. Hooper, as well as leading Indians.[30] The object of the book was 'to give moral support to those who are fighting for the liberties of mankind', for, if Hitler was to triumph, 'civilization would perish'. The book was 'an expression of our confidence in the spirit of freedom and equality which is the very foundation of the British Commonwealth of Nations'.

In the book, the man who was to become the first President of independent Mauritius, Seewoosagur Ramgoolam, claimed that the 'fundamental principle of the Hindu religion is loyalty to King and Country' and praised Sir Bede Clifford for his efforts to improve conditions for Indians.[31] Muslim loyalty was also in evidence. A. M. Osman's chapter was entitled 'We Shall be Victorious', and recorded that the 200 members of the Muslim Youth Brigade had offered their services to the MTF (in July 1943 the Jumma mosque in Port Louis held special prayers for the Royal and Merchant Navies).[32]

Despite these expressions of empire loyalty, Ramgoolam had impeccable credentials for a future opponent of British rule. He had spent time in Britain in the 1930s, attended the 1931 Round Table conference on the future of India, met Gandhi, and had become acquainted with Creech Jones. Upon his return to Mauritius he established the elite Indian newspaper *Advance*, was elected to the Port Louis municipal council and in 1940 was nominated for the Council of Government at a time when the Governor was courting the Indo-Mauritian elite to counter the MLP. But events in Mauritius during the war led Ramgoolam to become a leader of the Indian masses, calling for franchise extension, improvements in labour conditions and, eventually, for self-government.[33]

Another important expression of Indo-Mauritian awakening during the war was the Hindu cultural movement led by Bassdeo Bissoondoyal. His Jan Andolan movement was based on the Arma Samaj movement in India, where he had spent time, and influenced by the techniques and message of Gandhi (who had briefly alighted in Mauritius when returning from South Africa earlier in the century). The movement was similar to the independent church and schools movements that sprang up in other colonies to challenge local colonial authority.

The Bissoondoyal brothers led popular resistance to constitutional proposals that would have entrenched British and Franco-Mauritian authority in the Council of Government, and to other unpopular Government policies. For example, a lecture delivered by the Director of Education, W. E. F. Ward, at the Port Louis theatre in August 1943 was disrupted as 400 people filed out when Ward rose to speak. This was a demonstration against proposals to abolish Tamil and Hindi in schools. With overtones of the civil disobedience and Swadeshi movements in India, Jan Andolan demonstrated a capacity for the peaceful mobilization of tens of thousands of ordinary people. In December 1943 elements of the 2nd Battalion The Mauritius Regiment, the KAR and other security forces were on alert as a crowd estimated at 60 000 celebrated Maha Jag in Port Louis. North-Coombes recorded that his Battalion was 'mobilized overtly' for the 'coming monster Hindu meeting to be conducted at Port Louis by a fanatic missionary called Bissoondoyal'.[34] In February 1944 Bassdeo Bissoondoyal was tried for holding illegal public meetings and prosecuted under the Defence Regulations. In November 1944 he began a sentence of 12 months' hard labour. A petition with 10 000 signatures was delivered to the Governor and a day of prayer for Bissoondoyal held on 28 November 1944.

There were other 'agitators' for the Government to worry about. At the time of Bissoondoyal's trial, the Governor was about to detain the leader of the North and Central Riviere de Rempart (Industrial Employees) Association, Harryparsad Ramnarain. The Governor told the Colonial Office that he was an 'illiterate fanatic' in danger of becoming 'the next Bissoondoyal'. He had 'converted himself into a "holy man" and is strongly suspected of fomenting illegal strikes ... He has recently gone outside his area, [and] toured the whole island on an "anti-Allies" campaign'.[35] His touring among the workers had led to increasing absenteeism, and the Governor felt he had no option but to detain him.

Another headache was Dr Millien, editor of *L'Ouvre*. He had 'for months ... fomented intense racial feeling'.[36] As a result of his actions, press censorship was tightened. In January 1944 a mob of 1500 demonstrators had been dispersed by a police baton charge and the use of tear gas. The Secretary of State was perturbed by the news from Mauritius and the extremity of the measures the Governor had felt compelled to adopt. He urged the Governor to keep him informed, as 'individuals will probably contact Members of Parliament'.[37]

There were no Council of Government elections between 1938 and 1948 because of the war. The Council 'did not enjoy the trust of the common people who were conscious of the fact that the Council did not represent its interests'.[38] Though there was of course a long way to go until independence, and though Franco-Mauritian and British control of the legislative (through the Governor's nominated members) and executive was to remain for some time, a major point had been gained in the 1947 constitutional proposals and the 1948 election that saw them enacted:

> Control of the legislative had passed from the officials, planters, and large white commercial interests to those representing the labourers, small planters, and white-collared workers. Control also passed from the British, Franco-Mauritians, and Creole elements to the Indo-Mauritians.[39]

What the war had done was to speed things up, by forcing the British to put the constitution on the list of things for change. The Colonial Office and the Governor had preferred instead to direct attention towards economic reform as the medicine that would lead to a happier and healthier Mauritius; politics was considered, in characteristic British vein, to be the preserve of 'agitators' bent on misleading the public for selfish gain. Whitehall had tried to deflect attention from the issue of constitutional reform. In 1941 the Under Secretary of State for the Colonies, George Hall, agreed with the Governor that the throes of a world war were not the best times to 'raise what is without exception the most controversial issue in the politics of Mauritius'.[40] Two years later there was an exchange in the House of Commons after S. B. Emile had written to Creech Jones, and the indefatigable colonial campaigner raised the constitutional issue again. The Secretary of State, Oliver Stanley, said that he would look into the matter but cautioned that 'the Honourable gentleman must realize that Mauritius is still very close to the front line'.[41] However, despite official reservations, the constitution became the main course on the political menu due to wartime developments.

In 1943 came suggestions for a revised constitution, but by 1946 Governor Sir Donald Mackenzie Kennedy considered that what might have been acceptable then was no longer so.[42] Conditions in the 1930s and 1940s, and the activities of the likes of Ramgoolam, Ramnarain and Bissoondoyal meant that a new constitution – the first since 1885 – would have to embrace those previously denied electoral representation. The Governor and the Colonial Office wanted to keep the constitution off the political agenda, at least for the immediate future. But by the end of the war this was no longer a realistic goal, and this forcing of developments was an achievement of wartime political activity. 'Mauritians could be certain of one thing: the 1947 constitution had permanently and drastically altered the politics of the island'.[43] The 1948 elections saw only one Franco-Mauritian candidate returned among the elected members of the Council of Government. After 1948 the Franco-Mauritians increasingly looked to Britain for protection, opposing independence and arguing for a form of association to be maintained.

The economics of war

Information on the Mauritian war economy is scant and often conflicting. One writer concludes that 'when the 1939–45 World War came to an end, the economy of Mauritius was in a sad plight'.[44] In direct contradiction, another writes that 'war brought relative prosperity to the island'.[45] The complex series of public and private gifts, loans and tax increases that sent money from the colonies to the mother country in war time need to be disentangled from the money flowing in the other direction, in the form of grants-in-aid or development loans from the Imperial Exchequer. At the end of the day, one is left unsure as to whom was borrowing from whom.

According to Colonial Office figures, the colonial empire (i.e. not including India, the Dominions, the Sudan, and the HCTs), loaned the imperial government £48 846 000 during the course of the war. It gave the imperial government £24 014 948 as an outright gift. The Mauritian contribution is difficult to ascertain accurately. One official report puts it at £301 962 (gift money), and for comparison (using the same statistics) this figure was almost identical to that given by Uganda, twice as much as that given by Nyasaland and just £60 000 less than the Gold Coast's contribution.[46] Another official source says that the Mauritian contribution was greater than that of all the African colonies save Nigeria.[47] By 1944 Mauritius had raised £100 000 for Spitfires and by July 1943 gifts and loans sent to the Colonial Office totalled £550 000.[48]

By July 1940 the British Government had accepted Rs. 2 million (£150 037 – from 1934 the Mauritian rupee was detached from the Indian rupee and tied to the pound sterling at one shilling and six pence)[49] as a war gift, Rs. 160 000 (£12 000) from a special tax raised on that year's sugar crop voluntarily imposed by the planters themselves, and £150 000 from surplus balances.[50] In 1940 Mauritius made a gift of £163 000 and an interest-free loan of £300 000;[51] £2000 was voted to the Red Cross, and £11 000 for a Walrus seaplane for HMS *Mauritius* came from the 1892 Hurricane Loan Fund.[52] (Mess furnishings were also provided. The Governor Sir Bede Clifford, on a visit to London, caused embarrassment in Downing Street when trying personally to present a silver table-piece for the officer's mess depicting the Battle of Grand Port, to Churchill).[53] Rs. 100 000 (£7501) was subscribed in the first three months of war for comforts for the crew of HMS *Mauritius* and other war-related funds.[54] According to figures published by the Government of Mauritius, from the outbreak of war until the end of December 1940 gifts and loans from the colony to Britain amounted to £375 000 along with 2300 tons of scrap metal.

There existed a plethora of charitable organizations happy to accept gifts from the colonies, where they successfully appealed for donations as part of the British mobilization of its imperial population – funds for shipwrecked sailors, Anti-Aircraft Command Welfare, Merchant Navy Comforts, Aid to China, Warship Weeks, to name but a few. The first mobile canteens on the streets of blitzed London in the winter of 1940–41 were donated by the schoolchildren of Mauritius (vans from which sandwiches and cups of tea were dispensed).[55] 'Navy Weeks', gymkhanas and a variety of social events were organized to raise money. Maison de France acted as a focal point for efforts to aid the stricken power, a War Organization Fund was created, those who could afford to bought War Savings Certificates from 1941, the Lottery (HM Forces) Ordinance funded welfare provisions for Mauritian soldiers overseas (and later grants to ex-servicemen), and the Imperial Forces (Comforts) Ordinance funded the distribution of gifts and comforts. Britain benefited in other ways from its possession of a resourceful empire; Mauritius produced a lot of alcohol from its sugar, and during the war it was sent to Britain for the manufacture of gin (it was also used as a motor spirit).[56]

Of course, for the proverbial man and woman in the street, the most visible manifestation of the economic effects of war were worsening conditions on the home front. Shipping shortages meant there was less to buy, leading to inflation. Wages failed to keep pace, so the mass of people were worse off than before the war. As an official report put it:

> It is beyond controversy that the cost of living has risen enormously for every section, and that, in particular, the poorer classes have suffered seriously by the suspension of rice importation. In addition the cyclones of the early part of 1945 have considerably added to the economic difficulties.[57]

However, the impact on ordinary people was conflicting. Reference has been made to the comparative wealth that military pay brought the wives of serving soldiers. The people of Rodrigues, it was reported, endured rationing and the disappearance of some basic consumer items, but soldiers' pay and the sale of fish and eggs led to a cash flow 'such as has never been seen in the island'.[58]

As in Britain, the rich did not suffer so, and many became richer. The purchase of the sugar crop was guaranteed by the British Government. Prices for the crop increased throughout the war, according to figures given in the House of Commons in January 1945: 1939–8.3 shillings per hundredweight (s/cwt); 1940–10.6 s/cwt; 1941–11.11 s/cwt; 1942–13.0 s/cwt; 1943–13.6 s/cwt; 1944–14.6 s/cwt; and 1945–16.6 s/cwt.[59]

The sugar planters raised a voluntary tax on their crops as a contribution to the war effort. Direct taxation was imposed for the first time to help fund the war, though the Colonial Office was sure that this did not hurt the wealthier people required to pay it. As Twining noted, 'the prosperity of the Colony during the war period is resulting in the accumulation of a large volume of wealth for which at present there is no outlet'.[60] Tax on profits was high, and some critics suggested that money would be better spent on increased wages, thereby, perhaps, avoiding further rioting. In the year ending March 1943 Anglo-Ceylon and General Estates was the largest sugar producer on the island, and paid £180 000 in Excess Profit Tax and income tax to the Imperial Treasury out of profits of £240 924 (£134 199 of this figure from its Mauritian estates).[61]

As a fortress colony Mauritius had since the nineteenth century paid an annual sum to the Imperial Treasury as a contribution to the maintenance of British garrison troops. From the mid-1930s the Government of Mauritius also paid for the locally recruited MTF. The annual contribution for the Mauritius Garrison was naturally a disputed arrangement, some feeling that the garrison was there for imperial purposes – not specifically the defence of Mauritius – and should therefore be funded entirely from metropolitan coffers. 'Both politicians and Colonial Office bureaucrats realized that Mauritius had defence costs only because it was a "fortress" in an Empire that it never chose to join and whose shipping it had been elected to protect'.[62] Of course, imperial officials had a different outlook, and could not divine such a sharp divide between 'imperial' defence and 'local' defence, believing that the one was very much bound up with the other.

The Imperial Treasury assumed total responsibility for funding the island's defences from July 1942. Until then, the annual defence contribution was five-and-a-half per cent of Mauritian revenue (in 1938–39 this had amounted to £63 377).[63] Given escalating defence costs, the Governor tried to get the War Office to take over the whole burden, suggesting that the annual defence contribution be waived given the colony's heavy expenditure on local forces and defence works.[64] At first the Colonial Office was lukewarm, given the great burden that the British taxpayer was already bearing because of the war. It was pointed out that Mauritius made no contribution to naval defence though it was 'almost entirely dependent on Naval Defence ... Moreover, there is a good deal of evidence that the Mauritius Defence measures [the MTF] locally taken are bad value for money'.[65]

The Governor predicted that in the first year of hostilities the colony's war contribution would amount to £93 373. Most of this was for the Mauritius Garrison and the MTF. It also funded harbour defence, the supply control service, communications and the Censorship Department. The Governor offered to raise and fund further military units for defence of the Mauritian dependencies[66] and told the Colonial Office that Mauritius would pay for the MTF increase this entailed. However, the Colonial Office – though happy for the colony to continue making its peacetime contribution to its own defence – thought that the War Office should pay for these extra measures as they were clearly imperial defence commitments.[67]

This caused a Whitehall fracas between the two offices of state, in which the Treasury also became involved. The War Office agreed to pay, though was inclined to think in the circumstances that what might be considered 'imperial' defence measures were just as much a concern of the colonies.[68] The Treasury thought that Mauritius should pay as it had surplus balances. But the Colonial Office vigorously fought against the assumption that Mauritius was not really contributing to the war effort according to her means.[69] Contributions to date were recited; an outright gift to the British Government of £150 000, a £400 000 loan, £100 000 for Spitfires and an increase in defence expenditure met by increased taxation – £225 000 raised through direct tax increases alone. Apparently unimpressed, a Treasury official caustically noted that 'direct tax in the colony is still almost ridiculously low on the middle grade of income', and that there were six months' worth of accumulated reserves.[70] The Treasury was 'not convinced that Mauritius is taxing herself as heavily as she might'.[71]

This was a sentiment that appears to have been shared by the Government of Mauritius. It was predicted by the Financial Secretary in October 1940 that the colony would receive about Rs. 52 million (£3 900 975) for its sugar crop that year – 'the highest figure for fourteen years'.[72] This was to be used to finance its imports at enhanced prices, to pay increased wages, to finance the cost of a reserve stock of rice, and to reduce the colony's overdraft in London by £490 000.[73] The Financial Secretary noted that the repayment of debt by borrowers, if the money was borrowed in Mauritius, did not affect the colony's ability to finance a war loan. 'On Mr Leclezio's own showing, the commercial community will be £790 000 better off as a result of this year's crop and I consider that it can well afford to subscribe to a loan of £300 000'.[74]

The food situation

Food shortages were a grave wartime problem in Mauritius and led to rationing, dietary disruption and widespread malnutrition. The food situation was acknowledged as one of the major contributing factors to the 1943 riots. The situation was not surprising for, like Britain, Mauritius could not feed itself and was dependent on imports. The overriding need to feed British people given the loss of merchant shipping caused by the U-boat offensive led to direct Government control of agriculture, huge strides in mechanization and the cultivation of two million additional acres for food crops. Similarly, the U-boat offensive in the Indian Ocean led to direct Government intervention in agriculture and the enforced cultivation of food crops on one-quarter of all sugar estate land.

In August 1943 Governor Sir Donald Mackenzie Kennedy wrote to Oliver Stanley, Secretary of State for the Colonies, summarizing the position:

> Throughout the year 1942, the hardships of war, which had not been seriously felt before the entry of Japan into the conflict, bore more and more hardly on the people ... Rice, the principal diet of the population, began to fail and it became necessary to turn to unaccustomed foods, the cost of living was rising in spite of efforts to stabilize it, there was a shortage of popular transport, and generally, the situation of the great mass of the population was rapidly becoming more and more straitened ... In these circumstances there was naturally an intensification of the criticism of 'Government'. Arising out of a war psychosis, these criticisms were not sober, reasoned criticisms ... There are not lacking persons who see a hopeful political future for themselves, in their tendentious handling of present difficulties.[75]

In 1941 food cargoes continued to arrive. However, 'when Japan overran Burma and threatened India our rice imports shrank rapidly to negligible proportions'.[76] Japanese hostility also cut off supplies from India, the main source of edible oils. The Government had stockpiled supplies in anticipation of war, but these could not be adequate as there were 'special difficulties' in building large stockpiles in remote colonies like those in the Indian Ocean.[77] Before the war, of course, the calamities that were to bring the war so close and require such self-sufficiency were not expected – namely the fall of France (cutting off supplies from neighbouring islands) and the entry of Japan into the conflict.

Dietary essentials such as rice, flour, meat and edible oil had to be rationed. The introduction of rice rationing in October 1942 led to a 'disquietude of the population'.[78] In January 1943 the rice ration was reduced to 150 grammes per day. Rice disappeared from the island's diet in 1943, not to reappear until 1945 (in 1940 Mauritius had imported 60 668 tons of rice; in 1944 this figure had plummeted to 1491 tons).[79] Importers reaped huge profits and there was widespread profiteering and a thriving black market. The state attempted to marshal its resources. An Imports, Exports and Customs Powers (Defence) Ordinance was passed in 1939.[80] Ordinance No. 43 of 1940 empowered Government to assume full control over production, manufacture and trade in any foodstuffs. A Supply Board tried to control the import of foodstuffs and their distribution and a Profiteering Court punished offenders. A Food Controller was appointed at the outbreak of war and a Bulk Purchase Office established in 1941 to acquire essential materials from America under lend-lease.[81] The Government took control of all rice imports, leading to 'violent protests from the Indian traders'.[82] To control the price of rice the Food Controller purchased all stocks in the colony at cost price, selling them back to dealers at fixed prices. The Governor unsuccessfully asked for a 10 000-ton freighter to be placed at the disposal of Mauritius for supplies from Ceylon, India and Burma.

As well as the loss of supplies from Burma and India, the important inter-regional trade dried up, caused by the fall of France. Neighbouring enemy territories were blockaded, and Madagascar had been the main source of meat. The meat shortage became acute, and as meat imports dwindled, people began illegally slaughtering the remaining stock, leading to a sharp fall in milk supplies. The milk situation was officially described as 'appalling'.[83] There was resentment in Mauritius that trade with Madagascar had been cut off by the naval blockade, though the Government told traders that the stoppage was due to the intransigence of the Madagascar authorities.[84] The Vichy islands suffered even more, and supplies were used as bargaining counters in negotiations with Vichy authorities. The British ship *Tinhow* had supplies for Reunion, though these were kept in Mauritius until a deal was struck with the Vichy Governor, 35 000 bags of rice being exchanged for 300 British subjects (mostly Indian).[85]

Given this perilous food situation, efforts were made to become self-sufficient by encouraging the cultivation of private gardens and by the enforced transition of 27 per cent of sugar estates to food crops like maize (a new mill at Richelieu was opened in May 1943), sweet potatoes, manioc and potatoes. Despite the compulsory reduction in the acreage under sugar, the 1943 harvest was nearly a record.[86] A lack of shipping also stopped the supply of edible oils and copra from the Mauritian dependencies (the Agalega islands were the main sources).[87] The colonial steamer *Caraboa* was requisitioned and the *Zambezia* was laid up in dry dock. As the Governor cabled the Secretary of State, 'we cannot get copra without ships; we cannot reinforce food supplies of the garrison and the population of Rodrigues without ships; we cannot get meat without ships'.[88] Efforts to produce oil using peanuts in Mauritius were hampered by a lack of machinery for extracting the oil (the necessary machinery was ordered, but the ship bringing it to Mauritius was torpedoed 'almost within sight of the island').[89] Reconstruction of local plant was undertaken in 1941, and as a result a half of the island's oil requirements could be produced.

Pulses were the main source of protein for the majority vegetarian population. Supplies of pulses (dholls and lentils) which the Ministry of Food tried to send failed to reach the island (none arrived until 31 January 1944).[90] This contributed to the physical decline of the population. A 'critical state' with regard to edible oils was reached. The shortage, then the disappearance, of rice after the fall of Burma was a gaping hole in the island's staple diet. In its stead, bread was made, milled with 10 per cent maize meal to save flour, also in short supply. By March 1943 food supplies were 'practically exhausted'.[91] A Nutrition Demonstration Unit toured the island teaching new ways of cooking unfamiliar foods, how to make bread and to encourage vegetable planting. May Twining, heavily involved in every medical and welfare operation in wartime Mauritius, had a demonstration van attached to her Child Welfare team that would visit villages and demonstrate how best to use rations. A Hindu cook and two Voluntary Aid Detachment (VAD) workers travelled with it, as well as a goat so that milking technique could be demonstrated.[92] Improvization was the name of the game – one lesson was the use of shark-liver oil for vitamin A. With supplies of seeds cut off because of the war, the Agriculture Department had to learn how to produce its own, and three seed-production stations were created.[93]

A credible population easily swayed by rumours had to be targeted by the propaganda of the Information Office, for fear of more rioting. There was a rumour that the Government had stopped rice imports. It was pointed out that in 1939 Mauritius had consumed 700 000 bags of rice, and that in 1942 only 260 000 bags were available.[94] W. E. F. Ward, the Director of Education, was detailed to conduct a publicity campaign aimed at countering such rumours. He wrote that 'the food situation went from bad to worse. The poor ignorant villagers assumed that the Governor must have immense underground stores of rice; and there were hunger marches, begging him to release some of his abundance'.[95]

The press carried articles aimed at convincing the people that another prevalent rumour – that the Jewish people were absorbing vital food supplies – was untrue. There was a scarcity of milk, eggs, and fresh vegetables, and an acute shortage of onions and potatoes. Things were made worse in October and November 1941 by exceptional drought conditions.[96] The cyclones of early 1945 set the food situation back for the 'badly nourished population'. Most vegetable crops were destroyed and prices became exorbitant. The black market flourished, though if people tried to expose guilty traders they would not be able to buy goods they needed.[97]

Crisis was averted by the fact that the occasional life-saving cargo managed to get through to Mauritius, and that by 1944 the general situation had eased and supplies became available from old markets like Madagascar and new imperial markets. In 1943 reserves were nearly exhausted, but crisis was avoided by the diversion of 8000 tons of wheat in April 1943 and by the arrival in May of 12 000 tons of flour from Australia, along with 2000 tons of manioc starch from Madagascar. Trade relations were re-established with Madagascar, but this was to little avail in 1943. Only 1437 bullocks were imported that year, however in 1944 the number rose to 11 494.[98] The edible oils situation improved in 1945 when Southern Rhodesian and South American supplies became available. Copra from the Mauritian Oil islands reappeared, along with peanuts from India. Maize was available from East Africa from 1945, and flour arrived more regularly from Australia. Only pulses and fish remained in short supply. From 1943 the value of trade with South Africa increased more than tenfold (partly through South African wines replacing those no longer available from France). In 1939 imports from South Africa amounted to Rs. 682 000 (£51 162). By 1944 this figure had risen to Rs. 8 236 000 (£617 854).[99]

Given the scale of the difficulties facing Mauritius before the upturn in food imports in 1944, the Government's hope that its compulsory food-crop cultivation scheme would make the island self-sufficient by 1943 – from a position of almost zero self-sufficiency – appears fanciful. There was an 'earnest, but relatively unsuccessful attempt at large-scale production of maize and root crops' between 1942 and 1945.[100] Every planter with more than 20 acres was obliged to cultivate foodcrops on 20 per cent of his land (rising to 27.5 per cent in May 1943). Efforts were hampered by drought (causing a 40 per cent drop in the estimated maize crop in the first year) and the labour shortage caused by men being called up for war work and military service. Everyone was encouraged to join in through 'Dig for Victory' and 'Grow More Crops' campaigns, planting food crops wherever they could. The Food Adviser to the Colonial Office termed the scheme a 'partial success' rather than a failure.[101] The Food Adviser recommended a quick return to full sugar cultivation, and in February 1945 the Colonial Secretary agreed. However, the crops harvested from the island's efforts saved it from a disaster like the Bengal famine of 1942. Food shortages and rationing, as in Britain, carried over into a period of postwar austerity.

Development, health and education

In the words of Larry Butler:

> The British colonial state was transformed during the Second World War, and adopted a new commitment to economic and social development funded by the United Kingdom. Designed to pre-empt international and colonial criticism of colonial rule, this policy was affected by wartime debates within Britain on post-war social and economic reconstruction.[102]

During and immediately after the war Mauritius saw more official reports produced by the Government, the Council of Government and visiting experts than at any previous time in its history. This was a distinctly metropolitan-led outpouring, elicited by the promise of CDWA money, in which all manner of socio-economic problems were identified and remedies prescribed. However, it is no surprise that the improvements glimpsed in the pages of such reports often proved a mirage amid the poverty, squalor and developmental backwardness all too common in the colonies.

But try they might. The 60 million people of the colonial empire, 'had shared in the common struggle, and their expectations too had been raised by British wartime promises of a better life to come'. The CDWA of 1945 promised a slice of the New Jerusalem for the colonial empire as the age of welfare imperialism began (£120 million for the colonial empire over a period of 10 years). According to Joanna Lewis, 'a momentum towards genuine imperial moral and practical re-armament had been building up' since the 1930s, and the 'fall of Singapore in 1942 provoked the most coherent and penetrative call to recast the colonial state-social relations along the needs of local people'.[103] The Labour victory in the 1945 general election was 'received with acclamation here by the vast masses', wrote the adviser sent to Mauritius to advise on trades unions. His own presence was a mark of how the colonial world was changing and the extent to which metropolitan prescriptions were being foisted upon often unenthusiastic colonial governments (the Governor considered the union adviser, Kenneth Baker, a 'subversive').[104]

The first CDWA of 1940 led to the creation of a Development Committee instructed to formulate the colony's wish list of development goals and tactics for achievement, though it was not a real success as committee members were extremely busy with an increased war workload. Twining noted that the members were discouraged when it was discovered that Mauritius had been allotted a relatively paltry £30 000 per annum.[105] He confided to his wife that 'the Heads of Department caused me more trouble than the schemes'.[106]

However, in line with the rest of the colonial empire, the war years saw the preparation of detailed reports as a range of industrial, social and welfare matters were examined. One thing was certain to thrive, and that was the Government Press in Port Louis that reeled off official reports throughout the war. The hope was that postwar development and welfare funds would enable the Government to tackle the many problems facing Mauritian society. As elsewhere 'perhaps the worst effect of war in Mauritius was the fact that it held up development and reform of every kind'.[107] But the CDWA of 1940 and 1945 transformed thinking, as previously insoluble problems seemed conquerable if metropolitan money was forthcoming.

A memorandum of 1944 illustrates the extent of the Government's development and social welfare shopping list. On the economic front, emphasis was placed upon developing subsidiary industries (for example tea, dairy produce and cattle) and the creation of a class of peasant proprietors and smallholders engaged in food growing. Measures were considered for irrigation,[108] drainage, malaria relief, children's health, clinics and hospitals, schools, youth, culture, and religious activities, new crop campaigns, animal rearing, better houses, roads, social insurance, the tea industry,[109] and a groundnut scheme ('an emergency war-time measure' that became one of the Department of Agriculture's main concerns).[110] There was a lot of work to be done if aspects of Mauritian society that had received little Government attention since British rule began were to be genuinely improved. On arrival from Achimota College in the Gold Coast to fill the newly created post of Director of Education, W. E. F. Ward opined that 'education in Mauritius is defective in every respect'.[111] 'It was, not to put too fine a point on it, shamefully bad'.[112]

The Government identified the fundamental tasks facing Mauritius as improvement in the fields of education and the eradication of malaria, anaemia, dysentery and hookworm. Coupled with this, health standards were to be raised through improvements in sanitation, water, housing, nutrition and social services.[113] A major effort was to be made to counter malaria, a disease killing thousands of Mauritians each year.[114] 'The greatest single factor' accounting for the postwar increase in the rate of population growth was the eradication of the disease 'which in a single year reduced the death rate by 32 per cent'.[115] After his arrival in Mauritius as Director of the Medical and Health Department, Dr Adam Rankine was asked by the Governor to devise a scheme 'for the improvement of health conditions generally'.[116] In 1942 the mean death rate was 29.2 per 1000 people – 'a figure which is little short of double that of Trinidad', a similar tropical island colony.[117] Of the 11 927 deaths in 1942, 34.8 per cent were attributable to parasitic and infective disease, in the main, malaria.[118]

One beneficial result of the war was the effort to eradicate malaria.[119] 'The outbreak of the Second World War, necessitating the stationing in Mauritius of a considerable garrison representing all branches of His Majesty's Forces, provided the next impetus to malaria control'.[120] The most important initiator was the Admiralty, establishing a malaria control organization and spending over £116 000.[121]

In June 1942 medical officers began anti-malarial work in areas where naval personnel were to be accommodated. In January 1943 Surgeon Lieutenant Pilkington was sent from the naval base at Kilindini to inaugurate the work.[122] Surgeon Lieutenant David Keedy arrived in March 1943, and was 'employed assisting the local malaria control unit, as Medical Officer for naval personnel and responsible for maintaining anti-malarial measures in areas already occupied by the Navy'.[123] In 1942 the Government of Mauritius decided to initiate a major campaign across the whole island in conjunction with the Admiralty's efforts, and in 1943 a Malaria Control Committee was established, and the first use was made of the insecticide dichloro-diphenyl-trichloro-ethane (DDT).[124] Malarial Field Ambulance expeditions were undertaken throughout the island by members of the Red Cross.[125] In August 1942 May Twining was doing malarial survey work three days a week, travelling to the coast in a 'badly converted ambulance and examining hundreds of children'.[126] The Army also contributed – Major W. G. Jepson commanded the 26 (East African) Mobile Malaria Section, EAAMC.[127]

Malaria was not the only health problem on Mauritius. In 1945 there was an 'epidemic of acute poliomyelitis, unequalled in the annals of medicine for its explosive and spectacular incidence'.[128] The Director of Medical and Health Services said that the outbreak was 'a result of the conditions under which the people have been living'.[129] In the first six months of 1942 over 2000 children under the age of five died, which meant maternity care improvements were sorely needed. During the war May Twining's public health work was notable, earning her an OBE. Major Dr Arthur de Chazal (Medical Specialist at the EAAMC Military Hospital in Curepipe, President of the Mauritius Branch of the British Red Cross, and member of the Council of Government), wrote that she:

> has been Secretary of the Mauritius Maternity and Child Welfare Society ... and Superintendent of District Midwives. [A] Medical Officer of the Mauritius Red Cross Society she has been the first woman pioneer to train and initiate less expert and less remunerated personnel in other branches of Social Welfare, such as tropical hygiene, sanitation, and nutrition; and secure their cooperation in the most important of all measures for the development and welfare of this sub-tropical colony, namely the control of malaria.[130]

Franco-Mauritians

Mauritius does not receive the attention it merits as a unique settler society within the British empire. As in other territories, the white population both collaborated with the colonial government and resisted it, exasperating generations of British officials, making their wives feel socially inadequate and being, in British eyes, oh so *very* French. But the community was an effective collaborative elite through whom the British ruled the island from their takeover in 1810 until the postwar period. Sweetening the alliance was an economic relationship based on sugar and an empire market for its sale. During the war the Franco-Mauritian community continued to supervise the sugar economy and supported the British and Free French war efforts in a variety of ways.

It is clear that a minority of Franco-Mauritians were extremely pro-Vichy, to the extent of being considered anti-British, whilst others willingly donned British uniform. As an example of the former, Clement Robillard was imprisoned in Vacoas for his absolute refusal to 'serve under the English flag' and determination 'to obey only the authority of Marshal Petain'.[131] There are unsubstantiated stories of ardent Vichyites driving to the coast and signalling with headlamps to enemy shipping, and the Dodo Club in Curepipe was a pro-Vichy bastion. British authorities feared that pro-Vichy sentiment blunted the effectiveness of the locally raised armed forces and had a negative impact on the war effort of the non-white population.

Like French communities the world over, the Franco-Mauritians were divided along a Petain–de Gaulle fault line. Maladroit handling by local British officials, coupled with events like the British raid on Dakar or the tragic sinking of the French squadron at Mers-el-Kebir, understandably fanned the flames against perfidious Albion. The war heightened British exasperation with the Franco-Mauritians, and non-whites resented their status in the Army. But this was no 'crime' peculiar to the Franco-Mauritian community; in the 1940s the world was defined along racial lines, and throughout the British colonial empire a non-white officer was a very rare phenomenon indeed.

The Franco-Mauritians shared in the sense of shock and grief throughout the French world that greeted the fall of France. Franco-Mauritians naturally took the lead in wartime organizations on the home front. The Maison de France was opened in Curepipe in 1941 by Maurice Vigier de Latour, organizing charitable works and fund raising for the Free French war effort.[132] Raymond Hein was President of the Spitfire Fund and Sir Edouard Nairac was President of the Comité Mauricien de la France Libre.

The Franco-Mauritians made a most 'gallant and distinguished' contribution to the Armed Forces, particularly the SOE in occupied Europe (and Madagascar) and beyond, where they had the special advantage of being both British subjects and natural French speakers.[133] In France, Mauritian SOE members performed heroic deeds. For example, M. L. M. A. Larcher joined the SOE circuit 'Scientist' as a wireless operator, was parachuted into France in February 1944 and was killed in Calvados in July of that year.[134] The 'Scientist' circuit was run by another Mauritian, Claude de Baissac.[135] P. E. and E. P. Mayer, Mauritians 'like several of F section's most vigorous agents', ran the 'Fireman' circuit around Limoges.[136] 'Nearly 100 000 retreating Germans were cornered near Limoges by the forces the Mayer brother, Liewer, and Philippe de Vomecourt inspired'.[137] A third Mayer brother, J. A. Mayer, was 'caught working with 'Rover' and executed in Germany' at Buchenwald.[138]

Of particular importance was the 'Shipwright' circuit of Major Rene Amedee Louis Pierre Maingard de la Ville-es-Offrans. Parachuted into France in April 1942, he was in charge of communications between Britain and five departments of southwest France, responsible for blocking enemy communications and for sabotage operations before D-Day. 'In his area the resistance movement owed its existence, training and equipment to "Maingard" alone and virtually unaided – within a few weeks after D-Day he had over 5000 men under his command'.[139] A notable exploit was the assistance rendered by Maingard to an SAS team sent to hold up German reinforcements for Normandy.[140]

Franco-Mauritians also served in the RAF,[141] the MTF/MR and the Pioneer Corps. Some joined the Free French Forces, like Ignace Planche who enlisted with 60 other Franco-Mauritians in August 1941. They were sent to the Middle East to join the 1st Division, fighting at Alamein, Tobruk, and later taking part in the liberation of Toulon.[142] Georges Desmarais served in the Free French Navy.[143] Gerard du Plessis was 'fished out of the water at Dunkirk by a tug called *The Lord Cavan*, which had crossed over from Dover'.[144] At Dunkirk Captain Gustave Souchou, King's Royal Hussars, was serving with the British Army's French Liaison Pool, and Captaine Arnaud de la Roche du Ronzet, was serving with the French Mission to the British Army. Both were Franco-Mauritians who gave their lives.[145]

Lady Edith Kemsley was a Franco-Mauritian who had married the wealthy newspaper owner Lord Kemsley. She formed the 'Daily Sketch War Relief Fund' run from her London home, Chandos House. 'It was destined to become a vast organization with its own offices, and much later when I was in the Western Desert I was thrilled to receive parcels from it'. She also set up an organization for Mauritian volunteers arriving in London:

> A lot of Mauritians were arriving in London to volunteer into the various forces and my aunt Edith was a first port of call for them. When the numbers grew out of control she bought a house (in Gloucester Square) and set it up as an information and rest centre.[146]

Franco-Mauritians contributed in other ways. For example, Paul Vigureux (1903–99) joined the Admiralty Scientific Service in 1938 and was posted to the Portland naval base and the Anti-Submarine

Experimental Establishment on the Clyde, where he worked on developing 'a receiver to improve the detection of echoes returned by the hull of U-boats. The receiver was a success and, by the end of the war, had been installed in almost every ship in the Royal Navy'.[147]

The Jewish detainees

One of the most unusual episodes of the Mauritian war was the enforced sojourn on the island, for nearly five years, of over 1500 Central European Jews.[148] There was a British tradition of using remote islands for the exile of awkward political customers. During the war Mauritius played host to the former Prime Minister of Yugoslavia Milan Stoyadinovitch and the deposed Shah of Persia, Reza Khan Pahlevi arrived.[149] Mauritius was seriously considered as a destination for Greek refugees from Turkey in 1943, though the plan was eventually scuppered by the Greek Under Secretary of State.[150]

The Jews were also, in a sense, political prisoners. Detained not as enemy aliens, but as illegal immigrants to Palestine, they were kept in the Central Prison at Beau Bassin.[151] Their journey to Mauritius was a tragic epic. A convoy of four ships sailed down the Danube from Bratislava, capital of 'independent' Slovakia, on 4 September 1940. Those destined for Mauritius were on board the *Helios* and the *Schoenbrunn*. The *Helios* contained 300 Czechs, 300 Austrians and 500 Danzigers. The *Schoenbrunn* carried about 600 people from Vienna. Many had been in German concentration camps, and were 'released on the undertaking that they would leave the Reich at once'.[152]

The ships arrived in Romania where the passengers were transferred to the SS *Atlantic*. It sailed for Palestine via Istanbul, Crete and Cyprus. Illegal Jewish immigration into Palestine had been a highly sensitive political issue since the British promise of a Jewish 'homeland' in 1917. In the Second World War Jewish immigration became a most difficult issue. The British High Commissioner in Palestine suspected that German agents were among the Jews seeking admission in 1940. As an alternative, the Colonial Office investigated sending them to a British colony, and Mauritius was asked if it could 'as a matter of urgency provide accommodation for a considerable number of Jews who are endeavouring to enter Palestine illegally'.[153] The reasons why the Jews could not enter Palestine were clearly set out.[154] The Governor agreed to accept up to 4000 as 'long as they brought all their own bedding, crockery, chamber pots, etcetera, their own guards and doctors, and that they had been duly inoculated' (typhoid due to the conditions on board ship had already started to kill).[155]

The episode attracted the personal attention of Churchill, though his wish that the detainees be allowed to remain in Palestine was voiced too late to alter the deportation order. As the Jews were waiting to be shipped to Mauritius, tragedy struck on 25 November 1940; 267 perished in a bomb explosion as they boarded the ship that was to take them to Mauritius. This was the result of an attempt by Jewish terrorists to prevent the deportation. Despite this, they sailed onboard two Dutch ships, arriving at Port Louis on Boxing Day 1940; 1580 arrived in Mauritius.

The life of these unfortunate war migrants whilst on Mauritius has been described in detail elsewhere. Though the British authorities insisted that 'everything is being done to enable detainees to live as normal a life as possible', the Jews were to have many complaints.[156] It is towards the unpleasant aspects of the life of the detainees that recent accounts have naturally gravitated, with the British fulfilling their traditional villainous role, albeit in a slightly water-downed form.[157] The fact was that they were *detainees*, not free people. In December 1940 the Council of Government passed the precautionary European Detainees (Control) Ordinance 1940. This was specifically to prevent the Jews attempting to use the law to challenge their detention.[158] Personal liberty was denied in the camp life that they were to endure for five years, to the extent that for much of the time husbands and wives were not permitted to live together. The Jews were escorted whenever outside the camp, and there was special censorship. However, it must be recalled that news of the extermination of the Final Solution was still unknown, and as German-speaking inhabitants of enemy lands the British were understandably suspicious. As the Government maintained, at least their lives were not threatened whilst in Mauritius. Some softening in camp conditions did come with time, partly to offset negative reports received by Jewish communities elsewhere. In April 1945 the Jews left the island and were permitted – finally – to go to Palestine. In the graveyard of St Martin's at Beau Bassin are the 127 they left behind.

8
The End of the War and Strategic Transformation in the Indian Ocean

VE Day was greeted with all the paraphernalia of victory throughout the British empire. In Mauritius, the Council of Government held a special session and announced a two-day public holiday,[1] the cannons at Port Louis fired a salvo, church bells rang throughout the island, the Police Band entertained at the Champ de Mars, the Town Hall, the Luna Park and the Majestic were illuminated, there was a Chinese dragon procession, fireworks at Champ de Mars, bonfires at the Citadel and on Signal Mountain, and flags and bunting festooned the streets.[2] At Champ de Mars a huge Union Flag hung from the grandstand and the Governor, resplendent in the white dress uniform and pith helmet of the Colonial Service, took the salute. After the victory over Japan there were further celebrations. A reception was held at Le Reduit on 24 August, and a grand parade took place at Port Louis on 30 August; 6 September was declared a public holiday, and around 50 000 people attended a gathering at Champ de Mars.[3]

Yet as in Britain, the war's impact by no means ended with the firing of the last shot; colonial involvement in the war was too deep to allow for that. First of all, of course, there were the people whose relatives never came back, or returned disabled. It is difficult to put an exact figure on the Mauritian casualty list, though it can be no less than 350 dead.[4] Food shortages and price controls continued late into the 1940s, and thousands of soldiers remained overseas. On the announcement of the Japanese surrender the Governor cautioned that people could not 'expect immediate improvement in conditions in the colony ... [or] the immediate return of the thousands of soldiers still overseas'.[5] In the postwar years Mauritius continued to provide a base for the Royal Navy and to support a garrison of imperial troops, and the island and its scattered Indian Ocean dependencies remained strategic outposts in British and then American global defence.

Unforeseen events hindered the Mauritian emergence from the privations of war. Cyclones at the beginning of 1945 caused damage, hardship and economic difficulties.[6] They were responsible for a 30 per cent drop in the output of the sugar industry, killing 24, destroying 10 000 homes, sinking or damaging hundreds of fishing boats and thousands of fishing traps.[7] A Relief Fund was started and thousands of pounds subscribed, including contributions from the crew of HMS *Mauritius*, the British Army, Government of India, British Government, Seychelles Government, Reunion Government, Mauritian community in Madagascar, Trinity College, Cambridge, Messrs Blyth Green Jourdain and Company Ltd and the Anglo-Ceylon Company.[8] KAR engineers re-established road communications.

The soldiers return

Measures were put in place to try to ease the reabsorption of thousands of men into home society. Reabsorption was acknowledged in all colonies as a potential threat to postwar social stability. In 1942 the Director of Labour, Edward Twining, wrote that soldiers would 'return with a very much greater degree of skill than is usual in Mauritius. They will have become accustomed to high wages and there is little outlet in Mauritius for certain of the trades they have learnt'.[9]

The island's senior soldier felt a special responsibility towards the ex-servicemen. The OCT Colonel Ronald Yeldham said that employers should 'reinstate our men when they leave the Forces'.[10] He insisted that the Government had a 'definite moral obligation to them'.[11] However, it was not to be so easy. An Ex-Servicemen's Welfare Committee was established to help soldiers find employment and to administer a fund to which ex-servicemen could apply for small grants.[12] The Ex-Servicemen's Welfare Fund had been established by Ordinance early in the war, receiving funds from the Lotteries (HM Forces) Fund (today's National Lottery), from Government and from Earl Haig's Fund.[13]

Unlike many African Pioneers, Mauritians rarely had to endure a lengthy and troublesome demobilization period. A booklet entitled *Release and Resettlement* was issued to all men explaining the demobilization stages and what help they could expect upon repatriation.[14] Bell Village was to be the Dispersal Centre. The booklet outlined what items of kit the soldiers were allowed to keep. A week's pay in advance was issued, along with money for civilian clothing and the fare home.

A questionnaire was issued for use by the Employment Office (an Employment Exchange was created in 1944). There was information on Army gratuity entitlements, disability benefits and a section called 'Back to Civilian Life'.

George Andre Decotter was the Reabsorption Officer, based at the National Service Office in the Civil Hospital, Port Louis. By December 1946, the number of ex-servicemen registered at the Reabsorption Office had risen from 2000 to 10 000. The Reabsorption Officer reported a decrease in job opportunities for ex-servicemen in 1947. In that year the Ex-Servicemen's Committee considered 2107 applications for financial assistance. In 1948, 13 577 ex-servicemen seeking financial assistance were interviewed. Help could be given in the form of disbursements for a bicycle or tools to begin a small business, and in Port Louis a welfare and recreation centre for ex-servicemen was established.[15]

However the organization could not create jobs or provide pensions. It was estimated that in 1948 there were 2000 unemployed ex-servicemen on the island.[16] At the end of 1948, there were still 12 000 men in the Middle East. The fact that the men 'come back with a new turn of mind and new ideas has not made things easier'.[17] Army pay had raised standards of living among soldiers and their dependants and they were unable to find the equivalent in civilian life. The simple fact was that there were not enough jobs in Mauritius able to satisfy ex-soldiers who had high pay expectations and a desire to use new skills. Matters were made worse in the first 12 months of peace by the 'closing down of most of the War Services and the release from such services (Mauritius Labour Corps, Detainment Camp, Information Office, Mauritius Auxiliary Police, etc.) of some 8000 men'.[18]

The Public Works Department started emergency schemes that found 500 jobs, and Government tried to give priority to ex-servicemen in Government jobs. A Further Education and Training Scheme was able to find 24 scholarships overseas. Farming schemes were started in the hope of providing a livelihood for some ex-servicemen. At Montebello a mixed farming experiment was established on Crown lands to raise livestock and poultry. In 1942 there was a proposal for two estates to be 'purchased by Government to settle ex-soldiers after the war ... they would be a real contribution to the post-war ex-soldier problem'.[19]

As early as November 1944 the President of the MLP wrote to Arthur Creech Jones saying that unemployed ex-servicemen are 'getting filled with discontent'.[20] Given the situation, the only option for many of the men, and for others who had not served during the war, was (re-)enlistment in the Pioneer Corps. By the end of 1948, 33 per cent of released troops had re-enlisted. Between 1946 and 1949, 20 880 men were enlisted into the Pioneer Corps and 7706 released.[21] This went some way towards assuaging the unemployment problem, but by 1950 there were 20 000 ex-servicemen in Mauritius. This was a huge problem, reflecting the island's huge manpower contribution to the British Army.

There was little the Government could do beyond proffer advice. Today the ex-servicemen well remember the Government's admonishment not to be improvident upon their return, and to be self-reliant. The message was conveyed in a Creole proverb (*'Dans disable bet gette so lisie'*, or *'befs dans disable, sakene gette so lisie'*), as Roger Requin explains:

> This is a Creole saying which could be translated into English as 'in shifting and unreliable circumstances, one has to be constantly on the watch so as not to become 'blind' through lack of foresight or be outdone by others. Just as the ox on a sandy soil has to be vigilant to prevent grains of sand getting into its eyes or other oxen playing a trick over it. So the ex-servicemen (to whom this adage was addressed immediately after the war) had to be on the lookout for a job and not turn towards Government represented at the time by the Reabsorption Office for seeking employment for him'.[22]

Such advice was not welcomed by the soldiers. Monaf Fakira remembers them returning as proud men, smartly turned out in their demob suits with a lump sum in their pockets. '"We were nothing, now we are to be admired" was the attitude; before the Army, many did not wear shoes'.[23] Army service had wrought other changes. Though the hopes of British officials that the Army would engineer mass Anglicization were not fulfilled, some alterations in habits did take place. A famous *sega* (a national music of Mauritius) song describes the wife of a Pioneer noticing how her husband had changed, pronouncing words with an English accent, demanding bacon and eggs for breakfast, and approaching her romantically in an entirely new fashion ('Oh, my darling' etc).[24]

The end of the war meant a return to poverty for many ex-servicemen. Some chose to emigrate. Many men had been and seen overseas and the postwar period saw the start of the outflow of Mauritians that continues to this day. The war was a solvent that thawed former geographical rigidities and expanded the horizons of many thousands of Britain's colonial subjects. Sam Lingayah refers to the impulse that the war gave to migration, quoting an ex-serviceman who settled in Britain:

> As a result of the involvement, our knowledge of the UK, stimulated by war propaganda, news-reels shown in the cinema, and a mobile news van, which visited the towns and villages regularly, increased tremendously. Another source of our knowledge of Britain came from the Mauritian soldiers who had served overseas ... When they returned home, considerably more sophisticated and aware of developments in Britain and other countries, they usually rejoined the street-corner society and told us a great deal about life beyond the shores of our land, thereby making us progressively inquisitive and whetting our appetite for more information. As it was natural for our informers to feel psychologically good to tell us only about the most interesting parts of life overseas, particularly in Britain, we became excited and began to start thinking seriously about emigration.[25]

A continuing military role

The strategic imperatives of previous centuries of imperial warfare remained in the Indian Ocean at the end of the Second World War, and the dawning Cold War and nuclear age were to layer it with new significance. The KAR garrisoned Mauritius until the early 1960s. Continuing a tradition of withdrawing troops from the Mauritius Garrison when troubles arose in other corners of the empire, KAR soldiers left for the State of Emergency in Kenya from 1952. In 1960 150 years of the Mauritius Garrison came to an end.[26] But British military involvement in Mauritius and its dependencies was by no means over.

The island continued to send thousands of men to join the British Army in a period when African and Indian Ocean colonies were looked to for more troops to support the overstretched Regular Army after the loss of India and the Indian Army. As late as 1952 there were still 78 000 colonial troops in the British Army.[27] Mauritians became the Pioneer Corps backbone of Middle East Land Forces, remaining in the Middle East until the Suez Crisis of 1956; a new military force, the Special Mobile Force (SMF) was created, commanded by a British

Lieutenant Colonel until the mid-1970s; in 1965 and 1968 British troops were called in to suppress political unrest (a company of the 2nd Battalion The Coldstream Guards in May 1965 and two companies of the 1st Battalion The King's Shropshire Light Infantry in 1968);[28] the Royal Navy remained on the island until the mid-1970s; the Seychelles remained British until 1976; and the Mauritian dependency of Diego Garcia formed the heart of BIOT from 1965, which after Mauritian independence in 1968 was leased to America. Today it forms one of the most strategically significant military bases in the world.

The Royal Navy maintained a communications station on Mauritius until 1976 when the military base at Vacoas, formerly known as Abercromby Barracks but from 1962 known as the shore base HMS *Mauritius*, was paid off. Today, Abercromby Barracks are the headquarters of the Special Mobile Force (SMF). Mauritius had performed its traditional role as a facility for ships, and had seen its importance as a communications facility enhanced by the closure of the wireless station at Welisara in Ceylon.[29] In the pre-satellite age, long-distance military communications continued to rely on such relay stations, not least for the control of the new Polaris missile-armed nuclear powered submarines.

Strategically, Mauritius and its dependencies had an enduring role. As late as 1968 Mauritius and its Indian Ocean dependencies were of significance in Britain's east of Suez strategy.[30] With the rapid shrinking of empire, Aden remained one of only two main bases east of Suez, and the headquarters of MEC following withdrawals from Palestine, Egypt and Kenya and the failure to get the UN mandate of Libya (however Libya was under British and French military administration until 1949, and although Britain retained bases in Libya until the 1960s, a UN mandate would have enabled Libya to be used as a replacement for the Suez Canal Base). Political unrest in Aden threatened its utility as a base, so Socotra, the Seychelles, Mauritius and Diego Garcia were 'canvassed as possible alternatives'.[31] In a world of imperial contraction, Britain sought to pursue her traditional strategic ends and use imperial connections to provide footholds in the new world of Cold War defence.

As a contribution to Western defence, the Indian Ocean was to remain a 'British lake' and Britain was to police the states of the Arabian Gulf. In the 1960s Britain still had 'a special, and one might add jealously guarded, responsibility for the defence of the Indian Ocean and the Persian Gulf' (which since the Royal Navy switched from coal to oil in 1909 had become a strategic priority).[32] Though the

Raj had gone, Britain still felt an obligation to be in a position to offer defensive aid to India, Pakistan, Australia and New Zealand. Britain had a keen interest in the Indian Ocean rim, particularly the Middle East and Persian Gulf, and in retaining control of the oceanic 'gateways' to the Indian Ocean. The fear of Soviet penetration into regions of traditional British supremacy, and Britain's dependence on Gulf oil, meant that even in the decolonization age the Indian Ocean remained a strategic 'must have' for the British. New military technology and strategic thinking revived interest in Indian Ocean bases like Mauritius. As an example, the island staging post idea – that would see men and materials transported to distant troublespots by aircraft stopping off at British bases – involved islands like Ascension, Sal (in the Cape Verde Islands), Mauritius, Diego Garcia, Socotra and the Cocos Islands.

New strategic and technological imperatives required island supply bases for the carrier group that was to be stationed at Singapore and as stopovers to aid the rapid movement of strategic reserves by air. The 1957 Defence White Paper stressed Britain's role in East Africa and the East of Suez region. Britain would continue to fulfil her colonial and international commitments in the Middle East and Far East by means of carrier groups normally stationed in the Indian Ocean.[33] In the 1960s Aden was the main British base in the region, and a £5 million RAF base had been built on Gan in the Maldive Islands to replace facilities in Ceylon. The RAF maintained a staging post on Mauritius with a 6000-foot runway, and naval facilities were available. One of the island's chief attractions was its stable political situation. As late as 1968 Mauritius and the Cocos Islands were viewed as potential bases for F-111 long-range bombers to be used for the air policing of the Indian Ocean and beyond.[34] As the British Government contemplated the withdrawal of the carrier-based fleet that embodied Britain's East of Suez commitment, it was suggested that the role could be maintained and costs cut if air power took over.

Britain, even in the decolonization age, sought to honour its remaining colonial commitments, perform traditional and newly acquired international policing roles, safeguard its trading interests and patrol the sea routes. In the mid-1960s, Britain was the 'only power with the territorial resources to patrol the area ... The UK, with her carrier force based at Singapore, is at present the only power with a navy of any size in the Indian Ocean/Persian Gulf area'.[35] In 1963–64, two of Britain's three strike carriers and a commando ship were to be based in the Indian Ocean.[36]

It was announced in 1965 that Mauritius would soon be granted independence, though the islands of the Chagos Archipelago were excluded from the deal and £3 million paid to resettle the 1300 Ilois inhabitants in Mauritius. The Chagos Archipelago (with Diego Garcia at its core) was detached, and together with the Seychelles islands of Aldabra, Farquhar and Desroches, formed BIOT. It was considered that this would make Britain's forthcoming withdrawal from Aden more palatable to the Americans (today the Government of Yemen affords naval facilities to the Americans in the port of Aden), and be viewed favourably in the light of Britain's non-involvement in the Vietnam War. Given the American war effort, bases in the region were highly valued.

Finally withdrawing from Mauritius and its dependencies at the end of the 1960s when the East of Suez commitment was terminated, Britain 'was willing to disengage in the Indian Ocean, but intended to confide guardianship of the West's interests in the region to the United States'.[37] America granted a rebate on the cost of Polaris in partial return for the lease of Diego Garcia.[38] At first it was to be a naval communications centre, but from 1975 became a fully fledged naval and air base. It is now considered to be one of America's most important overseas military installations, establishing and supporting American power in the Indian Ocean, Asia, the Gulf and beyond. It has recently seen action in the Gulf War, the 1992 intervention in Somalia, action in Afghanistan against Osama bin Laden, and 600 sorties were flown from the island during the 1999 bombing of Iraq.[39] Diego Garcia and similar bases are viewed as essential to American air power and its ability to react to crises the world over; simply put, American bombers, even the latest B-2s, cannot conduct all of their operations from the continental United States.[40]

The status of Diego Garcia has remained a bone of contention between Britain, America and Mauritius. The deported Ilois recently won a High Court case against the British Government permitting them to return to the archipelago.[41] The Government of Mauritius maintains its claim to sovereignty.[42] Though it remains a matter of international debate, it is unlikely that America will give up what is considered to be an integral part of its worldwide military structure.[43] It is a 'military fortress' and in the late 1980s was a 'key site for the American Strategic Defence Initiative (Star Wars).[44] A 1990 White Paper 'noted that the strategy of US forces was to be able to strike any point in the world from only three bases – one in the US, another on the Pacific island of Guam, and a third on Diego Garcia'.[45]

Indian Ocean islands acted as bases during a period of Anglo-French international rivalry and world wars in the eighteenth and nineteenth centuries, before Britain established a hegemony that was to remain unchallenged until the twentieth century when further world wars arose to threaten British power. British paramountcy remained until the beginning of the 1970s, when the mantle was taken up by America. Thus the Indian Ocean has maintained, through centuries of war and empire, a role in the changing arena of global strategy and defence.

As for the Second World War, what had been the result of it all? Well, the Royal Navy had done its job and kept the sea lanes open, and Mauritius had not endured the enervating blockade imposed upon the neighbouring islands of Reunion and Madagascar. Though imports had suffered and malnutrition was widespread, famine was avoided. Mauritius and its dependencies were not invaded by the Japanese, a fate that would have been far worse than any perceived hardships borne under British rule. The war years witnessed political awakenings – often stimulated by war and the hardships that trailed in its wake – that were to lead to a radical shift in the island's political landscape. Perhaps more importantly, the Colonial Office had finally grasped the need to try and engineer fundamental change in Mauritius; the palliatives of the 1930s would no longer do. As the Governor recognized in May 1945, 'the war has had at least one good effect; it has opened the eyes of all of us to the social conditions of our people and to the necessity for raising the general standard of living'.

Mauritian society, like that of other colonies, had been mobilized and regimented in a completely novel way. Mauritius was on the winning side, albeit in a war that it had neither caused nor asked to become involved in. But that was the reality of the mid-twentieth century when almost every small country was under the formal rule or informal sway of a larger one. If Mauritius and the other Indian Ocean islands had not been British or French in 1939, they would have been colonies of another great power. In the global age it would have been unrealistic for any corner of the world to expect political, economic, social or military exemption in such a conflict. In world wars, one did not stop to ask if subject peoples objected to their territories becoming involved or their resources allocated, and by 1939 the British had come as far as any power ever has to garnering the active participation of a vast empire in a world war without resort to brutal means. This is the remarkable fact underpinning the material examined in this book. Mauritius was not forced into the war. Local elites collaborated, and the common people enthused, resisted or acquiesced, much as they did back in Britain. Despite British worries about the 'Frenchness' of the island and the failure of successive governments to adequately Anglicize the population, something appears to have rubbed off, and Mauritians accepted the facts and the need to stand against tyrannies incomparable in their methods of rule to the empire under which they lived. The call of France in her hour of need was a clear rallying point for the 10 000 Franco-Mauritians, and for the many Creoles who looked to France and French civilization. Furthermore, the appeal of imperial Britain was not entirely without a sympathetic audience. As Abdool Amode writes:

> We Mauritians were proud to be British subjects. At school children proudly sang 'God Save The King' and 'Three Cheers for the Red, White, and Blue'. On Empire Day ... there was a public holiday. School children waving the Union Jack gathered at certain schools. The Governor in full ceremonial dress came to deliver a speech. After unveiling a portrait of His Majesty King George VI, they sang heartily 'God Save The King'. The children were served cakes and lemonade. On one such Empire Day a leaflet was distributed to the children. The leaflet said, "Children, you belong to the Empire. Love it. Serve it. Defend it. The Empire belongs to you". Being then loyal subjects of His Majesty the King, Mauritians heartily responded to the appeal of their King to defend the Empire and the world from totalitarian powers.[46]

The view of one individual and not to be taken as representative of all British Indian Ocean islanders, to be sure. But it at least enables one to glimpse a fact too readily forgotten today by a general public often led to believe that empire equalled unmitigated evil, and that its only legacy is guilt and the enduring condemnation of the descendants of those over whom our forefathers ruled. And the fact is that a common imperial citizenship was not only an ideal that was floated, but one that actually had some purchase, and one that Britain could better have pursued for the sake of its own position in the world and the upliftment of those over whom it ruled.

As was the case elsewhere in the empire, local elites were loyal to the imperial connection but in opposition to the local colonial regime on a number of issues. The main issue was, of course, participation in the operation of power, and the social and economic status that accompanies such power. In 1943 a Mauritian journalist despaired of 'those many officials who are still to learn that the Empire is being rebuilt and defended by citizens of all races'.[47] The true solvent of empire was not the fact of the link between colonies and the metropole, but the relationship of indigenous people to the peripheral face of imperial rule. There was not enough effort to create opportunities for participation in the imperial project, and for too many people the injustices of colonial society blended with the glass-ceiling that divided the two levels of the colonial world. But it could not really have been any other way, for empire depended upon such a divide; you were either ruler or ruled.

Notes

Introduction: War and Empire

1. Alfred North-Coombes, *The Island of Rodrigues* (Port Louis: Mauritius Advertising Bureau, 1971). See Naval Historical Branch (henceforth NHB), Ministry of Defence, London. Commander-in-Chief (henceforth C-in-C) Eastern Fleet War Diary, volume 11, p. 76.
2. K. Hazareesingh, *History of Indians in Mauritius* (London: Macmillan Press – now Palgrave, 1978), p. 119.
3. Sir Alan Burns, 'The Future of the Colonial Service', quoted in A. H. M. Kirk-Greene, *On Crown Service: a History of HM Colonial and Overseas Civil Service, 1837–1997* (London: I. B. Tauris, 1999), p. 211. For an interesting angle on the empire at war, see Robert Holland, 'Anti-Imperialism', in I. C. B. Dear (ed.) *The Oxford Companion to the Second World War* (Oxford: Oxford University Press, 1995).
4. 'Loyalty' as a colonial response was the prevalent official view of the empire's reaction to Britain's declaration of war. Though this is of course questionable in many ways (for example, South Africa's delay in declaring war), it is true that men were found for the Army and home populations mobilized without the need for British coercion. Indigenous elites procured the necessary support – and for the British, this was good enough to count as loyalty.
5. Ronald Robinson and John Gallagher (with Alice Denny), *Africa and the Victorians: the Official Mind of Imperialism* (London: Macmillan Press – now Palgrave, 1961) and A. G. Hopkins and P. J. Cain, *British Imperialism*, 2 volumes (Harlow: Longman, 1993).
6. For a critique of this view, see Ashley Jackson, *Botswana 1939–45: an African Country at War* (Oxford: Clarendon Press, 1999).
7. Susan Briggs, *Keep Smiling Through: the Home Front, 1939–45* (London: Weidenfeld & Nicolson, 1975), p. 170.
8. For the history of some of the lesser known imperial units, see James Lunt, *Imperial Sunset: Frontier Soldiering in the Twentieth Century* (London: Macdonald Futura, 1981).
9. Keith Jeffery, 'The Second World War', in Judith Brown and William Roger Louis (eds) *The Oxford History of the British Empire, Volume IV: the Twentieth Century* (Oxford: Oxford University Press, 1999), p. 307.
10. John Gallagher, *The Decline, Revival, and Fall of the British Empire: the Ford Lectures and Other Essays*, ed. Anil Seal (Cambridge: Cambridge University Press, 1982).
11. Written by the Resident Commissioner of the Bechuanaland Protectorate during a tour of the Ngamiland region in March 1940. A. Jackson, *Botswana 1939–45*, p. 51.
12. K. Jeffery, 'The Second World War', p. 307. See Ronald Hyam, 'Churchill

187

and the British Empire', in Robert Blake and Wm Roger Louis (eds) *Churchill* (Oxford: Oxford University Press, 1993).

13. John Darwin, 'A Third British Empire? The Dominion Idea in Imperial Politics', in J. M. Brown and Wm Roger Louis (eds) *The Oxford History of the British Empire*, p. 64.
14. K. Jeffery, 'The Second World War', p. 307.
15. See N. J. Westcott, 'British Imperial Economic Policy During the War', in David Killingray and Richard Rathbone (eds) *Africa and the Second World War* (London: Macmillan Press – now Palgrave, 1986).
16. Michael Havinden and David Meredith, *Colonial Development: Britain and its Tropical Colonies, 1850–1960* (London: Routledge, 1993).
17. Public Record Office (henceforth PRO), London. CO 167/919/18. Compulsory Military Service. China's defeat and occupation by Japan had a profound impact on the Chinese community of Mauritius who had actively supported Chiang Kai-Shek's war efforts. The Chinese community was opposed to the establishment of the communist regime in China, and this widened the gulf with the mother country. Travel between China and Mauritius was stopped by the Japanese occupation of the Chinese ports. For the Chinese community see Huguette-Ly-Tio-Fane-Pineo, *Chinese Diaspora in Western Indian Ocean* (Rose Hill: Editions de l'Océane Indiene, 1985).
18. By the end of 1940, 2300 tons of scrap metal had been promised and 490 tons shipped. Mauritius National Archives (henceforth MNA), *Advance*, 3/4/41.
19. See for example, Rhodes House Library (henceforth RHL), Oxford. Mss. Brit. Emp. s. 365, Fabian Colonial Bureau (henceforth FCB) Papers, box 170.
20. See for example, Larry Bowman, *Mauritius: Democracy and Development in the Indian Ocean* (London: Dartmouth, 1991), pp. 27–33.
21. D. A. Low, *Eclipse of Empire* (Cambridge: Cambridge University Press, 1991), p. 70.
22. A. Jackson, 'Franco-Mauritians and Indo-Mauritians as Intermediaries of Empire', seminar paper, St Antony's College, Oxford, 6/6/00.
23. PRO. CO 968/24/3. A. J. L. Phillips, Director of Local Defence, War Cabinet, 'Defence Plan for Mauritius and Rodrigues', 14/4/43.
24. PRO. CO 167/920/2. Formation of Mauritius Coastal Defence Squadron. Governor to Secretary of State, 30/12/41.
25. PRO. CO 968/131/2 and 3. National Register of 100 000 males aged 16 to 50 for defence, defence construction, and local food production.
26. The 'Chagos victory' was given extensive coverage in the British press. See *The Times*, 4/11/00. The return of the Ilois people will not affect the American military base, for the island of Diego Garcia remains out of bounds.
27. BBC Radio 4 news report, 16/7/00.
28. *The Times*, 24/12/98.
29. Raymond D'Unienville to A. Jackson, 22/8/00.

1   Mauritius and the Indian Ocean in Imperial Wars and Imperial Strategy: from the Eighteenth Century to the Interwar Years

1. See the classic statement of sea power and empire, Gerald Graham, *The Politics of Naval Supremacy: Studies in British Maritime Ascendancy* (Cambridge: Cambridge University Press, 1965). In particular, chapter 2, 'The Indian Ocean: From the Cape to Canton'.
2. For an interwar Army appreciation of imperial defence see D. H. Cole, *Imperial Military Geography: General Characteristics of the Empire in Relation to Defence* (London: Sifton Praed, 1928).
3. PRO. CO 167/909/15. Governor's Broadcast after Outbreak of War. It was felt that the Governor 'could have chosen a happier phrase'. Colonial Office minute, 6/9/39.
4. Senoo Babajee, *A Concise History of Mauritius* (Bombay: Hind Kitabs, 1950), p. 94.
5. See Robert Scott (a former Governor of Mauritius), *Limuria: the Lesser Dependencies of Mauritius* (Oxford: Oxford University Press, 1961). Annual visits to the islands by the Assistant Magistrate were meticulously reported to the Governor, and reports forwarded to the Secretary of State for the Colonies. See PRO. CO 167/911/11. St Brandon Islands Visit by Magistrate, 1940, and CO 167/916/14. Agalega Islands Visit by Magistrate.
6. Lance Davis and Robert Huttenback, *Mammon and the Pursuit of Empire: the Economics of Imperialism* (Cambridge: Cambridge University Press, 1988), p. 114.
7. F. D. Ommanney, *The Shoals of Capricorn* (London: Longmans, Green and Company, 1952), p. 56
8. See Robert Kubicek, 'Empire and Technological Change', in Andrew Porter (ed.) *The Oxford History of the British Empire Volume III: the Nineteenth Century* (Oxford: Oxford University Press, 1999), map 12.1.
9. Ronald Hyam, 'The Primacy of Geopolitics: the Dynamics of British Imperial Policy, 1765–1963', in Robin Kilson and Robert King (eds) *The Statecraft of British Imperialism: Essays in Honour of Wm Roger Louis* (London: Frank Cass, 1999), p. 41.
10. P. M. Kennedy, 'Imperial Cable Communications and Strategy, 1870–1914', *English Historical Review* (October 1971).
11. RHL. Sir Hilary Blood Papers. 'Mauritius: Its Position in the Empire', address by Honourable Roger Pezzani at a Meeting of the Committee of the Empire Parliamentary Association, Westminster Hall, 31/7/40. 'Mauritius as an Air Base', p. 14. The Governor was keen to see regular air stop-offs in Mauritius. See PRO. CO 968/55/5.
12. Ben Warlow, *Shore Establishments of the Royal Navy: Being a List of the Static Ships and Establishments of the Royal Navy* (Liskeard: Maritime Books, 1992).
13. Interview with Peter Millar, Curepipe, July 1999. Millar has photos showing many Navy ships in Mauritian ports, as well as Hurricanes and flying boats.
14. John Shuckburgh, 'Colonial Civil History of the Second World War' (London: Colonial Office, 1949), p. 13.

15. Philippe La Hausse de Lalouviere (ed.) *Coastal Fortifications: Proceedings of an International Conference on Coastal Fortifications Held in Mauritius 18–21 June 1996* (Mauritius: Heritage, 1998). Allister Macmillan, *Mauritius Illustrated: History and Descriptive, Commercial and Industrial, Facts, Figures, and Resources* (London: W. H. & L. Collingridge, 1914). On p. 56 an excellent panorama of Port Louis shows the Line Barracks. A picture on p. 258 shows the Hong Kong and Singapore Battalion at the Line Barracks, and p. 259 shows all the men of the 5th Northumberland Fusiliers at a farewell outing in 1906.

16. A. R. Mannick, *Mauritius: the Development of a Plural Society* (Nottingham: Spokesman, 1979), p. 29.

17. C. Northcote Parkinson, *War in the Eastern Seas, 1793–1815* (London: Allen & Unwin, 1954), p. 14.

18. J. Addison and K. Hazareesingh, *A New History of Mauritius* (London: Macmillan Press – now Palgrave, 1984), p. 41.

19. F. D. Ommanney, *The Shoals of Capricorn*, p. 49.

20. Sydney Selvon, *Historical Dictionary of Mauritius* (London: Scarecrow, 1991), p. 8. For Mauritius and imperial warfare in this period, see Raymond D'Unienville, *Letters of Sir John Abercromby, September 1810–April 1811* (Quatre Bornes: Michel Robert, 1969); D'Unienville, *Last Years of the Ile de France (1800–14) Through Texts* (Port Louis: Mauritius Printing Company, 1959), and Patrick O'Brian's novel, *The Mauritius Command* (London: HarperCollins, 1996 edition). The Mauritius Underwater Group regularly dives the wreck of HMS *Sirius* in Grand Port.

21. The classic texts are C. Northcote Parkinson, *War in the Eastern Seas*, particularly chapter 21, 'The Battle of Grand Port', and chapter 22, 'The Capture of Mauritius', and H. C. M. Austen, *Sea Fights and Corsairs of the Indian Ocean, Being the Naval History of Mauritius from 1715 to 1810* (Mauritius, 1934).

22. Paul Langford, *Modern British Foreign Policy: the Eighteenth Century 1688–1815* (London: Adam & Charles Black, 1976), p. 233.

23. Quoted in J. M. Brown and Wm Roger Louis (eds) *The Oxford History of the British Empire*, p. 2.

24. L. Davis and R. Huttenback, *Mammon and the Pursuit of Empire*, p. 114.

25. Peter Burroughs, 'The Mauritius Rebellion of 1832 and the Abolition of British Colonial Slavery', *Journal of Imperial and Commonwealth History,* IV (1976).

26. See map 'Imperial Defence: Naval Bases, Stations and Army Garrisons', in P. Burroughs, 'Defence and Imperial Disunity', in A. Porter (ed.) *The Oxford History of the British Empire*, p. 321.

27. L. A. M. Tyack, *Treasures of the Indian Ocean: Mauritius and its Dependencies* (Lausanne: France Inter Press, 1965) and 'Star and Key of the Indian Ocean', *Libertas*, 7, 3 (1947).

28. P. J. Barnwell and A. Toussaint, *A Short History of Mauritius* (London: Longmans, Green and Company for the Government of Mauritius, 1949), p. 213.

29. E. Babajee, 'Indian Troops in Mauritius', *United Empire: Journal of the Royal Empire Society*, VXLV, 5 (1954).

30. Lawrence James, *Raj: The Making and Unmaking of British India* (London: Abacus, 1997), p. 246.

31. Malcolm Page, *KAR: A History of the King's African Rifles* (London: Leo Cooper, 1998). p. 3. In 1905 the Central African Rifles was merged with the Uganda Rifles and East African Rifles to create the KAR.

32. See Timothy Parson, *The African Rank-and-File: Social Implications of Colonial Military Service in the King's African Rifles, 1902–1964* (Oxford: James Currey, 1999), p. 158.

33. PRO. WO 192/182. Fort Record Book.

34. Hugh Seton-Watson, *The Decline of Imperial Russia 1855–1914* (London: Methuen, 1952), p. 183.

35. RHL. KAR Papers, Mss. Afr. s. 1715. Box 17, item 273.

36. For an excellent discussion see Wm Roger Louis, *Great Britain and Germany's Lost Colonies* (Oxford: Oxford University Press, 1967).

37. Sir Charles Lucas, *The Empire at War, Volume IV, Africa* (London: Oxford University Press, 1924), Part V, 'African Islands', Section I, 'Mauritius', p. 550. The author compiled the chapter from notes sent by the Assistant Colonial Secretary.

38. B. Warlow, *Shore Establishments of the Royal Navy*, p. 116.

39. PRO. WO 192/182. Fort Record Book.

40. C. Lucas, *The Empire at War*, p. 538.

41. Royal Commonwealth Society (henceforth RCS) Library, University of Cambridge. Robert Edward-Hart, *Les Volontaires Mauriciens aux Armées 1914–18* (Port Louis: General Printing & Stationery Company, 1919). This remarkable book provided biographical details of the 520 British and French Mauritians who served in Europe.

42. C. Lucas, *The Empire at War*, p. 537.

43. Philippe La Hausse de Lalouviere (ed.) *Coastal Fortifications*, pp. 64–5. PRO. WO 192/182. Fort Record Book.

44. Alan Villiers, *The Indian Ocean* (London: Museum Press, 1952), p. 221.

45. Jacques Mordal, *Twenty Five Centuries of Sea Warfare* (London: Abbey Library, 1970), chapter 23, 'The Cruise of the *Emden*'. For a map showing her cruise, see Bernard Ireland, *Naval History of World War Two* (London: HarperCollins, 1998), p. 12. For the *Konigsberg*, see Kevin Patience, *Konigsberg: A German East African Raider* (Bahrain: Dar Akhbar, 1994); and Patience, *Zanzibar and the Loss of HMS Pegasus, 20 September 1914* (Bahrain: Dar Akhbar, 1996).

46. RCS. Hesketh Bell Collection, photographs.

47. C. Lucas, *The Empire at War*, p. 536.

48. Ibid., p. 539.

49. J. Shuckburgh, 'Colonial Civil History', p. 13. This paragraph draws on Shuckburgh's study.

50. Antoine Chelin, *Maurice: Une Ile et Son Passe* (Reunion: Bibliothèque Indienocéanienne, 1989), note 233.

51. PRO. CO 167/907/1. Visits of HM Ships.

52. Ibid.

53. J. Shuckburgh, 'Colonial Civil History'.

54. PRO. CAB 11/199. Mauritius Defence Scheme.

2   Defence of Empire and the Sea Lanes: the Royal Navy and the British Indian Ocean World

1. N. A. M. Rodgers presentation, Oxford Commonwealth History seminar, Michaelmas Term 1999.
2. See Anthony Clayton, *The British Empire as a Superpower, 1919–39* (London: Macmillan Press – now Palgrave, 1886). For an overview of twentieth-century imperial defence, see Clayton, '"Deceptive Might": Imperial Defence and Security, 1900–1968', in J. M. Brown and Wm Roger Louis, (eds) *The Oxford History of the British Empire*.
3. See Gerald Graham, *Great Britain in the Indian Ocean, 1810–1850: a Study in Maritime Enterprise* (Oxford: Clarendon Press, 1967) and L. C. F. Turner, H. R. Gordon-Cumming and J. E. Beltzer, *War in the Southern Oceans, 1939–45* (Cape Town: Oxford University Press, 1961).
4. Barry Gough, 'Profit and Power: Informal Empire, the Navy, and Latin America', in Raymond Dumett (ed.) *Gentlemanly Capitalism and British Imperialism: the New Debate on Empire* (London: Longman, 1999), p. 73. The potential for naval history to illuminate the study of imperial history is present on every page of Gerald Graham's classic *The Politics of Naval Supremacy*.
5. Michael Simpson (ed.) with John Somerville, *The Somerville Papers: Selections from the Private and Official Correspondence of Admiral of the Fleet Sir James Somerville* (Aldershot: Scolar Press for the Naval Records Society, 1995), p. 356.
6. H. P. Willmott, *Grave of a Dozen Schemes: British Naval Planning and the War Against Japan 1943–45* (London: Airlife, 1996), p. 154.
7. NHB. C-in-C Eastern Fleet War Diary, volume 11, p. 76. Singapore conference, 18/12/41.
8. H. P. Willmott, *Grave of a Dozen Schemes*, pp. 155–56.
9. Quoted in B. B. Schofield, *British Sea Power: Naval Policy in the Twentieth Century* (London: B. T. Batsford, 1967), p. 163.
10. Ibid., p. 110.
11. See Arthur Marder, *Old Friends, New Enemies: the Royal Navy and the Imperial Japanese Navy – Strategic Illusions 1936–1941* (Oxford: Clarendon Press, 1981).
12. N. A. M. Rodgers to A. Jackson, January 2000.
13. Carl Boyd lecture, 'German and Japanese Cooperation in World War Two', All Souls, Oxford, 10/2/00.
14. Suki Dockrill (ed.) *From Pearl Harbor to Hiroshima: the Second World War in Asia and the Pacific, 1941–45* (London: Macmillan Press – now Palgrave, 1994), p. 161.
15. Gerhard Weinberg, *A World At Arms: a Global History of World War II* (Cambridge: Cambridge University Press, 1994), p. 307.
16. NHB. C-in-C Eastern Fleet War Diary.
17. See W. David McIntyre, *Rise and Fall of the Singapore Naval Base, 1919–1942* (London: Macmillan Press – now Palgrave, 1979) and Ian Hamill, *The Strategic Illusion: the Singapore Strategy and the Defence of Australia and New Zealand* (Singapore: Singapore University Press, 1981).
18. G. Weinberg, *A World At Arms*, p. 292.

19. Jurgen Rohwer and G. Hummelchen, *Chronicle of the War at Sea 1939–45: the Naval History of World War Two* (London: Greenhill, 1992), p. 50. French Somaliland information from I. C. B. Dear (ed.) *The Oxford Companion to the Second World War* (Oxford: Oxford University Press, 1995), p. 422.
20. A. Clayton, '"Deceptive Might"', p. 285.
21. Stephen Roskill, *The War at Sea 1939–1945, Volume II* (London: HMSO, 1954), p. 238.
22. G. Weinberg, *A World At Arms*, p. 324.
23. Ibid., p. 324.
24. John Keegan, *The Price of Admiralty: the Evolution of Naval Warfare* (London: Penguin, 1990), p. 193.
25. See Nicholas Tarling, *The Fall of Imperial Britain in South East Asia* (Singapore: Oxford University Press, 1993); Tarling, *British South East Asia and the Onset of the Pacific War* (Cambridge: Cambridge University Press, 1996); and Tarling, *British South East Asia and the Onset of the Cold War, 1945–50* (Cambridge: Cambridge University Press, 1998).
26. Ronald Lewin, *Slim: the Standard Bearer. A Biography of Field-Marshal Viscount Slim* (Hertfordshire: Wordsworth Editions, 1999), p. 99.
27. M. C. O'Neill (ed.) *The History of the Second World War: Volume II* (London: Odhams, 1951), p. 263.
28. Ibid., p. 264.
29. S. Woodburn Kirby, *The War Against Japan, Volume I: The Loss of Singapore* (London: HMSO, 1957), p. 251. The point is made forcefully in a letter from Churchill to Roosevelt, dated 15/4/42, and quoted in M. Simpson, *The Somerville Papers*, p. 356
30. Martin Kolinsky, *Britain's War in the Middle East: Strategy and Diplomacy 1936–42* (London: Macmillan Press – now Palgrave, 1999), p. 6.
31. F. H. Hinsley, *British Intelligence in the Second World War* (London: HMSO, 1993), p. 386.
32. John Keegan, *The Second World War* (London: Pimlico, 1988), p. 94.
33. NHB. C-in-C Eastern Fleet War Diary, volume 10.
34. Ibid., volume 9, pp. 362 and 296.
35. Correlli Barnett, *Engage The Enemy More Closely: the Royal Navy in the Second World War* (London: Hodder & Stoughton, 1991), p. 868.
36. See Paul Haggie, *Britannia at Bay: the Defence of the British Empire Against Japan, 1931–1941* (Oxford: Clarendon Press, 1981).
37. NHB. C-in-C Eastern Fleet War Diary, volume 9.
38. Bernard Ireland, *Jane's Naval History of World War Two* (London: HarperCollins, 1998), p. 242.
39. B. Schofield, *British Sea Power*, p. 78.
40. NHB. C-in-C Eastern Fleet War Diary, volume 11, March 1942.
41. See Donald MacIntyre, *Fighting Admiral: the Life of Admiral of the Fleet Sir James Somerville* (London: Evans Brothers, 1961); and S. Roskill, *The War at Sea 1939–1945, Volume I* (London: HMSO, 1954), p. 555.
42. NHB. C-in-C Eastern Fleet War Diary, volume 10, p. 305.
43. S. Woodburn Kirby, *The War Against Japan, Volume I*, p. 251.
44. M. C. O'Neill (ed.) *The History of the Second World War*, pp. 263–4.
45. NHB. C-in-C Eastern Fleet War Diary, volume 10, p. 308.

46. Richard Hough, *The Longest War At Sea 1939–45* (London: Weidenfeld & Nicolson, 1986), p. 147.
47. Ibid., p. 151.
48. M. Simpson, *The Somerville Papers*, p. 358.
49. NHB. C-in-C Eastern Fleet War Diary, volume 10, p. 301.
50. M. Kolinsky, *Britain's War in the Middle East*, p. 202.
51. NHB. C-in-C Eastern Fleet War Diary, volume 11, p. 165.
52. M. Simpson, *The Somerville Papers*, p. 403.
53. Ibid.
54. S. Roskill, *The War At Sea 1939–45, Volume II*, p. 22.
55. R. Lewin, *Slim*, p. 112.
56. M. Simpson, *The Somerville Papers*, p. 363.
57. S. Roskill, *The War At Sea 1939–45, Volume II*.
58. M. Simpson, *The Somerville Papers*, p. 364. Mauritius had a special relationship with its namesake ship, HMS *Mauritius*, a Fiji class cruiser armed with twelve 6-inch and eight 4-inch guns, launched in 1939, displacing 10 350 tons (fully loaded). [NHB. *Naval Staff History of the Second World War: War With Japan: Volume II, Defensive Phase* (London: Admiralty Historical Section, 1954)]. The island bought her Walrus seaplane, a piano and a table centrepiece in silver depicting the Battle of Grand Port off Mauritius in 1810. On service with the Eastern Fleet, HMS *Mauritius* regularly visited the colony. She had an engagement with German destroyers in the Bay of Biscay. In 1943 she was withdrawn from the Eastern Fleet and transferred to the Mediterranean where she took part in the invasion of Sicily and the Anzio landings. [*Naval Staff History of the Second World War: War With Japan: Volume III, The Campaigns in the Solomons and New Guinea* (London: Admiralty Historical Section, 1956), p. 115]. The following year HMS *Mauritius* took part in the D-Day bombardment, flying the flag of Rear Admiral Patterson, Commander of the 2nd Cruiser Squadron, anchored in the bay of the Sienne. Bombardment Force D, of which she was a part, consisted of HMS *Ramillies, Warspite, Roberts, Frobisher, Arethusa, Danae*, the Polish ship *Dragon* and 13 destroyers. [Eric Grove, *Sea Battles In Close Up, World War Two*, volume II (Surrey: Ian Allan, 1993), p. 150.
The ship was broken up in March 1965. [B. Warlow, *Shore Establishments of the Royal Navy*]. A scale model is in the Musée pour la Paix at Caen and its battleflag is in the Naval Museum, Mahebourg, Mauritius. For a photo, see Eric Grove, *Vanguard to Trident: British Naval Policy Since World War Two* (London: Bodley Head, 1987), p. 154. For the eight Fiji class cruisers, see M. J. Whitley, *Cruisers of World War Two: an International Encyclopaedia* (London: Arms & Armour, 1995) and H. T. Lenton, *British and Empire Warships of the Second World War* (London: Greenhill, 1998), p. 68.
59. S. Roskill, *The War at Sea 1939–45, Volume II*, p. 423.
60. PRO. ADM 223/523.
61. H. P. Willmott, *Grave of a Dozen Schemes*.
62. S. Roskill, *The War at Sea 1939–45, Volume III*.
63. M. Simpson, *The Somerville Papers*, p. 364.
64. B. Ireland, *Jane's Naval History of World War Two*, p. 216.
65. PRO. ADM 12/1376. War Cabinet 31/3/42: Defence plans for bases in the Indian Ocean.

66. J. R. M. Butler (ed.) *History of the Second World War* (UK Military Series); S. Woodburn Kirby, *The War Against Japan: Volume II, India's Most Dangerous Hour* (London: HMSO, 1958), p. 58 – see chapter 7, 'Japan's Naval Raids on Ceylon' and chapter 8, 'Madagascar'.
67. S. Roskill, *The War At Sea 1939–45, Volume II*, p. 33.
68. NHB. *Naval Staff History of the Second World War: War With Japan: Volume IV, The South East Asia Operations and Central Pacific Advance* (London: Admiralty Historical Section, 1957), p. 181.
69. P. J. Barnwell and A. Toussaint, *A Short History of Mauritius*, p. 233.
70. See Arthur Hezlet, *The Electron and Sea Power* (London: Peter Davies, 1975).
71. PRO. ADM 116/4964. Mauritius Naval W/T Station: Meeting at the Admiralty 25/4/43.
72. PRO. ADM 12/1736.
73. PRO. CO 968/24/8.
74. PRO. CO 968/24/3. Admiralty to Colonial Office, 2/9/43. WO 106/3797. Indian Ocean Bases.
75. RHL. *Mauritius Colonial Annual Report 1948* (London: HMSO, 1949) p. 93.
76. Interview with Peter Millar, Curepipe, June 1999. See I. C. B. Dear, *The Oxford Companion*, p. 740.
77. Joseph Lawrence, *The Observers Book of Aircraft* (London: Frederick Warne & Coy, 1949). The Catalina flew at 196mph at 7500 feet. It was armed with 0.5-inch machine guns in side blisters and a 1.3-inch machine gun in the nose. Thanks to Matt Jackson for this reference.
78. RHL. *Mauritius Colonial Annual Report 1948*, p. 93.
79. PRO. ADM 199/609. Operations East African Theatre, 1940–43.
80. NHB. C-in-C Eastern Fleet War Diary, volume 10, p. 348. See Somerville's diary entry for 9/5/42, p. 418.
81. PRO. CO 968/24/7. Provision of six-inch Guns for Diego Garcia. Protection of anchorages in event of Far Eastern war, C-in-C East Indies, 31/10/41.
82. M. Simpson, *The Somerville Papers*, p. 427.
83. PRO. WO 106/3719. Report on Diego Garcia by Major E. Crogham visiting the island 29 March to 12 April 1942. PRO. WO 106/3797. Indian Ocean Bases April 1942 to November 1943.
84. NHB. C-in-C Eastern Fleet War Diary, volume 10, p. 233.
85. Ibid., volume 10, p. 246.
86. I. C. B. Dear, *The Oxford Companion*, p. 754.
87. NHB. C-in-C Eastern Fleet War Diary, volume 10, p. 247.
88. PRO. WO 106/3719. Report on Diego Garcia by Major E. Crogham.
89. PRO. WO 106/3797. Indian Ocean Bases April 1942 to November 1943.
90. PRO. WO 106/3719. Report on Diego Garcia by Major E. Crogham.
91. NHB. C-in-C Eastern Fleet War Diary, volume 10, p. 347.
92. Ibid., volume 10, p. 237.
93. PRO. WO 106/3797. Indian Ocean Bases April 1942 to November 1943.
94. NHB. C-in-C Eastern Fleet War Diary, volume 10, p. 121.
95. Ibid., p. 377.
96. Ibid., p. 78.
97. NHB. *Naval Staff History of the Second World War: War With Japan: Volume I, Background to the War* (London: Admiralty Historical Section, 1956), p. 53.

98. NHB. C-in-C Eastern Fleet War Diary, volume 12.
99. Ibid., volume 10, p. 15.
100. Ibid., volume 10, p. 44.
101. Ibid., volume 11.
102. Robert Aldrich, *Greater France: a History of French Overseas Expansion* (London: Macmillan Press – now Palgrave, 1996), p. 84.
103. Gustav Lenoir and M. Carosin interview, Dodo Club, Curepipe, 13/7/99.
104. J. Rohwer and G. Hummelchen, *Chronicle of the War at Sea*, p. 6.
105. H. P. Willmott, *Grave of a Dozen Schemes*, p. 157.
106. For the Channel in this period see PRO. ADM 199/1404.
107. On 26 April 1943, south of Mauritius, the German submarine U-180 transferred the rebel Indian National Army leader Subhas Chandra Bose to the Japanese submarine I-29 on route to Penang. Jurgen Rohwer and G. Hummelchen, *Chronicle of the War at Sea*, p. 205.
108. F. H. Hinsley, *British Intelligence in the Second World War*, p. 386.
109. Ibid., p. 386.
110. PRO. ADM 223/8.
111. Patrick Beesly, *Very Special Intelligence: the Story of the Admiralty's Operational Intelligence Centre 1939–1945* (London: Hamish Hamilton, 1977), chapter 9, 'June to December 1942: the Indian Ocean and Torch'.
112. T. Parsons, *The African Rank-and-File*, p. 35.
113. Jurgen Rohwer and G. Hummelchen, *Chronicle of the War at Sea*.
114. RHL. Flora Moody Diaries, item 4. *Hoi How* was employed as a supply ship to Islands Bases administered by Flag Officer East Africa. C-in-C Eastern Fleet War Diary, volume 12. For the sinking see PRO. ADM 199/1404.
115. NHB. Indian Ocean D 191 II, November 1942–May 1945. Reported attacks and sinkings, pp. 62–3. Detailed German documents removed from the German naval headquarters at the end of the war show the German reports relating to such sinkings. See NHB, PG ('pinched documents') 30168, war diary of U-181.
116. Rainer Busch and Hans-Joachim Roll, *German U-Boat Commanders of World War Two: a Biographical Dictionary* (London: Greenhill Books, 1999), p. 182.
117. B. Ireland, *Jane's Naval History of World War Two*, p. 42.
118. NHB. Indian Ocean II, D 191. November 1942 to May 1945. Log of reported sinkings and attacks, p. 69.
119. *Lloyd's War Losses, Second World War, Volume I, British, Allied, and Neutral Merchant Vessels Sunk or Destroyed by War Causes 1942–45*.
120. Thanks to Ann Waswo for this information.
121. Carl Boyd lecture, 'German and Japanese Cooperation in the Second World War'.
122. NHB. C-in-C Eastern Fleet War Diary, volume 10, p. 343.
123. S. Roskill, *The War At Sea 1939–45, Volume II*, p. 271.
124. See R. Lewin, *The Other Ultra* (London: Hutchinson, 1982), chapter 9, 'A Broken Axis: the Blockade Runners' Ruin'.
125. I. C. B. Dear (ed.) *The Oxford Companion*, see map on p. 452 showing Indian Ocean sinkings of the two ships.
126. John Winton, *Ultra at Sea* (London: Leo Cooper, 1988), p. 7.
127. See 'Auxiliary Cruisers' in I. C. B. Dear (ed.) *The Oxford Companion*.

128. HMS *Cornwall* was a Kent class cruiser launched in 1926. On 7 May 1941 as a result of a distress message from the tanker *British Emperor* she was ordered to search for a German raider, which was sighted by the cruiser's aircraft. Her disguise was penetrated and she was identified as the *Pinguin*. A salvo caused her to blow up; 58 German and 25 British survivors were rescued. In March 1942 *Cornwall* was attached to 4th Cruiser Squadron of the new Eastern Fleet. On 5 April she was sunk by 50 dive bombers off the south coast of Ceylon with the loss of 190 men. NHB. 'HMS *Cornwall*: Summary of Service'.

129. Jurgen Rohwer and G. Hummelchen, *Chronicle of the War at Sea*, p. 62.

130. NHB. Battle Summary Reports.

131. B. Schofield, *British Sea Power*, p. 192.

132. John Winton, *Ultra at Sea*, pp. 37–8.

133. PRO. CAB 106/345. *London Gazette*, 9/7/48, 'Actions Against Raiders'. See also H. P. Willmott, *Grave of a Dozen Schemes*.

134. PRO. ADM 223/38. NHB. *Naval Staff History of the Second World War: War With Japan: Volume IV*, p. 188.

135. PRO. ADM 223/8 and ADM 223/38.

136. PRO. ADM 223/39. East Indies Station 1944 Fleet and Miscellaneous Operations.

137. J. Rohwer and G. Hummelchen, *Chronicle of the War at Sea*, p. 6. Disguised raiders were also a threat in the region, like the auxiliary cruisers *Schiff 33/Pinguin* and *Schiff 16/Atlantis*. Crew members have written fascinating accounts. See Ulrich Mohr, *Atlantis: the Story of a German Surface Raider* (London: Werner Laurie, 1955) and Bernhard Rogge (captain of the *Atlantis*), *Under Ten Flags: the Story of the German Commerce Raider Atlantis* (London: Weidenfeld & Nicolson, 1955).

138. H. P. Willmott, *Grave of a Dozen Schemes*, p. 160.

139. NHB. C-in-C Eastern Fleet War Diary, volume 10, p. 120.

140. Ibid., volume 12.

141. PRO. ADM 223/523. Commander-in-Chief East Indies Station to Admiralty, 27/9/41. See also ADM 223/678. Operation Ration.

142. NHB. C-in-C Eastern Fleet War Diary, volume 9, p. 27. See also PRO. ADM 223/678 for Operation Ration, the interception of a French convoy.

143. Ibid., volume 10, p. 275.

144. Ibid., volume 9, p. 283.

145. *Leander*, a light cruiser of the Royal New Zealand Navy, had on the outbreak of war deposited two dummy 4.7–inch guns at Fiji, indicative of the pressure that world war put upon the empire's military resources and the importance attached to the appearance of imperial protective inclusivity. K. Jeffery, 'The Second World War' in J. M. Brown and Wm Roger Louis (eds) *The Oxford History of the British Empire*, p. 306. Even imperial fortresses of the first order were ill-defended; Gibraltar boasted two 3-inch anti-aircraft guns, and Malta none. B. Schofield, *British Sea Power*, p. 134.

146. NHB. C-in-C Eastern Fleet War Diary, volume 9.

147. PRO. CO 969/24. Prize Case: Mauritius – SS *Charles L. D.* Also CO 969/50, CO 969/92, CO 969/25, CO 969/138.

148. NHB. C-in-C Eastern Fleet War Diary, volume 9, p. 347.

149. Ibid., volume 9, pp. 356 and 362.

150. Ibid., volume 9, p. 10.
151. B. Schofield, *British Sea Power*, p. 207.
152. The term is used by Martin Thomas in 'Captives of Their Countrymen: Free French and Vichy French POWs in Africa and the Middle East, 1940–43', in Bob Moore and Kent Fedorowich (eds) *Prisoners of War and Their Captors in World War Two* (Oxford: Berg, 1996), p. 93. Thanks to Martin Thomas for his reading suggestions. See also his 'Imperial Backwater or Strategic Outpost? The British Takeover of Vichy Madagascar in 1942', *Historical Journal*, 39, 4 (1996).
153. PRO. ADM 223/550. Operation Ironclad. ADM 223/564 Operation Stream (Majunga), Line (Tananarive), and Jane (Tamatave). See S. Woodburn Kirby, *The War Against Japan: Volume II*, chapter 8, 'Madagascar April–November 1942'.
154. Louis Grundlingh, 'The Role of Black South African Soldiers in the Second World War: A Contested Contribution', conference paper delivered at St Antony's College, Oxford (April 1998), p. 6.
155. PRO. ADM 12/1736.
156. PRO. HS 3/14. Mauritius was designated operational HQ for SOE operations against Reunion and Madagascar. K. E. Robinson to Julius Hanau (Caesar), 22/12/41.
157. PRO. HS 3/9. SOE Abyssinia/East Africa/Madagascar 1941–43. This file details the outstanding contribution of Mayer and his wife. See also Ted Harrison, 'British Subversion in French East Africa, 1941–42: SOE's Todd Mission', *English Historical Review* (April 1999).
158. Imperial War Museum (henceforth IWM). SOE Sound Archive. Accession 15320. Interview with Peter Simpson-Jones, recorded 1995. See also Kate Johnson (ed.) *The SOE Sound Archive Oral History Recordings* (London: IWM, 1998).
159 Sir Bede Clifford had made a careful study of the harbour on his way to Mauritius, and offered the government advice on its capture during the war. Bede Clifford, *Proconsul: Being Incidents in the Life and Career of The Honourable Sir Bede Clifford* (London: Evans Brothers, 1964), p. 227.
160. Martin Thomas, *The French Empire at War 1940–45* (Manchester: Manchester University Press, 1998), p. 5.
161. Ibid., p. 52.
162. NHB. C-in-C Eastern Fleet War Diary, volume 10, p. 162.
163. M. Thomas, *The French Empire at War*, p. 152.
164. NHB. C-in-C Eastern Fleet War Diary, volume 10, p. 163.
165. M. Thomas, *The French Empire at War*, p. 46.
166. I. C. B. Dear, *The Oxford Companion*, p. 705.
167. W.G. Beasley, *The Rise of Modern Japan* (London: Weidenfeld & Nicolson, 1990), p. 202.
168. Ann Waswo to A. Jackson, 20/9/99.
169. M. Thomas, *The French Empire at War*, p. 153.
170. PRO. HS 3/9. SOE Abyssinia/East Africa/Madagascar, 1941–43. High Commissioner South Africa to Dominions Office, 12/2/42.
171. RHL. *Mauritius Colonial Annual Report 1946*, p. 127.
172. Eric Rosenthal, *Japan's Bid for Africa: Including the Story of the Madagascar Campaign* (South Africa: Central News Agency, 1944).

173. Bill Nasson, 'National Mobilization and Military Effectiveness in the Union of South Africa, 1939–45', conference paper delivered at St Antony's College, Oxford (April 1998), p. 8.
174. Thanks to Donal Lowry for this information.
175. E. Rosenthal, *Japan's Bid for Africa*, p. 97.
176. See map 'War at Sea in South African Waters', in I. B. B. Dear (ed.) *The Oxford Companion*, p. 1025.
177. B. Nasson 'National Mobilization', p. 11.
178. Paul Auphan and Jacques Mordal, *The French Navy in World War Two* (Annapolis, Maryland: US Naval Institute, 1952), p. 203.
179. Alain Mathieu, 'The Failure of the Mauritian Spies and the Taking of Reunion in 1942', Mauritius History Society Paper, 23/10/42. Thanks to Raymond D'Unienville and Alain Mathieu for a copy of this lecture, and Marina Carter for translating it. The paper also contains the report of the 'Judgement Given by the Permanent Tribunal at Tananarivo, Constituted as a Court Martial, 19 June 1942'.
180. Arthur Stamberg, *Footprints on a Winding Road: Recollections of an Old Jerseyman* (Jersey: La Haule, 1998), chapter 16, 'Mauritius'.
181. IWM. Simpson-Jones interview.
182. NHB. C-in-C Eastern Fleet War Diary, volume 10, 20/11/42.
183. Ibid., volume 10, pp. 265 and 292. PRO. CO 968/86/3. France and French Possessions: Reunion Operations. Governor to Secretary of State, 29/11/42.
184. P. Auphan and J. Mordal, *The French Navy in World War Two*, p. 162.
185. NHB. *Naval Staff History of the Second World War: War With Japan: Volume IV*, p. 181.

3   Defending the Home Front: Local and Imperial Defence Measures

1. J. Shuckburgh, 'Colonial Civil History,' p. 13.
2. For the British Home Guard, see S. P. Mackenzie, *The Home Guard: the Real Story of 'Dad's Army'* (Oxford: Oxford University Press, 1996).
3. MNA. *Government Gazette*. Notice 494.
4. RHL. Clive Watt Papers. Mss. Brit. Emp. s. 291.
5. PRO. CO 968/24/1. Colonial Office passing on views of the Overseas Committee, 28/7/41. Scale of Attack estimates.
6. PRO. CO 968/24/2. Governor to Secretary of State, 23/7/42.
7. PRO. CO 968/24/1. Governor to Secretary of State, 18/12/41.
8. PRO. CO 968/24/3. Governor to Secretary of State, 14/8/43.
9. PRO. CO 968/24/1. Mauritius Defence. The Colonial Office gave the Admiralty a nudge and the minesweepers were built in Calcutta. PRO. CO 968/24/3. E. E. Sabben-Clare to Admiralty, 16/8/43.
10. Ibid. Governor to Secretary of State, 21/1/42.
11. PRO. WO 106/3719.
12. A shortage of weapons for the Home Guard led to the requisitioning of private weapons without compensation. MNA. *Advance*, 18/2/42.
13. PRO. CO 968/24/2. Governor to Secretary of State, 18/3/42.

14. PRO. CO 968/24/3. Governor to G. E. J. Gent, Colonial Office, 15/12/42.
15. PRO. CO 968/24/1. Colonial Office, 28/7/41.
16. NHB. C-in-C Eastern Fleet War Diary, volume 12.
17. PRO. CO 968/24/3. Secretary of State to Governor, 11/8/43.
18. Ibid., 20/12/43.
19. PRO. ADM 199/609. Operations East African Theatre, 1940-43.
20. Laurence Grafftey-Smith, *Hands to Play* (London: Routledge and Keegan Paul, 1975), p. 73.
21. NHB. C-in-C Eastern Fleet War Diary, volume 9, p. 41.
22. Ibid., volume 10, p. 66.
23. Ibid., volume 12, p. 222.
24. Ibid., volume 10, p. 298.
25. PRO. CO 968/147/2. Governor to Secretary of State, 26/1/43.
26. PRO. CO 968/24/3. GOC-in-C East Africa to War Office, 3/2/43.
27. Ibid. War Office to GOC-in-C East Africa, 5/2/43.
28. Manning O'Brine, *Dodos Don't Duck* (London: Hammond & Hammond, 1953), p. 132.
29. PRO. CO 968/147/2. Governor to Secretary of State, 28/1/43, and Control of Local Forces, Mauritius. GOC-in-C East Africa to War Office, 24/1/43.
30. PRO. WO 192/40. Fort Record Book.
31. PRO. CO 968/147/2. Governor to Secretary of State, 3/5/43.
32. PRO. CO 968/104b/8 (file released at author's request from FCO April 1994). Mauritius: Post-Occupational Activities Secret Defence 1942–45.
33. PRO. CO 167/920/11. Mauritius Civil Labour Corps. Secretary of State to Governor, 26/2/43. See CO 968/147/2. Control of Local Forces. Secretary of State to Governor, 26/2/43.
34. PRO. CO 968/24/1 War Office to Commander-in-Chief India, 28/12/41.
35. PRO. CO 968/24/3. Governor to Secretary of State, 31/5/43.
36. MNA. *Le Cerneen-Le Mauricien-Advance*, 4/3/43.
37. Twining Papers. 'Oddments, 1939–46'. May Twining letter, 12/8/42.
38. PRO. CO 968/131. Manpower Mauritius. Governor to Secretary of State, 27/5/44.
39. Ibid. Minute, 12/5/44.
40. 'Privations and the Military Regime', *L'Express*, 19/1/97.
41. Abdool Cader Amode, 'Mauritius During World War Two', 1/2/91. Newspaper article.
42. D'Unienville Papers, private collection of Raymond D'Unienville. Colony of Mauritius, *Air Raids: What You Must Know and What You Must Do* (Port Louis: Government Printer, 1941).
43. MNA. *Government Gazette 1939*, general notice 787.
44. Interview with Nick Bouchet's aunt, Vacoas, 27/6/99.
45. RHL. FCB Papers. Box 170. *Annual Report of the Labour Department 1942* (Port Louis: Government Printer, 1943), p. 15. PRO. CO 968/72/7. Civil Defence Progress Report, S. Moody to Secretary of State, 6/5/42.
46. PRO. CO 167/928/9. Passive Defence: Fire Fighting. Governor to Secretary of State, 23/9/43.
47. RHL. *Mauritius Colonial Annual Report 1948* (London: HMSO, 1949), p. 87.
48. PRO. CO 167/920/2. Formation of Mauritius Coastal Defence Squadron. Governor to Secretary of State, 30/12/41.

49. PRO. CO 167/917/16. Police: Enlistment for War Period.
50. PRO. CO 968/24/4. Governor to Secretary of State for the Colonies, 16/2/41.
51. See Christopher Bayly, *Imperial Meridian: the British Empire and the World 1780-1830* (Harlow: Longman, 1989).
52. PRO. CAB 106/308. *What the British Empire Has Done: Facts and Figures on the Empire at War* (London: Ministry of Information, March 1944). RHL. KAR Papers. Box 16, item 245.
53. RHL. Mss. Brit. Emp. r. 9 and 10. A. Walter, 'Echoes of a Vanishing Empire: the Memoirs of a Meteorologist and Civil Servant in the Colonial Empire, 1897–1947', two volumes, p. 304. Walter travelled to Rodrigues from Mauritius on a whaler requisitioned by the Royal Navy and named HMS *Mastiff.*
54. A. Chelin, *Maurice: Une Ile et Son Passe.*
55. South African Department of Defence Archive, Pretoria. CGS (Chief of General Staff) War. Box 283/58/6. Colonel C. M. Ross to Quarter Master General, 31/10/44. Thanks to Kent Fedorowich for this reference.
56. Ibid. Quarter Master General to Colonel C. M. Ross.
57. PRO. CO 968/147/2. Governor to Secretary of State, 8/2/43.
58. PRO. CO 167/920/11. Civil Labour Corps. Mr. Hibbert minute, 24/9/42.
59. PRO. CO 167/902/10. Labour Conditions.
60. The Governor had passed a Labour Ordinance in 1938, without Colonial Office approval. 'Very extraordinary that we've heard nothing' an official minuted – yet another example of Sir Bede Clifford acting upon and beyond his own gubernatorial authority. PRO. CO 167/907/10. Labour Ordinance.
61. RHL. FCB Papers. Box 170. Aborigines Protection Society to Fabian Colonial Bureau, November/December 1944.
62. Ibid. Governor to Secretary of State, 30/5/42.
63. PRO. CO 167/919/18. Compulsory Military Service.
64. RHL. *Mauritius Colonial Annual Report 1946,* p. 13.
65. PRO. CO 968/131/3. Manpower Mauritius: Pioneer Corps. Officer Commanding Troops to Commander-in-Chief Middle East, 9/5/42.
66. PRO. CO 968/131/2. Manpower Mauritius. Extracts from notes of a discussion held at the Colonial Office with Mr Twining, Director of Labour, 4/8/43.
67. RHL. *Annual Report of the Labour Department 1943* (Port Louis: Government Printer, 1944).
68. Monica Maurel Papers, private collection. A. North-Coombes Diary, p. 190.
69. PRO. CO 968/147/2. A. R. Thomas minute, 6/5/43.
70. IWM. Colonel Reginald Yeldham interview, accession no. 003960/05. Predecessors in the position included General Charles Gordon, the martyr of Khartoum, who in 1882 was Garrison Commander of Mauritius. He is reported to have relayed the following anecdote: 'They say that HRH in one of his furies with someone said to the Adjutant General, "send him to hell". The AG said, "We have no station there, your Royal Highness"; on which HRH said, "Then send him to Mauritius".' Alexander J. Ward, *The Call of Distant Drums* (Edinburgh: Pentland Press, 1992), p. 131.

71. P. J. Barnwell, *Visits and Despatches 1598–1948* (Port Louis: Standard Printing Establishment, 1948), p. 296. This fascinating book contains a list of all the regiments that served in the garrison, up to the Indian Army's 17th Loyals in 1915. For the history of the QAIMNS see Juliet Piggott, *Queen Alexandra's Royal Army Nursing Corps* (London: Leo Cooper, 1975).
72. Graeme Crew, *Royal Army Service Corps* (London: Leo Cooper, 1970), pp. 259–60.
73. PRO. CO 968/24/2. Moody to Secretary of State, 2/5/42.
74. PRO. CO 968/147/2. Moody to Secretary of State, 21/6/45.
75. Ibid. Minute, 3/8/45.
76. PRO. CO 968/24/2. T. I. K. Lloyd, Colonial Office to H. W. Dinwiddie, War Office, 9/7/42.
77. Ibid. Governor to Secretary of State, 26/11/41.
78. PRO. CO 167/919/18. Compulsory Military Service. Also CO 167/920/11. Civil Labour Corps.
79. PRO. CO 167/919/18. Compulsory Military Service. Minute, 28/11/41.
80. Ibid. A. B. Acheson minute, 28/11/41.
81. Rex Salisbury Woods, *Cambridge Doctor* (London: Robert Hale, 1962), p. 171. See chapter 19, 'Escape to Mauritius'.
82. RHL. KAR Papers. Box 11, Item 182, Edward Mayne, typescript p. 10.
83. J. F. C. Harrison, *Scholarship Boy: a Personal History of the Twentieth Century* (London: Rivers Oram Press, 1995).
84. A. North-Coombes Diary, p. 114.
85. Ibid., p. 130.
86. Guy Sauzier, 'The Events Which Marked the Arrival of the Mauritian Battalion at Diego Suarez in 1943', lecture given to the Mauritius Historical Society, 23/5/98, p. 2.
87. Alfred Pitray and Guy Morel, 'War Memories', lecture to the History Society, 5/11/95.
88. Philippe La Hausse de Lalouviere, *Coastal Fortifications*.
89. Gustav Lenoir, 'Memories of a Former Gunner', lecture to the History Society, 13/5/95.
90. Interview with Gustav Lenoir and M. Carosin, Dodo Club, Curepipe, 13/7/99.
91. PRO. WO 192/182. Fort Record Book.
92. Alfred Pitray and Guy Morel, 'War Memories'.
93. 'Privations and the Military Regime', *L'Express*, 19/1/97.
94. A. Chelin, *Maurice: Une Ile et Son Passe*.
95. A. North-Coombes, *The Island of Rodrigues*, chapter 19, 'The Magistrates (1938–50)', p. 215.
96. Ibid., p. 216.
97. Ibid., 9/12/43.
98. See David Stafford, *Secret Agent* (London: BBC Worldwide, 2000) and the accompanying television series.
99. See T. Harrison, 'SOE's Todd Mission'.
100. William Mackenzie, *The Secret History of SOE: The Special Operatons Executive, 1940–1945* (London: St Ermin's Press, 2000) fails to mention the Mauritian SOE team. Thanks to M. R. D. Foot for the reference.

101. PRO. CO 968/104b/8. Mauritius: Post-Occupational Activities Secret Defence 1942–45. W. R. Rolleston minute, 16/6/42.
102. Ibid., T. I. K. Lloyd minute 24/2/42.
103. Documents supplied by Duncan Stuart, SOE Adviser to the Foreign and Commonwealth Office. Duncan Stuart to A. Jackson, 8/3/01.
104. Ibid.
105. PRO. CO968/104b/8. Governor to Secretary of State, 11/2/42.
106. Ibid., Colonel B. M. Clarke to T. I. K. Lloyd 3/6/42. Darrell Bates, *A Gust of Plumes: a Biography of Lord Twining of Godalming and Tanganyika* (London: Hodder & Stoughton, 1972), p. 127.
107. PRO. CO 968/104b/8. Colonel B. M. Clarke, to T. I. K. Lloyd, 27/6/42.
108. Ibid. T. I. K. Lloyd to Smith, 18/7/42
109. Ibid. Colonel B. M. Clarke to T. I. K. Lloyd, 9/8/42.
110. Ibid. T. I. K. Lloyd to Colonel B. M. Clarke, 22/6/42.
111. PRO. CO 968/146/5. Defence Scorched Earth Policy, Mauritius: Denial Scheme, 1943.
112. PRO. CO 968/81/11. Scorched Earth Policy. Byatt to Thomas, 28/7/42.
113. Ibid. Governor to Secretary of State, 21/3/42.
114. PRO. CO 968/81/11. Scorched Earth Policy. Minute 2/9/42.
115. Ibid. Governor to Secretary of State, 27/3/42.
116. Ibid. Governor to Secretary of State, 29/4/42.
117. Ibid. Moody to Secretary of State, 23/6/42.
118. Ibid. Secretary of State to Governor, 2/4/42.
119. Ibid. R. N. Byatt, Ministry of Economic Warfare (Far Eastern Section) to A. R. Thomas, Colonial Office.
120. PRO. CO 968/104b/8. Major T. Benham to Anthony Lincoln, 12/11/43.
121. PRO. CO 968/147/2. Governor to Secretary of State, 2/11/44.

4 Colonial Military Labour in Europe and the Middle East

1. For the role of Bletchley Park intelligence in the African and Italian campaigns, see F. W. Winterbotham, *The Ultra Secret: the Inside Story of Operation Ultra, Bletchley Park, and Enigma* (London: Weidenfeld & Nicolson, 1974).
2. Vichy France aided the Germans, selling Rommel all French lorries in Africa, providing ships and permitting the use of the port of Bizerta. Martin Van Creveld, *Supplying War: Logistics From Wallenstein to Patton* (Cambridge: Cambridge University Press, 1977), p. 186.
3. For example the official UK Military Series volumes, I. S. O. Playfair, C. J. C. Malony and W. Jackson, *The Mediterranean and Middle East*, 6 volumes (London: HMSO, 1954–88); Neil Orpen, *War in the Desert*, volume III of *South African Forces in World War Two* (Cape Town: Purnell, 1971); Anthony Farrar-Hockley, *The War in the Desert* (London: Faber & Faber, 1969); James Lucas, *War in the Desert: the Eighth Army at El Alamein* (London: Arms & Armour, 1982); Roger Parkinson, *The War in the Desert* (London: Hart-Davis, MacGibbon, 1976); and Barry Pitt, *Crucible of War: Western Desert 1941* (London: Jonathan Cape, 1980) and *Crucible of War: Year of Alamein 1942* (London: Jonathan Cape, 1982).

4. Wm Roger Louis, 'Introduction', in J. M. Brown and Wm Roger Louis (eds), *The Oxford History of the British Empire*, p. 24.
5. Ibid., p. 24.
6. Ibid., p. 179.
7. The supply dumps that littered the desert battlefields required prodigious efforts on the part of Pioneers. There were huge dumps at Belhammed and Tobruk. Sometimes dumps fell to the enemy, like that at Benghazi in January 1942.
8. I. C. B. Dear, *The Oxford Companion*, p. 874. George Forty, *British Army Handbook 1939–1945* (Stroud: Sutton Publishing, 1998), p. 42.
9. I. C. B. Dear, *The Oxford Companion*, p. 874.
10. G. Forty, *British Army Handbook*, p. 42
11. Ibid.
12. Ibid.
13. See M. Van Creveld, *Supplying War*. Chapter 6 examines Rommel's logistical problems. Julian Thompson's study, *Lifeblood of War: Logistics in Armed Conflict* (London: Brassey's, 1991) does not mention Pioneers.
14. Correlli Barnett, *The Desert Generals* (London: Cassell & Co, 1999), p. 28.
15. E. R. Elliott, *Royal Pioneers 1945–1993* (Hanley Swan, Worcestershire: Self Publishing Association, 1993), p. 9. E. H. Rhodes-Wood, *A War History of the Royal Pioneer Corps 1939–45* (Aldershot: Gale & Polden, 1960).
16. E. R. Elliott, *Royal Pioneers*, p. 14.
17. See K. W. Mitchinson, *Pioneer Battalions of the Great War: Organized and Intelligent Labour* (London: Leo Cooper, 1997).
18. Wm Roger Louis and J. M. Brown (eds), *The Oxford History of the British Empire*, p. 671.
19. See Michael Summerskill, *China on the Western Front: Britain's Chinese Workforce in the First World War* (London: M. Summerskill, 1982). It numbered 140 000.
20. See Robin Kilson, 'Calling Up The Empire: the British Military Use of Non-White Labour in France, 1916–1920', Ph.D Thesis (Harvard University, 1990). For South Africa, see Brian Willan, 'The South African Native Labour Contingent, 1916–18', *Journal of African History*, 19, 1 (1978); Norman Clothier, *Black Valour: the South African Native Labour Contingent 1916–18 and the Sinking of the Mendi* (Pietermaritzburg: University of Natal Press, 1987); and Albert Grundlingh, *Fighting Their Own War: South African Blacks and the First World War* (Johannesburg: Ravan Press, 1987).
21. D. Killingray, 'Labour Exploitation for Military Campaigns in British Colonial Africa, 1870–1945', *Journal of Contemporary History*, 24, 3 (1989), p. 493.
22. E. R. Elliott, *Royal Pioneers*, p. 15.
23. Ibid., p. 76. See 'No Labour, No Battle', *British Army Journal*, 4 (1950).
24. Ibid., p. 15. In 1993 the RPC was merged with other service branches to form today's Royal Logistics Corps.
25. G. Forty, *British Army Handbook*, p. 135.
26. PRO. WO 253/1.
27. E. R. Elliott, *Royal Pioneers*, p. 24.
28. Ibid., p. 32.
29. J. Shuckburgh, 'Colonial Civil History,' part II, 'Use of Colonial Manpower'.

30. The use of African fighting units was to go far beyond the envisaged reserve role with possible deployment in North Africa or the Middle East. East and West African troops were to the fore in the campaigns against the Italians in Eritrea, Somaliland and Abyssinia. They were used in the invasion of Madagascar, in Ceylon, and extensively in the Burma campaign – General Wingate even using a Nigerian brigade in his famous Chindits Long Range Penetration Force. See J. Shuckburgh, 'Colonial Civil History', for figures and unit details.

31. The records of all colonial servicemen are kept at the Ministry of Defence's Records department, Hayes, Middlesex. There are 200 linear metres of records. Each file contains the subject's Attestation Paper, Military History Record, Medical Examination/History Sheet, Service and Casualty Form, Qualification and Record Card and Conduct Sheet. Mrs J. M. Keel, Defence Records, Ministry of Defence to A. Jackson, 27/8/99.

32. E. H. Rhodes-Wood, *A War History of the Royal Pioneer Corps 1939–45* (Aldershot: Gale & Polden, 1960), p. 157.

33. G. Forty, *British Army Handbook*, p. 136.

34. Ibid., p. 129.

35. Ibid., pp. 129–30.

36. E. H. Rhodes-Wood, *A War History of the Royal Pioneer Corps*, p. 115.

37. France R. Domingo, *Les Mauriciens dans la Deuxième Guerre Mondiale: La 8eme Armée au Moyen-Orient et en Italie (1941–45)* (Moka: Editions de l'Océan Indien, 1983). See part 1, 'The 741 A. W. Company RE at Work in the Western Desert'.

38. RHL. *Mauritius Colonial Annual Report 1946*, p. 12.

39. PRO. CO 968/106/1. Report of Governor on Visit to Seychelles Troops in the Middle East, 1945.

40. PRO. CO 968/131/3. Manpower Mauritius: Pioneer Corps.

41. RCS. Command 6423, Major G. St J. Orde Brown, *Labour Conditions in Ceylon, Mauritius, and Malaya* (London: HMSO, 1943), p. 57.

42. Monaf Fakira interview, Grosvenor Hotel, London, 23/2/99.

43. MNA. *Advance*, 28/2/41.

44. *Le Corps Royal de Pionniers* issued by the British Army, copy in possession of Ex-Servicemen's Association (Mauritius), Port Louis HQ. The separate RPC Association (Mauritius Branch) has been based at Plaza Yard, Rose Hill since 1949. The RPC Association estimated its membership in 1999 to be 4000. Meeting at RPC HQ, 7/7/99.

45. RHL. Moody Papers. Item 3, p. 94, 1/9/41.

46. Ibid., p. 95.

47. PRO. CO 968/131. Major D. G. Pirie, 'Notes on Mauritius Pioneers and Artisans', 1/1/44.

48. PRO. CO 968/133/7: Family Allowances: Mauritius, Seychelles, St Helena, Falkland's, and Ceylon. Governor to Secretary of State, 9/6/44.

49. PRO. CO 968/38/6. Tour by Assistant Deputy Adjutant General Middle East. Cape Town, 18/4/41.

50. *L'Express*, 12/1/97.

51. MNA. *Advance*, 21/1/41.

52. MNA, *Advance*, 20/3/41.

53. G. Forty, *British Army Handbook*, p. 318.

54. PRO. CO 968/38/6. Governor to Secretary of State, 22/4/41.
55. B. Burrun, 'Mauritius and the Second World War', *Week-End*, 16/10/91.
56. PRO CAB 106/308. *What the British Empire Has Done: Facts and Figures on the Empire at War* (London: Ministry of Information, March 1944).
57. PRO. CO 968/38/6. Tour by Assistant Deputy Adjutant General Middle East. Cape Town, 18/4/41.
58. Jean-Michel Domingue, 'The Experience of the Mauritian and Seychellois Pioneers in, and Contribution to, the Egyptian and Western Desert Campaigns, 1940-43', MA Thesis (SOAS: University of London, 1994), p. 34.
59. PRO. CO 167/920/8. Hostel Facilities for Mauritius and Seychelles troops, Middle East. A. Acheson to S. Moody, Mauritius Colonial Secretary, 31/12/41.
60. Twining Papers. Strictly Confidential: Notes on Labour and Related Problems in Mauritius, c. 1942, pp. 4 and 34.
61. PRO. CO 167/920/8. Mauritian Troops in the Middle East. S. Moody to A. B. Acheson, 22/4/42.
62. For a discussion of some aspects of racial tension in the Pioneer Corps, see A. Jackson, 'African Soldiers and Imperial Authorities: Tensions and Unrest During the Service of HCT Soldiers in the British Army, 1941–46', *Journal of Southern African Studies*, 25, 4 (1999).
63. At the end of July 1950, 12 Mauritians and 2 Seychellois were commissioned after 18 months training at the Officer Cadet Training Wing, Geneifa, which had been especially established for the Indian Ocean Pioneers. E. R. Elliott, *Royal Pioneers*, p. 182.
64. Ibid. 1506 (Mauritius) Company War Diary.
65. PRO. CO 968/131. Major D. G. Pirie, 'Notes on Mauritius Pioneers and Artisans', 1/1/44.
66. J. Domingue, 'The Experience of the Mauritian and Seychellois Pioneers'.
67. Ibid. p. 33.
68. See Prynne's articles on establishing the base in *The Royal Pioneer* (1949).
69. E. H. Rhodes-Wood, *A War History of the Royal Pioneer Corps*, p. 34.
70. For a recent study, see Frank Harrison, *Tobruk: the Great Siege Reassessed* (London: Arms & Armour, 1997).
71. T. Parsons, *The African Rank-and-File*, pp. 27 and 208.
72. Ibid.
73. RPC. 1501 (Mauritius) Company War Diary. Entry, 13/4/41.
74. J. Lee Ready, *Forgotten Allies: the Military Contribution of the Colonies, Exiled Governments, and Lesser Powers to the Allied Victory in World War Two. Volume I: The European Theatre* (Jefferson, NC: McFarland & Co, 1985), pp. 48-9.
75. J. Lee Ready, *World War Two Nation by Nation* (London: Arms & Armour, 1995), p. 201.
76. RPC. 1503 (Mauritius) Company War Diary. The first diary entry saw the Company working at the railhead at Mischifa in February 1942. It then moved to Fort Capuzzo, and in March it was working at the railhead and on salvage.
77. J. Lee Ready, *Forgotten Allies, Volume I*, p. 111.
78. E. H. Rhodes-Wood, *A War History of the Royal Pioneer Corps*, p. 152.
79. The Mauritian POWs form part of a novel written by George Andre

Decotter, *'Le Jour N'en Finit Plus'!* (Port Louis: Editions Grand Océan, 1995).
80. C. Barnett, *The Desert Generals*, p. 166. For Mauritian accounts, see Louis Roger Medar to A. Jackson; Nathaniel Fanchin, 'Issa Somir, Former Soldier in the Second World War in the Hell of Tobruk,' *5-Plus*, 4/12/96; 'Father Guy Mammet Recounts his Imprisonment in a German Concentration Camp', *Week-End*, 7/5/95; and B. Burrun, 'Mauritius and the Second World War', *Week-End*, 30/10/91.
81. David Killingray, 'Africans and African Americans in Enemy Hands', in B. Moore and K. Fedorowich (eds) *Prisoners of War and Their Captors*, p. 193.
82. Ibid., p. 193. The quote is taken from Ian Gleeson, *The Unknown Force: Black, Indian, and Coloured Soldiers Through Two World Wars* (Johannesburg: Rivonia, 1994).
83. Ibid., p. 193.
84. E. H. Rhodes-Wood, *A War History of the Royal Pioneer Corps*, p. 154.
85. Ibid., p. 154.
86. E. H. Rhodes-Wood, *A War History of the Royal Pioneer Corps*, p. 188.
87. Ibid., p. 189.
88. IWM Miscellaneous 713. Reminiscences by Paul L'Hoste on his service with 163 GT (Mauritius) Company RASC in the Eighth Army in Egypt in 1941, giving an excellent picture of the tasks performed by Pioneers.
89. RPC. 1501 (Mauritius) Company War Diary. Entry, 18/4/41.
90. Ibid. 1508 (Mauritius) Company War Diary. Entry, 7/3/42.
91. Ibid. Entry, 30/5/42.
92. Ibid. Entry, 28/6/42.
93. Ibid. 1504 (Seychelles) Company War Diary. Entry, 14/3/42.
94. E. H. Rhodes-Wood, *A War History of the Royal Pioneer Corps*, p. 198.
95. RPC. 1507 (Rodrigues) Company War Diary. Entry, 27/2/43.
96. E. H. Rhodes-Wood, *A War History of the Royal Pioneer Corps*, p. 202.
97. J. Lee Ready, *Forgotten Allies*, p. 202.
98. Ibid., p. 202.
99. E. H. Rhodes-Wood, *A War History of the Royal Pioneer Corps*, p. 223.
100. RPC. 1505 (Mauritius) Company War Diary.
101. Ibid. Entry, 1/1/44 and 31/1/44.
102. Ibid. Entry, 21/9/43.
103. Ibid. Entry, 9/2/44.
104. For welfare, see A. Jackson, *Botswana 1939-45*.
105. T. Parsons, *The African Rank-and-File*, p. 35.
106. At all levels from GHQ down to brigade HQ there were three staff departments that assisted the commander: General (G) Staff, Adjutant General (A) Staff, and Quartermaster (Q) Staff. G – operations, intelligence, tactical and training matters. A – personnel and discipline. Q – supplies, quartering and movements. G. Forty, *British Army Handbook*.
107. PRO. CO 968/131. Major D. G. Pirie, 'Notes on Mauritius Pioneers and Artisans', 1/1/44.
108. PRO. CO 167/920/8. S. Moody to A. B. Acheson, 22/4/42. There was a plan to set up a hostel especially for Mauritians on leave. PRO. CO 167/920/8. Hostel Facilities Mauritius and Seychelles Troops, Middle East.
109. Soldiers of 1506 made a flag; in three of the quartered sections they

embroidered the coats of arms of Mauritius, the Seychelles and Rodrigues. They asked one of the officers, Captain Russell, if he had a coat of arms that could be used in the fourth and final quarter, and he gave them the coat of arms of his home town, Haslinden in Lancashire. His son returned the flag to Mauritius in 1997. Private correspondence with Mr Russell, April 1999. See articles in the *Mauritius News*, May, June, July 1997.

110. PRO. CO 167/920/9. Appointment of Liaison and Welfare Officer. Governor to Secretary of State, 17/1/42.
111. PRO. CO 968/131. Major D. G. Pirie, 'Notes on Mauritius Pioneers and Artisans', 1/1/44.
112. E. R. Elliott, *Royal Pioneers*, p. 182.
113. Mauritius Ex-Servicemen's Association interviews, Port Louis.
114. For a postwar example of unrest among Mauritian troops, see RCS. *Mauritian Troops in Egypt and Cyrenaica: Report of the Delegation of the Legislative Council*, sessional paper No. 12 (Port Louis: Government Printer, 1951).
115. RHL. *Mauritius Colonial Annual Report 1946*, p. 40.
116. Wm Roger Louis, 'The Dissolution of the British Empire', in J. M. Brown and Wm Roger Louis (eds) *The Oxford History of the British Empire*, p. 339.
117. E. R. Elliott, *Royal Pioneers*, p. 212.
118. Ibid., p. 181.
119. Ibid., p. 182.
120. E. R. Elliott, *Royal Pioneers*, p. 177.
121. Ibid., p. 178.
122. Ibid., p. 44.
123. Ibid., p. 117.
124. See Michael Cohen, *Fighting World War Three From the Middle East: Allied Contingency Plans, 1945-54* (London: Frank Cass, 1997), chapter 3, 'The Middle East in British Global Strategy'.
125. Ibid., p. 92. From PRO, CAB 129/43. Minute by Ernest Bevin, 27/11/50.
126. E. R. Elliott, *Royal Pioneers*, p. 185.
127. Ibid., p. 185.
128. Ibid., p. 189.
129. Ibid.
130. See A. Jackson, 'Imperial Military Authorities'.

5   The Mauritius Regiment and the Madagascar Mutiny

1. MNA. *Le Cerneen-Le Mauricien-Advance*, 14/10/43.
2. Despite this imperial relationship of metropolitan authority and peripheral subordination, local elites in the colonies had real power to influence the decisions and methods of Britain's proconsuls and the Colonial Office. Though Britain ruled imperially in Mauritius and the Council of Government had no constitutional authority whatsoever, it could influence the Governor, express indigenous political sentiment and after the war it was central to the colony's constitutional advance.
3. D. Killingray, 'The Idea of a British Imperial African Army', *Journal of African History*, XX (1979).

4. For the RWAFF, see A. Haywood and F. A. S. Clarke, *The History of the Royal West African Frontier Force* (Aldershot: Gale & Polden, 1964).
5. J. Shuckburgh, 'Colonial Civil History', 'Use of Colonial Manpower'.
6. Ibid.
7. Lawrence James, *Mutiny: Mutinies in British and Commonwealth Forces 1797–1950* (London: Buchan & Enright, 1987).
8. IWM. Colonel Ronald Yeldham interview, accession 3960.
9. I. C. B. Dear, *The Oxford Companion*, p. 771.
10. Interview with Ramsing Kusrutsing, Louis Maxim Labour, Frank Roger Requin and Pierre Tonta. Mauritius Ex-Servicemen's League, Port Louis, 9/7/99.
11. 'A Tyrant in Colonel's Uniform', *L'Express*, 26/1/97.
12. A. Chelin, *Maurice: Une Ile et Son Passe.*
13. J. Shuckburgh, 'Colonial Civil History', p. 57.
14. Ibid.
15. Monica Maurel Papers, private collection. Alfred North-Coombes Diary, 11/10/43.
16. J. F. C. Harrison, *Scholarship Boy*, p. 109.
17. Malcolm Page, *KAR*, p. 131. Page lifts his brief account of the mutiny from Harrison.
18. Pierre Tonta interview, Port Louis, 9/7/99.
19. A. North-Coombes Diary, p. 109.
20. Roger Requin survey return.
21. PRO. CO 968/147/3. Mauritius Regiment: Employment in Madagascar or East Africa, Governor to Secretary of State, 21/9/43.
22. J. F. C. Harrison, *Scholarship Boy*, p. 108.
23. PRO. CO 968/147/3. Secretary of State to Governor, 27/9/43 and Governor to Secretary of State, 14/9/43.
24. PRO. CO 968/84/6. Control of Local Forces: Mauritius and Seychelles.
25. PRO. CO 167/919/18. Compulsory Military Service. Minute, 8/10/41.
26. Ibid. P. J. Cole minute, 9/10/41.
27. Ibid. Mr Halder, 10/10/41.
28. Ibid. A. B. Acheson minute, 10/10/41. A case of *fait accompli* was the 1938 Defence Order in Council (Indemnity) Ordinance – the Colonial Office could not see why it was needed at all, but it had already gone through. See PRO. CO 167/908/3.
29. Ibid. Edgar Laurent and Raoul Rivet to Governor, 29/10/43.
30. Ibid. Governor to Laurent and Rivet, 4/11/43.
31. Ibid.
32. Ibid.
33. Ibid.
34. Ibid.
35. Ibid. Quoted in Governor to Secretary of State, 31/1/42.
36. Ibid. Governor to Secretary of State, 23/3/42.
37. Ibid.
38. Ibid.
39. Ibid. Governor to Secretary of State, 31/1/42.
40. See *Parliamentary Debate (Hansard), Volume 380, Session 1942–43* (London: HMSO, 1943).

41. PRO. CO 167/919/18. Compulsory Military Service.
42. Ibid. Governor's letter, 31/1/42.
43. Ibid.
44. Ibid. Governor to Major G. E. J. Gent, 6/11/43.
45. Ibid.
46. Conversation with Suchita Ramdin, Head, Department of Folklore and Oral Traditions, Mahatma Gandhi Institute, Moka, 29/6/99.
47. Maxime Labour survey return.
48. Ramsing Kusrutsing survey return.
49. PRO. CO 167/919/18. Compulsory Military Service. A. B. Acheson minute, 22/5/42.
50. Ibid. Minute, 31/3/42.
51. J. F. C. Harrison, *Scholarship Boy*, p. 114.
52. Sam Lingayah, *A Comparative Study of Mauritian Immigrants in Two European Cities (London and Paris): an Investigation into the Process of Adaptation* (London: Mauritius Welfare Association, 1991), p. 201.
53. Twining Papers. Twining to mother, 5/1/44.
54. Ibid. Strictly Confidential: Notes on Labour and Related Problems in Mauritius, c. 1942.
55. K. Hazareesingh (ed.) *Selected Speeches of Sir Seewoosagur Ramgoolam* (London: Macmillan Press – now Palgrave, 1979), p. 73.
56. Mauritius Ex-Servicemen's Association interviews, Port Louis, 9/7/99.
57. Roger Requin survey return.
58. T. Parsons, *The African Rank-and-File*, p. 31.
59. Roger Requin survey return.
60. RHL. FCB Papers. Box 170, Emile to Parkinson, 18/10/43.
61. A. North-Coombes Diary, 3/2/44.
62. RHL. KAR Papers. Box 19, item 307.
63. IWM. Colonel Ronald Yeldham interview. Accession 3960.
64. A. North-Coombes Diary, 27/12/43.
65. Ibid. Attached letter to North-Coombes, November 1987.
66. Guy Sauzier, 'The Events Which Marked the Arrival of the Mauritian Battalion at Diego Suarez in 1943', p. 3.
67. Ibid., p. 140. There was evidence that equipment was poorly maintained as well. North-Coombes noted on 17/2/44 that Royal Electrical and Mechanical Engineers (REME) were reporting to HQ Sub-Area (in Diego Suarez) regarding the 'awful state' of 2MR weapons. North-Coombes also recorded in his diary that old spare lorry parts were being bought cheaply, swapped for parts from new Army lorries, then the new parts were being 'sold to the public at a hell of a price'.
68. A. North-Coombes Diary, p. 19.
69. Rex Salisbury Woods, *Cambridge Doctor*, p. 167, chapter 18, 'Diego Suarez', and chapter 19, 'Escape to Mauritius'. See P. J. Barnwell's obituary, *L'Express*, 20/10/86.
70. A. North-Coombes Diary, 11/12/43.
71. Ibid., p. 173.
72. Ibid., 8/2/44.
73. Groogobin Pem, 'Mutiny and the Dissolution of the 1st Battalion The Mauritius Regiment', *Le Mauricien*, 14/10/99.

74. RHL. Flora Moody Papers. Box 2, item 5, diary entry 15/8/45, p. 164. Victory Day.
75. J. F. C. Harrison, *Scholarship Boy*, p. 113.
76. G. Sauzier, 'The Events Which Marked the Arrival of the Mauritian Battalion'.
77. 'A Tyrant in Colonel's Uniform', *L'Express*, 26/1/97. The eyewitness account is that of a former Mauritius Regiment lance-corporal. He remembers that on the march to Orangea, the KAR military band was called in but 'the groans of the men drowned out the music'.
78. Mauritius Ex-Servicemen's interviews, Port Louis, 9/7/99.
79. A. North-Coombes Diary.
80. Monaf Fakira interview, Grosvenor Hotel, London, 23/2/99.
81. Interview with Royal Pioneer Corps Association, Rose Hill, 7/7/99.
82. G. Sauzier, 'The Events Which Marked the Arrival of the Mauritian Battalion', p. 3.
83. J. F. C. Harrison, *Scholarship Boy*, pp. 108 and 114.
84. Interview with J. F. C. Harrison, Cheltenham, 22/1/99.
85. J. F. C. Harrison, *Scholarship Boy*, p. 109.
86. G. Sauzier, 'The Events Which Marked the Arrival of the Mauritius Battalion', p. 3.
87. A. North-Coombes Diary, 9/10/43.
88. PRO. CO 968/147/2. Governor to Lieutenant Colonel K. Anderson, GOC EAC, 11/4/45.
89. PRO. CO 968/147/3. Lt. Col. Rolleston to Major Lord Mancroft, 8/2/44
90. L. James, *Mutiny: Mutinies in British and Commonwealth Forces*, p. 176.
91. Ibid., p. 176.
92. PRO. CO 968/147/4. Mauritius Regiment: Employment in Madagascar and Attitude of 1st Battalion (Diego Saurez Incident). Platt to War Office, 23/12/43.
93. Ibid. Governor to Secretary of State, 28/12/43.
94. Ibid. Lieutenant General Platt to OCT Mauritius and War Office, 31/12/43.
95. A. North-Coombes Diary, p. 156.
96. G. Sauzier, 'The Events Which Marked the Arrival of the Mauritius Battalion', pp. 4–5.
97. Geoffrey Elcoat to A. Jackson, 30/1/99.
98. Ibid.
99. Geoffrey Elcoat, 'Some Memories of a War-Time KAR Officer', *Rhino Link: Newsletter of the King's African Rifles and East African Forces Dinner Club*, 12 (1997). Geoffrey Elcoat to Jackson, 30/1/99. See also Elcoat's letter in *Rhino Link*, 15 (1998).
100. Ibid.
101. Tom Higginson, 'Mutiny in Madagascar', *Rhino Link*, 15 (1998).
102. RHL. KAR Papers. Box 5, item 138 (released on author's request).
103. Major General Rowley Mans to A. Jackson, 16/11/99.
104. Pierre Tonta survey return.
105. Michael Rose, interview with Royal Pioneer Corps Association, Rose Hill, 7/7/99.
106. Roger Requin survey return.

107. PRO. CO 968/147/4. Lieutenant General Platt to War Office, 16/1/44.
108. Major General Rowley Mans to A. Jackson, 16/11/99
109. Ramsing Kusrutsing survey return.
110. Mauritius Ex-Servicemen's Association interviews, Port Louis, 9/7/99.
111. 'A Tyrant in Colonel's Uniform', *L'Express*, 26/1/97.
112. PRO. CO 820/56/1 and 2. Discipline Mauritius. Petition signed by about nineteen ex-servicemen, 7/8/45.
113. 'A Tyrant in Colonel's Uniform', *L'Express*, 26/1/97.
114. Tom Higginson, 'Mutiny in Madagascar', *Rhino Link*, 15 (1998).
115. G. Sauzier, 'The Events Which Marked the Arrival of the Mauritius Battalion', p. 6.
116. 'Mutinerie et dissolution du 1er Bataillon du Régiment Mauricien', letter from Groogobin Pem to *Le Mauricien*, 14/11/99.
117. Ibid.
118. Rowley Mans to A. Jackson, 16/11/99.
119. PRO. CO 968/147/4. Lieutenant General Platt to War Office, 8/8/44.
120. G. Sauzier, 'The Events Which Marked the Arrival of the Mauritius Battalion', p. 7.
121. Ibid. Governor to Secretary of State, 23/8/44.
122. PRO. CO 968/147/2. Governor to Lieutenant Colonel K. Anderson, GOC EAC, 11/4/45.
123. Ibid.
124. A. North-Coombes Diary, 1/2/44.
125. Ibid., p. 179.

6   The Secret War: Censorship, Propaganda and Code-Breaking

1. See Michael Smith, *Station X: The Codebreakers of Bletchley Park* (London: Macmillan Press – now Palgrave, 1998) and the accompanying Channel 4 television series. See also F. W. Winterbotham, *The Ultra Secret: the Inside Story of Operation Ultra, Bletchley Park, and Enigma* (London: Weidenfeld & Nicolson, 1974). This book revealed to the wider public the astonishing secret of the intelligence war centred upon Bletchley Park.
2. I. C. B. Dear, *The Oxford Companion*, p. 1004.
3. See Rosaleen Smyth, 'Britain's African Colonies and British Propaganda During the Second World War', *Journal of Imperial and Commonwealth History*, XIV, 1 (1985).
4. 'Privations and the Military Regime', *L'Express*, 19/1/97.
5. Hugh Denham, 'Bedford-Bletchley-Kilindini-Colombo', in F. H. Hinsley and Alan Stripp (eds) *Code Breakers: the Inside Story of Bletchley Park* (Oxford: Oxford University Press, 1993), p. 270.
6. Michael Smith, *The Emperor's Codes: Bletchley Park and the Breaking of Japan's Secret Ciphers* (London: Bantam, 2000), p. 129.
7. NHB. C-in-C Eastern Fleet War Diary, volume 10, p. 219.
8. M. Smith, *The Emperor's Codes*, p. 283.
9. This is well documented in M. Smith, *The Emperor's Codes*.
10. Alan Stripp, *Codebreaker in the Far East: How the British Cracked Japan's Top*

Secret Military Codes (Oxford: Oxford University Press, 1995), p. 93.
Chapter 4, 'Delhi'; chapter 7, 'Japanese Codes and Ciphers: What Were
They Like?'; and chapter 10, 'How Were They Intercepted?'.
11. M. Smith, *The Emperor's Codes*, p. 199.
12. Ibid., p. 199.
13. PRO. DEFE 1/333 and 334. *History of the Postal and Telegraph Censorship
    Department 1938–46* (London: Home Office, 1949), two volumes. See
    'Mauritius', p. 545.
14. Martin Thomas, 'Signals Intelligence and Vichy France, 1940–44:
    Intelligence in Defeat', in David Alvarez (ed.) *Allied and Axis Signals
    Intelligence in World War Two* (London: Frank Cass, 1999), p. 190.
15. Air Chief Marshal Sir Frederick Rosier's foreword in Aileen Clayton, *The
    Enemy is Listening: the Story of the Y Service* (London: Crecy Books, 1993),
    p. 11.
16. M. Smith, *The Emperor's Codes,* chapter 2, 'Borrowing the Cables'.
17. D. Bates, *A Gust of Plumes.*
18. For Mayer's contribution, see PRO. HS 3/9. SOE Abyssinia/East
    Africa/Madagascar, 1941–43. He was awarded the OBE for his endeavours
    and decorated by the King after a Colonial Office debate as to whether it
    could be awarded to a 'foreigner', resolved when it was discovered that he
    was born in Mauritius.
19. PRO. HS 3/10. SOE East Africa 1940–43. Minute, 28/11/41. The file on
    'Mauritians in Madagascar' (CO 167/920/16 is listed as 'not transferred
    from department of origin'.
20. Twining Papers. 'Oddments, 1939–1946', Twining to May Twining, Cape
    Town, 2/9/40.
21. PRO. DEFE 1/333 and 334. *History of the Postal and Telegraph Department,*
    p. 257.
22. Ibid., p. 258.
23. PRO. CO 968/104b/8. Mauritius: Post-Occupational Activities Secret
    Defence 1942–45. Minute by Anthony Lincoln, 17/11/43.
24. PRO. DEFE 1/333 and 334. *History of the Postal and Telegraph Department,*
    p. 257.
25. Twining Papers. E. S. Herbert (Postal and Telegraph Censorship
    Department) to E. F. Twining, 24/5/45 and 20/10/45.
26. NHB. C-in-C Eastern Fleet War Diary, volume 10, p. 345.
27. John Fletcher-Cooke entry in the *Dictionary of National Biography, 1961–70*
    (Oxford: Oxford University Press, 1981), p. 1027.
28. Twining Papers. Twining to mother, 21/12/43.
29. Ibid. *The Times,* 8/6/44.
30. D. Bates, *A Gust of Plumes,* p. 123.
31. Ibid., p. 119.
32. Twining Papers.
33. Ibid. Twining to mother, 10/4/42.
34. Ibid. 'Oddments 1939–1946'. Twining to May, 26/11/41.
35. I. C. B. Dear, *The Oxford Companion,* p. 847.
36. See Malcolm Muggeridge, *Chronicle of Wasted Time II: the Infernal Grove*
    (London: Collins, 1973), chapter 3, 'On Secret Service'. John Bright-
    Holmes (ed.) *Like It Was: the Diaries of Malcolm Muggeridge* (London:

Collins, 1981).
37. Twining Papers. Twining to May Twining, Cape Town, 2/9/40.
38. NHB. C-in-C Eastern Fleet War Diary, volume 10, p. 144.
39. Ibid., volume 10, p. 177.
40. Twining Papers. 'Oddments 1939–1946'. Twining to May Twining, 1/11/42.
41. NHB. C-in-C Eastern Fleet War Diary, volume 9, p. 123.
42. Ibid., volume 10, p. 344.
43. NHB. C-in-C Eastern Fleet War Diary, volume 9, p.125.
44. Ibid., volume 9, p. 308.
45. PRO. ADM 223/551. Naval Section Censorship London.
46. PRO. DEFE 1/283.
47. PRO. ADM 223/22.
48. NHB. C-in-C Eastern Fleet War Diary, volume 9, pp. 312–313.
49. M. Smith, *The Emperor's Codes*, p. 226.
50. *Dictionary of Mauritian Biography*, 54 (October 2000), p. 1785.
51. M. Smith, *The Emperor's Codes*, p. 199.
52. Twining Papers. May Twining to Agatha, 17/8/41.
53. D. Bates, *A Gust of Plumes*, p. 121.
54. PRO. DEFE 1/333 and 334. *History of the Postal and Telegraph Censorship Department*, p. 546.
55. Twining Papers. Memoir written in the 1970s by Evelyn du Buisson.
56. PRO. ADM 223/505. Thanks to Dominic Sutherland of the BBC for providing a copy of this document.
57. Ibid.
58. Twining Papers. Twining to May Twining, 9/4/41.
59. PRO. CO 968/27/9. Governor to Secretary of State, 31/7/41.
60. Mrs M. E. Richards (wife of C. A. L. Richards) to A. Jackson, 24/8/99.
61. 'Echoes of St George's Day', *L'Express*, 13/5/96.
62. Arthur Stamberg, *Footprints on a Winding Road*.
63. C. Lucas, *The Empire at War*, p. 550.
64. B. Warlow, *Shore Establishments of the Royal Navy*, p. 116.
65. PRO. ADM 116/4964. Mauritius Naval W/T Station.
66. Anthony Clayton to A. Jackson 23/10/99, and phone conversation 27/10/99. See A. Clayton, *Forearmed: a History of the Intelligence Corps* (London: Brassey's, 1993), p. 167, 'Security in the Colonial Empire and on Shipping Routes'.
67. PRO. DEFE 1/333 and 334. *History of the Postal and Telegraph Censorship Department*.
68. Twining Papers.
69. Ibid.
70. PRO. CO 968/69/2. Security Arrangements Mauritius.
71. D. Bates, *Gust of Plumes*, p. 120.
72. Michael Malim, *Island of the Swan: Mauritius* (London: Longman, 1952), p. 84.
73. A. Chelin, *Maurice: Une Ile Sons Passe*.
74. MNA. *Le Cerneen-Le Mauricien-Advance*, 25/3/43.
75. MNA. *Mauritius and the War* (Port Louis: Indian Cultural Association, 1940).

76. PRO. CO 968/24/3. Minute, 24/8/43.
77. RHL. *Mauritius Colonial Annual Report 1948*, p. 121.
78. RHL. FCB Papers. Box 170, 13/2/43, Colonial Office Press Section release.
79. RHL. *Mauritius Colonial Annual Report 1948*, p. 122.
80. PRO. CO 167/909/15. Governor's Broadcast.
81. S. Selvon, *Historical Dictionary of* Mauritius, p. 118. Carnegie Library, Curepipe: Edouard Nairac, *Causeries du Mercredi* (Port Louis: General Printing, 1943) and *Deuxième Série des Causeries Radiodiffusees de Sir Edouard Nairac* (Port Louis: Government Printer, 1942).
82. RHL. *Mauritius Colonial Annual Report 1946* (London: HMSO, 1948). See Part 1, chapter 1, 'General Review of the Period 1939–45'.
83. W. Mackenzie, *The Secret History of SOE*, p. 327.
84. Raymond D'Unienville to A. Jackson, 26/7/00.
85. Carnegie Library, Curepipe. J. R. Pillet, *Entre Nous: Bulletins de Propagande du Poste Radio St Denis (November 1940 – February 1942)* (St Denis: Editions du Bureau de la Presse, 1942).
86. PRO. CO 968/24/1. H. T. Bourdillon minute, 24/12/41.
87. D'Unienville Papers. M. Barre to Edward Twining, 13/7/41.
88. D'Unienville Papers. C. A. L. Richards, Information Officer, to Press Office, Vacoas, 'Fighting French Propaganda', 28/8/42.
89. France D'Unienville to A. Jackson, 9/10/99.
90. PRO. HS 3/9.
91. Twining Papers. Twining to mother, August 1941.
92. Ibid. Evelyn Du Buisson memoir.
93. France D'Unienville to A. Jackson, 4/8/99.
94. De Gaulle to F. D'Unienville, 18/7/40. Thanks to France D'Unienville.
95. France D'Unienville to A. Jackson, 4/9/99. *La Maison de France* is a book describing the work of the institution established in Curepipe to espouse and support the Free French cause. Its archive is in possession of Patrick Millar of Curepipe. *Dialogues d'un Temps Trouble* is a rousing patriotic book. Francois Marrier D'Unienville, *Dialogues d'un Temps Trouble* (Port Louis: General Printing, 1943). Thanks to Raymond D'Unienville for a copy of this.
96. D'Unienville Papers. C. A. L. Richards to F. D'Unienville, 5/9/41.
97. Ibid. Twining to H. Paturau, 2/9/42. Also C. A. L. Richards, Information Officer, to Press Office, Vacoas, 'Fighting French Propaganda', 28/8/42.
98. Ibid., quoted.

7   The Effects of War on the Home Front

1. There are many books about the British home front during the war. See, for example, Angus Calder, *The People's War 1939–45* (London: Panther, 1971); Susan Briggs, *Keep Smiling Through: the Home Front 1939–45* (London: Weidenfeld & Nicolson, 1975); and Raynes Minns, *Bombers and Mash: the Domestic Front 1939–45* (London: Virago Press, 1980).
2. See for example Larry Bowman, *Mauritius: Democracy and Development in the Indian Ocean* (London: Dartmouth, 1991), pp. 27–33.
3. The literature on this subject is large. See, for example, J. M. Lee and

Martin Petter, *The Colonial Office, War and Development Policy: Organization and Planning of a Metropolitan Initiative 1939–45* (London: Institute of Commonwealth Studies, 1982); Robert Pearce, *The Turning Point: British Colonial Policy, 1938–1948* (London: Frank Cass 1982); M. Havinden and D. Meredith, *Colonialism and Development*; J. M. Lee, '"Forward Thinking" and War: the Colonial Office During the 1940s', *Journal of Imperial and Commonwealth History*, VI (1977); and Robert Pearce, 'The Colonial Office and Planned Decolonization in Africa', *African Affairs*, 83, 330 (1984).

4. A. Clayton and Donald Savage, *Government and Labour in Kenya 1895–1963* (London: Frank Cass, 1974), p. 184.

5. Adele Simmons, *Modern Mauritius: the Politics of Decolonization* (Bloomington: Indiana University Press, 1982), p. 57.

6. See for example, Paul Rich, *Race and Empire in British Politics* (Cambridge: Cambridge University Press, 1986), chapter 4, 'The Widening Critique of Empire,' and Nicholas Owen, 'Critics of Empire in Britain', in Wm Roger Louis and J. M. Brown (eds), *The Oxford History of the British Empire*.

7. RHL. FCB Papers. *Empire: Journal of the Fabian Colonial Bureau*, 6, 3 (1943).

8. Ibid. Box 170, S. B. Emile to W. Paling, 30/7/40. The Governor described Emile to the Secretary of State as 'a notoriety-seeking busybody'. (PRO CO 820/56/2. Discipline Mauritius. Governor to Secretary of State, 8/6/46). The thing was that, in the new climate of imperial relations that developed in the 1930s and 1940s, Governors could no longer just dismiss local leaders and politicians in this way, bang them up if they got too uppity, and wait for things to blow over. They were becoming too well supported both in their colonies and, more importantly, in Whitehall.

9. India Office Library (henceforth IOL), British Library. Extract from *Hansard*, 30/7/41.

10. Kenneth Morgan, 'Imperialists at Bay: British Labour and Decolonization', in R. Kilson and R. King (eds) *The Statecraft of British Imperialism*, p. 238.

11. J. Addison and K. Hazareesingh, *A New History of Mauritius*, p. 89.

12. P. J. Barnwell and A. Toussaint, *A Short History of Mauritius,* 'The Second World War', p. 236.

13. RCS. 'The Mauritius Riots, 1943', *The Anti-Slavery Reporter and Aborigines' Friend*, 5, 4 (January 1945), p. 67.

14. Richard Titmuss and B. Abel-Smith, *Social Policies and Population Growth in Mauritius: Report to the Government of Mauritius* (London: Methuen, 1960), p. 68.

15. P. J. Barnwell and A. Toussaint, *A Short History of Mauritius*, p. 236.

16. PRO. CO 167/917/15. Riots, September 1943. Governor to Secretary of State, 6/10/43.

17. PRO. CO 167/924/11. Riots 1943. *The Economist*, 30/12/44. For Orde-Brown's report, see RCS. Command 6423, Major G. St J. Orde Brown, *Labour Conditions in Ceylon, Mauritius, and Malaya*.

18. PRO. CO 167/930/1. Conditions in Mauritius.

19. Ibid. Governor to Secretary of State, telegram, 14/4/44.

20. Senoo Babajee, *A Concise History of Mauritius* (Bombay: Hind Kitabs, 1950), p. 92.

21. IOL. L/PJ/8/184. *Review of Important Events Relating to or Affecting Indians*

in Different Parts of the British Empire. For Indian representatives see L/PJ/8/180. Appointment of Representatives of the Governments of India and Pakistan in East Africa, Fiji, Mauritius, and the British West Indies.

22. IOL. V/27/820/14. *Report on Deputation to Mauritius 1925* (Delhi: Government of India Press, 1925).
23. IOL. S. Ridley, *Report on the Conditions of Indians in Mauritius, 1940* (New Delhi: Government of India Press, 1941).
24. IOL. L/PJ/8/270. Minute, 16/5/40.
25. PRO. CO 167/914/14. Condition of Indian Labourers. In 1940 an article on the 'Plight of Islam in Mauritius' appeared in the *Daily Herald* and *Hindusthan Standard* in India, with the subtitle 'Treated Worse Than Slaves'. The Government of Mauritius wrote to the Colonial Secretary, Malcolm Macdonald, in an attempt to head off trouble. The article had done the rounds; Cure and Anquetil had sent a memorandum to the President of the Natal Indian Congress. This was after (according to police enquiries) Pandit Ranema, an MLP member, had been Nehru's guest on a visit to India where he had been introduced to the President of the Natal Indian Congress.
26. Ibid.
27. PRO. CO 167/920/7. Accounting Control War Measures.
28. PRO. CO 167/921/5. The Administrative Machine in Mauritius, August 1943.
29. RCS. Command 7228, *Revision of the Constitution of Mauritius: Correspondence between the Governor and the Secretary of State for the Colonies* (London: HMSO, 1947), p. 12. RCS. *Report on District Administration in Mauritius for 1949* (Port Louis: Government Printer, 1950), p. I. See also *Report of the Select Committee Appointed to Examine Mr J. B. Swinden's Report on Local Government in Mauritius* (Port Louis: Government Printer, 1947).
30. MNA. *Mauritius and the War.*
31. Ibid. S. Ramgoolam, 'Our Duties to the Empire'.
32. MNA. *Le Cerneen-Le Mauricien-Advance,* 9/7/43. Moomtaz Emrith, *History of the Muslims of Mauritius* (Port Louis: The Regent Press, 1967).
33. For wartime speeches, see K. Hazareesingh (ed.) *Selected Speeches of Sir Sewoosagur Ramgoolam* (London: Macmillan Press – now Palgrave, 1979).
34. A. North-Coombes Diary, 12/12/43, p. 82. For the Bissoondoyal movement, see Uttama Bissoondoyal, *Promises to Keep* (New Delhi: Wiley Eastern, 1990).
35. IOL. L/PJ/8/270. Governor to Secretary of State, 20/1/44.
36. Ibid.
37. Ibid. Secretary of State to Governor, 25/1/44.
38. Anand Mulloo, *The Road to Independence* (Port Louis: Standard Printing, 1968), p. 39.
39. Burton Benedict, *Mauritius: the Problems of a Plural Society,* p. 61.
40. RHL. FCB Papers. Box 170. G. Hall to A. Creech Jones, 1/1/41.
41. MNA. *Le Cerneen-Le Mauricien-Advance,* 7/8/43.
42. RCS. Command 7228, *Revision of the Constitution of Mauritius* and *Summary of Proposed Constitutional Arrangements Presented to the Council of Government* (Port Louis: Government Printer, 1947).
43. A. Simmons, *Modern Mauritius,* p. 101.

44. M. V. M. Herchenroder, 'High-Lights of Mauritius Economy 1946–56', *Revue Agricole et Sucrière de l'Ile Maurice*, 36, 1 (February 1957), p. 8.
45. R. Titmuss and B. Abel-Smith, *Social Policies*, p. 9.
46. Bodleian Library. Command 7167, *The Colonial Empire 1939–1947* (London: HMSO, 1947), appendix II, p. 115.
47. PRO. CAB 106/307. E. E. Sabben-Clare, 'Colonial Military Forces in the Second World War', p. 56.
48. PRO. CAB 106/308. *What the British Empire Has Done*. See PRO, CO 167/919/4. Contributions to the War Effort.
49. J. Maurice Paturau, *Histoire Economique de l'Ile Maurice* (Port Louis: Les Pailles, 1988), p. 252.
50. PRO. CO 167/914/18. Mauritius: Contributions to War Effort.
51. PRO. CO 167/919/19. Estimates 1942–43. Minute, 28/7/42.
52. RHL. 912 r. 52. *Debates of the Mauritius Council of Government*, 5/12/39, p. 1054.
53. PRO. CO 167/914/18. Mauritius: Contribution to the War Effort.
54. RHL. *Debates of the Mauritius Council of Government*, 5/12/39. p. 1054.
55. RHL. *Mauritius Colonial Annual Report 1946*, p. 4. See the illustration on a 'Thank you, Dominica' poster in S. Briggs, *Keep Smiling Through*, p. 193.
56. RHL. *Mauritius Colonial Annual Report*, p. 58.
57. RCS. *Report of the Civil Service Commission 1945* (London: Crown Agents, 1946), volume I, p. 24.
58. A. North-Coombes, A History of Rodrigues.
59. RHL. FCB Papers. Box 170. FCB to S. B. Emile, from Hansard 31/1/45.
60. Twining Papers. Strictly Confidential: Notes on Labour and Related Problems in Mauritius, c. 1942.
61. RHL. FCB Papers. Box 170, Aborigines Protection Society to Colonial Office, 10/2/44.
62. L. Davis and R. Huttenback, *Mammon and the Pursuit of Empire*, p. 116.
63. PRO. CO 167/903/15. Military Contribution. See also CO 167/917/10 Governor's Speeches and CO 167/916/21. Estimates 1942–43 and 1943–44. CO 167/916/7. Military Contribution.
64. PRO. CO 968/147/2. Council of Government extract, 22/4/43.
65. PRO. CO 167/919/19. Estimates 1942–43. Minute, 27/7/42.
66. PRO. CO 167/968/24/5. Governor to Secretary of State, 3/5/41.
67. Ibid.
68. PRO. CO 167/916/18. Estimates 1941–42. E. V. Luke to H. H. Hobbs, War Office, 26/1/42.
69. PRO. CO 968/24/10. A. B. Acheson to C. H. M. Wilcox, 9/3/42 and vice versa 16/3/42.
70. Ibid. Minute, 28/7/42.
71. PRO. CO 167/916/21. Estimates 1942–43. W. H. Wilcox to J. B. Sidebotham, 20/1/43. See also PRO. CO 167/916/18. Estimates 1941–42. A. B. Acheson, 1/10/41.
72. RHL. Clive Watt Papers. Note to Governor, 4/10/40, Folio 178.
73. Ibid.
74. Ibid.
75. PRO. CO 167/916/20. Estimates 1943–44. Mackenzie Kennedy to Oliver Stanley, 4/8/43.

76. Ibid., p. 3.
77. J. Shuckburgh, 'Colonial Civil History,' part III: Colonial Economic Policy, 'Import, Export, and Exchange Controls', p. 92.
78. A. Chelin, *Maurice: Une Ile Sons Passe.*
79. RCS. A. Osman (foreword, no author cited), *The Production of Foodcrops in Mauritius During the War, 1939–45* (Port Louis: Government Printer, 1947), appendix II.
80. RHL. *Debates of the Mauritius Council of Government*, 1938–39.
81. RCS. *Report of the Commission of Inquiry into the Supplies Control Department* (Port Louis: Government Printer, 1949), p. 5.
82. J. Shuckburgh, 'Colonial Civil History'.
83. RHL. FCB Papers. *Milk Production and Distribution, Creameries, Ghee Refineries, Demonstration Poultry Farm, Lard Factory 1944* (Port Louis: Government Printer, 1945) and *Milk Production and Distribution: Steps to Implement Recommendations of 1944* (Port Louis: Government Printer, 1946).
84. RHL. *Mauritius Annual Report, 1940*, pp. 76–7.
85. E. Rosenthal, *Japan's Bid for Africa*, pp. 131–2.
86. RHL. FCB Papers. *Annual Report of the Labour Department 1943* (Port Louis: Government Printer, 1944).
87. John Eppstein (ed.) *Mauritius*, British Survey Popular Series, No. 146 (London: British Society for International Understanding, 1956), p. 21.
88. RCS. A. Osman, *The Production of Foodcrops in Mauritius*, p. 8.
89. Ibid., p. 8.
90. Ibid., p. 7.
91. Ibid., p. 7.
92. Twining Papers. 'Oddments, 1939–46'. May Twining letter, 11/11/43.
93. RCS. G. A. North-Coombes and J. H. Julien, *Production of Vegetable Seeds in Mauritius 1943–46* (Port Louis: Government Printer, 1949).
94. MNA. *Le Cerneen-Le Mauricien-Advance*, 4/3/43.
95. RHL. Mss. Ind. Ocn. s. 273. W. E. F. Ward, 'Education in Mauritius 1941–45', p. 34.
96. MNA. *Advance*, 22/1/41.
97. RHL. FCB Papers. Kenneth Baker, Trades Union adviser, to Rita Hinden, 16/5/45.
98. RCS. A. Osman, *The Production of Foodcrops in Mauritius*, p. 7.
99. Ibid., p. 7.
100. Ibid. Preface.
101. RCS. Dr W. M. Clyde, *Local Production of Foodstuffs* (Port Louis: Government Printer, 1944).
102. L. J. Butler, 'Reconstruction, Development, and the Entrepreneurial State: the British Colonial Model, 1939–51', *Contemporary British History*, 13, 4, (1999), p. 29.
103. Joanna Lewis, '"Tropical East Ends" and the Second World War: Some Contradictions in Colonial Office Welfare Initiative', *Journal of Imperial and Commonwealth History*, 28, 2 (2000).
104. RHL. FCB Papers. Box 170, file 170/2, Kenneth Baker to Rita Hinden, 11/8/45. The 'subversive' reference is from A. Simmons, *Modern Mauritius*, p. 83. For Baker's report, see Kenneth Baker, 'Trade Unionism' series of

talks on Mauritius Broadcasting Corporation (Port Louis: Government Printer, 1945) and Baker, *Co-operation in Mauritius* (Port Louis: Government Printer, 1945). There was also an adviser on forming co-operative societies sent to Mauritius during the war, producing the inevitable report. W. K. I. Campbell, *'Co-operation' Series of talks on Mauritius Broadcasting Corporation* (Port Louis: Government Printer, 1945).

105. Twining Papers. Strictly Confidential: Notes on Labour and Related Problems in Mauritius, c. 1942.

106. Ibid. 'Oddments, 1939–46'. Twining to mother, 14/4/40.

107. RHL. *Mauritius Colonial Annual Report 1946.*

108. A. R. Mannick, *Mauritius: the Development of a Plural Society,* p. 79. *Irrigation Proposals (Development and Social Welfare)* (Port Louis: Government Printer, 1945).

109. RHL. Mss. Ind. Ocn s. 81, E. De Mowbray, 'Mauritius Tea Industry'. During the war attempts were made to foster the tea industry by restricting import licenses.

110. RHL. Mss. Ind. Ocn s. 104, Emmenez De Charmoy, 'Groundnuts', includes a handwritten and undated paper entitled, 'The Production of Vegetable Seeds in Mauritius'. RCS. *Report of the Industrial Development Advisory Committee* (Port Louis: Government Printer, 1945). See N. R. Brouard, *A History of the Woods and Forests in Mauritius* (Port Louis: Government Printer, 1963), pp. 65–7. See also 'A Statement of Empire Forestry and the War, Mauritius', a report given to the Empire Forestry Conference, 1947. RCS. *Inaugural Meeting of Central Development and Welfare Committee 1 March 1945* (Port Louis: Government Printer, 1945).

111. RHL. FCB Papers. *Annual Report of Education Department for Year Ending 30 June 1944* (Port Louis: Government Printer, 1944).

112. RHL. Mss. Ind. Ocn. s. 273. W. E. F. Ward, 'Education in Mauritius 1941–45', p. 31. See also RCS. A. E. Nichols, *A Report on Secondary Education in Mauritius* (Port Louis: Government Printer, 1949).

113. RHL. *Mauritius Colonial Annual Report 1946,* p. 7.

114. RCS. A. Rankine, *Malaria in Mauritius with Suggestions of Future Policy in Regard to This Disease* (Port Louis: Government Printer, 1951).

115. B. Benedict, *Mauritius: the Problems of a Plural Society,* p. 4.

116. RCS. A. Rankine, *Report on Health Conditions in Mauritius* (Port Louis: Government Printer, 1944), p. 1.

117. Ibid., p. 2.

118. In 1867–8 malaria killed 78 000. A. R. Mannick, *Mauritius,* p. 47.

119. The war had other good effects; Vaughan (the Assistant Censor and botanist) and Wiehe did all they could to obtain measures for the protection of the remaining indigenous vegetation, threatened because of fuel shortages. Their efforts resulted in the Ancient Monuments and National Reserves Board in 1944. *Dictionary of Mauritian Biography,* 54 (October 2000), p. 1785.

120. A. Rankine, *Malaria in Mauritius,* p. 9.

121. NHB. C-in-C Easter Fleet War Diary, volume 12, p. 25.

122. Keedy Papers, private collection in possession of David Keedy. R. L. Grant, Naval Officer-in-Charge, Mauritius to Flag Officer-in-Charge, East Africa, 29/11/43. Subject: RNAS Medical Officers.

123. Personal correspondence with David Keedy, May 1999.
124. M. A. C. Dowling, 'The Malaria Eradication Scheme', *Corona: Journal of His Majesty's Colonial Service*, II, 12 (1950).
125. RHL. Moody Papers for an account of an Expedition, see item 4, p. 1–8, 4/8/42.
126. Twining Papers. May to Agatha, 12/8/42.
127. Jepson was also the head of the Bureau of Information at Radio Maurice.
128. Mauritius Institute, Port Louis. Box file M900, 'History, Geography, Travels', Major Arthur de Chazal (Medical Specialist, Military Hospital, Mauritius, EAAMC). The outbreak was 'unsurpassed in virulence in any other part of the world'. RHL. FCB Papers. Box 170, Secretary of State for the Colonies, 31/3/45, reporting Council of Government debate, 27/3/45. *Memorandum on Rehabilitation and Resettlement of Mauritian Ex-Servicemen* (Port Louis: Government Printer, 1945).
129. RHL. *Debates of the Mauritius Council of Government*, 27/3/45.
130. Twining Papers. Testimonial from Dr Chazal, 22/5/44.
131. Alfred Pitray and Guy Morel, 'War Memories'. See also Andre Masson, *5 Mois: Souvenirs Amusant de 5 Mois de Captivité* (Port Louis: Esclapon, 1955).
132. See Joseph Le Roy, *La Maison de France: Ile Maurice 1941–46* (Port Louis, 1946).
133. D'Unienville Papers. C. M. Woods, SOE adviser Foreign and Commonwealth Office, to Raymond D'Unienville, 15/11/87.
134. Ibid., p. 409. P. Bonieux (brother of Maurice Larcher) to A. Jackson, 11/11/99.
135. D'Unienville Papers. C. M. Woods, SOE adviser Foreign and Commonwealth Office, to Raymond D'Unienville, 15/11/87. See M. R. D. Foot, *SOE in France*, p. 199.
136. M. R. D. Foot, *SOE in France*, p. 380. Jacques Mayer to A. Jackson, 29/2/00.
137. Ibid., p. 413.
138. Ibid., p. 380.
139. Jan Maingard de la Ville-es-Offrans to A. Jackson, 22/10/99. Maingard Papers, private collection in possession of Jan Maingard. Sheet 30a, 'Shipwright Circuit'; Army Form W. 3121, DSO recommendation, Lieutenant General Gale, Chief Administrative Officer, 14/3/45. For a summary of Maingard's war record, see B. Burrun's article in *Week-End*, 4/8/91.
140. Paul McCue, *SAS Operation Bulbasket: Behind the Lines in Occupied France* (London: Leo Cooper, 1996).
141. Interview with Sir Maurice Rault, Quatre Bornes, 29/6/99. See his book, *Navigateur D'Occasion* (Port Louis: Athevre D'Imprimer, 1985). Also, Mel Rolfe, *To Hell and Back* (London: Grub Street, 1998), chapter 20, and Maurice Paturau, *Agents Secrets Mauricien en France, 1940–45*.
142. F. R. Domingo, *Les Mauriciens*.
143. Lorraine Lagesse to A. Jackson, 28/10/99.
144. Herbert du Plessis, 'Mauritians in London Prepare for War', memoir to A. Jackson, 3/6/00.
145. Raymond D'Unienville to A. Jackson, 4/3/00.
146. Herbert du Plessis, 'Mauritians in London Prepare for War'.
147. Entry for *Dictionary of Mauritian Biography*. *Times* obituary, 31/5/99.

148. The definitive studies of this episode have been written by Aaron Zwergbaum, 'Exile in Mauritius', *Yad Washem: Studies on the European Jewish Catastrophe and Resistance*, IV (Jerusalem, 1960); also by the same author, 'From Internment in Bratislava and Detention in Mauritius to Freedom', in A. Dagan (ed.) *The Jews of Czechoslovakia*, Volume II (New York, 1971), pp. 594–654. Other relevant works include Bernard Wasserstein, *Britain and the Jews of Europe 1939–45* (Oxford: Clarendon Press, 1979), and Israel Gutman (ed.) *Encyclopaedia of the Holocaust*, Volume II (New York: Simon and Schuster, 1990), p. 943 entry on Mauritius. See also Genevieve Pitot, *The Mauritian Shekel: the Story of the Jewish Detainees in Mauritius 1940–45* (Port Louis: Editions Vizavi, 1998), and Karl Lenk, *The Mauritius Affair: the Boat People of 1940–41* (Brighton: R. S. Lenk, 1993).
149. NHB. C-in-C Eastern Fleet War Diary, volume 10, p. 132. They were transported by the Royal Navy from Bombay to Mauritius, arriving on 16 October 1941. See PRO, CO 968/46/11. Ex-Shah of Persia.
150. PRO. CO 167/920/10. Greek Refugees in Turkey: Reception in Mauritius.
151. A. Zwergbaum, 'Exile in Mauritius', p. 191.
152. Ibid., p. 194.
153. B. Wasserstein, *Britain and the Jews*, p. 63.
154. Ibid., p. 64 reproduces the official British statement.
155. Ibid.
156. Mauritius Institute, Port Louis. H. J. Armitage, *Interim Report on the Detainment Camp For the Period 1 October 1941 to 30 September 1942* (Port Louis: Government Printer, 1942); *Memorandum on the Personal Services Rendered to Detainees* (Port Louis: Government Printer, 1943); and *Interim Report on the Detainment Camp for the Period October 1 1943 to September 30 1944* (Port Louis: Government Printer, 1945).
157. See G. Pitot, *The Mauritian Shekel*, and the fictional account by Maureen Earl, *Boat of Stone*. See 'Boat of Stone: American Novel Recounts the Life of Prisoners at Beau Bassin During World War II', *Week-End*, 20/3/94. See the critique of it by a former Detainment Camp guard, Philippe Oh San, 'The (Jewish) Detainment Camp (as seen by an eye witness)', *Week-End*, 17/4/94.
158. RHL. *Mauritius Colonial Annual Report 1946*, p. 126.

8   The End of the War and Strategic Transformation in the Indian Ocean

1. RHL. *Debates of the Mauritius Council of Government*, 9/5/45.
2. RHL. Moody Papers. Item 5, p. 155, 8/5/45.
3. Article in *L'Express*, 7/5/95.
4. P. Escaplon, *Roll of Honour: Mauritians Who Gave Their Lives 1939–45* (Port Louis: Escaplon, 1957).
5. RHL. *Debates of the Mauritius Council of Government*, 14/8/45.
6. See K. Hazareesingh, *The Story of the 1945 Cyclones* (Port Louis: Government Printer, 1948).
7. Ibid. RHL. FCB Papers. File 170/2, 'Tackling Cyclone Havoc in Mauritius', Colonial Office Public Relations Department.

8. See K. Hazareesingh, *The Story of the 1945 Cyclones* (Port Louis: Government Printer, 1948).
9. Twining Papers. Strictly Confidential: Notes on Labour and Related Problems in Mauritius, c. 1942, p. 18.
10. RHL. *Debates of the Mauritius Council of Government*, 19/6/45.
11. RHL. FCB Papers. *Inaugural Meeting of the Central Development and Welfare Committee 1 March 1945*, p. 6.
12. PRO. CO 167/929/1. Committee to Assist Ex-Servicemen in Mauritius. Also CO 167/920/13.
13. RHL. FCB Papers. *Annual Report of the Labour Department 1948* (Port Louis: Government Printer, 1949).
14. Mauritius Institute, Port Louis. Box file M900, 'History, Geography, Travels', *Release and Resettlement: Issued by the Government of Mauritius for the Information of Mauritians and Rodriguans in the Forces* (Port Louis: Government Printer, 1945).
15. RHL. *Mauritius Colonial Annual Report 1948* (London: HMSO, 1949).
16. RCS. *Report on the Activities of the Re-Absorption Office for the Year 1948* (Port Louis: Government Printer, 1949).
17. Ibid. *Report on the Activities of the Re-Absorption Office for the Year 1949* (Port Louis: Government Printer, 1950), p. 1.
18. Ibid., p. 3.
19. Twining Papers. Strictly Confidential: Notes on Labour and Related Problems in Mauritius, c. 1942, p. 12.
20. RHL. FCB Papers. Box 170, J. E. Anquetil to A. Creech Jones, 13/11/44.
21. RCS. *Report on the Activities of the Re-Absorption Office for the Year 1949*, report appendix B.
22. Roger Requin, Secretary, Ex-Service Association of Mauritius, to A. Jackson, 2/11/99.
23. Monaf Fakira interview.
24. Thanks to Marina Carter for this information.
25. S. Lingayah, *A Comparative Study of Mauritian Immigrants in Two European Cities (London and Paris)*, chapter 2, 'Origins of Mauritian Migrants in Britain'.
26. L. A. M. Tyack, *Treasures of the Indian Ocean*, p. 60.
27. Phillip Darby, *British Defence Policy East of Suez 1947–1968* (London: Oxford University Press, 1973), p. 42.
28. John Pimlott (ed.) *British Military Operations, 1945–1984* (London: Hamlyn, 1984), pp. 149 and 150.
29. NHB. J. Brown, 'Admiralty House and the Royal Navy at Trincomalee, 1810–1957' (1980), p. 6. HMS *Mauritius* was opened in February 1962, handed over in March 1966 and closed in 1975. B. Warlow, *Shore Establishments of the Royal Navy*.
30. See Neville Brown, *Arms Without Empire* (London: Penguin, 1968). Thanks to Neville Brown for a copy of his book.
31. Gillian King, *Imperial Outpost – Aden: its Place in British Strategic Policy* (London: Chatham House, 1964).
32. Ibid., p. 5.
33. G. King, *Imperial Outpost*, p. 5.
34. N. Brown, *Arms Without Empire*.

35.   G. King, *Imperial Outpost*, pp. 36 and 39.
36.   E. Grove, *Vanguard to Trident*, p. 264.
37.   Robert Aldrich and John Connell, *The Last Colonies* (Cambridge: Cambridge University Press, 1998), p. 178.
38.   Ibid., p. 179. See also 'Wilson's Stealthy US Deal That Banished 2000', *The Times*, 4/11/00.
39.   *Mauritius News*, August 2000, p. 3.
40.   See Barry Watts, 'American Air Power', in Williamson Murray (ed.) *The Emerging Strategic Environment: Challenges of the Twenty-First Century* (Westport, CT: Praeger, 1999).
41.   See 'The Enduring Claim of Mauritius Over the Chagos', *Mauritius News*, March 2000. 'Diego Garcia, 1975: the Debate Over the Base and the Island's Forever Inhabitants', Hearings Before the Special Sub-Committee on Investigations of the Committee on International Relations, House of Representatives (Washington: US Government Printing Office, 1975); 'Diego Garcia: the Islander's Britain Sold', *Sunday Times*, 21/9/75. BBC Radio 4 news headline, 14/7/00.
42.   Peter Chellen, 'The Battle for the Chagos Archipelago', *Mauritius News*, August 2000.
43.   See Jooneed Khan, 'Diego Garcia: the Militarization of an Indian Ocean Island', in Robin Cohen (ed.) *African Islands and Enclaves* (London: Sage Publications, 1983); Timothy Lynch, 'Diego Garcia: Competing Claims to a Strategic Isle', *Case Western Reserve Journal of International Law*, 16 (1984); Vivian Forbes, 'British Indian Ocean Territory: Chagos Archipelago', *The Indian Ocean Review* (March 1992); Iain Walker, *Zaffer Pe Sanze: Ethnic Identity and Social Change Among the Ilois of Mauritius* (Vacoas, 1986); John Madeley, *Diego Garcia: a Contrast to the Falklands* (London: Minority Rights Group, 1985); K. S. Jawatkhar, *Diego Garcia in International Diplomacy* (New Delhi: Sangam Books, 1983); Joel Larus, 'Diego Garcia: Political Clouds Over a Vital US Base', *Strategic Review*, 10 (1982); and Larus, 'Negotiating Independence? Mauritius and Diego Garcia', *The Round Table*, 294 (1985).
44.   R. Aldrich and J. Connell, *The Last Colonies*, pp. 180 and 182.
45.   Ibid., p. 182.
46.   Abdool Cader Amode, 'Mauritius During World War Two', newspaper article, 1/2/91.
47.   MNA. *Le Cerneen-Le Mauricien-Advance*, 25/3/43.

Select Bibliography

Primary sources

Papers have been consulted in the following collections:
Rhodes House, Oxford.
Royal Commonwealth Society, University Library, Cambridge
Naval Historical Branch, Ministry of Defence Library, London
Royal Pioneer Corps Museum, Camberley
Imperial War Museum, London
India Office Library, British Library, London
Public Record Office, London
Carnegie Library, Curepipe
Mauritius National Archives, Coramandel
Mauritius Institute, Port Louis

The following private papers have been consulted:
D'Unienville papers
Keedy papers
Maingard papers
North-Coombes diaries
Twining papers

Secondary sources

Books

Addison, J. and Hazareesingh, K. *A New History of Mauritius* (London: Macmillan Press – now Palgrave, 1984).

Aldrich, Aldrich, *Greater France: a History of French Overseas Expansion* (London: Macmillan Press – now Palgrave, 1996).

____, and Connell, John, *The Last Colonies* (Cambridge: Cambridge University Press, 1998).

Alvarez, David (ed.) *Allied and Axis Signals Intelligence in World War Two* (London: Frank Cass, 1999).

Austen, C. M. *Sea Fights and Corsairs of the Indian Ocean, Being the Naval History of Mauritius from 1715 to 1810* (Mauritius, 1934).

Babajee, Senoo, *A Concise History of Mauritius* (Bombay: Hind Kitabs, 1950).

Barnett, Correlli, *The Desert Generals* (London: Cassell and Company, 1999).

____, *Engage The Enemy More Closely: the Royal Navy in the Second World War* (London: Hodder & Stoughton, 1991).

Barnwell, P. J. *Visits and Despatches 1598–1948* (Port Louis: Standard Printing Establishment, 1948).

____, and Toussaint, A. *A Short History of Mauritius* (London: Longman for the

Government of Mauritius, 1949).

Bates, Darrell, *A Gust of Plumes: a Biography of Lord Twining of Godalming and Tanganyika* (London: Hodder & Stoughton, 1972).

Bayly, Christopher, *Imperial Meridian: the British Empire and the World 1780–1830* (Harlow: Longman, 1989).

Beasley, W. G. *The Rise of Modern Japan* (London: Weidenfeld & Nicolson, 1990).

Beesly, Patrick, *Very Special Intelligence: the Story of the Admiralty's Operational Intelligence Centre 1939–1945* (London: Hamish Hamilton, 1977).

Bennet, Pramila, *Mauritius* (Oxford: Clio Press, 1992).

Burton Benedict, *Mauritius: the Problems of a Plural Society* (London: Pall Mall Press, 1965).

____, *Indians in a Plural Society* (London: HMSO, 1961).

Bissoondoyal, Basdeo, *The Truth About Mauritius* (Bombay: Bharatiya Vidya Bhavan, 1968).

Bissoondoyal, S. *A Concise History of Mauritius* (Bombay: Bharatiya Vidya Bhavan, 1963).

Bissoondoyal, Uttama, *Promises to Keep* (New Delhi: Wiley Eastern, 1990).

Bowman, Larry, *Mauritius: Democracy and Development in the Indian Ocean* (London: Dartmouth, 1991).

Briggs, Susan, *Keep Smiling Through: the Home Front 1939–45* (London: Weidenfeld & Nicolson, 1975).

Bright-Holmes, John (ed.) *Like It Was: the Diaries of Malcolm Muggeridge* (London: Collins, 1981).

Brown, Judith and Roger Louis, William (eds) *The Oxford History of the British Empire, Volume IV: The Twentieth Century* (Oxford: Oxford University Press, 1999).

Brown, Neville, *Arms Without Empire* (London: Penguin, 1968).

Busch, Rainer and Roll, Hans-Joachim, *German U-Boat Commanders of World War Two: a Biographical Dictionary* (London: Greenhill, 1999).

Butler, L. J. *Industrialization and the British Colonial State: West Africa 1939–51* (London: Frank Cass, 1997).

Cain, P. J. and Hopkins A. G. *British Imperialism,* two volumes (Harlow: Longman, 1993).

Calder, Angus, *The People's War, 1939–45* (London: Panther, 1971).

Chelin, Antoine, *Une Ile et Son Passe: Ile Maurice, 1507–1947* (Port Louis: Mauritius Printing, 1973).

Clayton, Aileen, *The Enemy is Listening: the Story of the Y Service* (London: Crecy Books, 1993).

Clayton, Anthony, *The British Empire as a Superpower, 1919–1939* (London, 1986).

____, *Forearmed: a History of the Intelligence Corps* (London: Brassey's, 1993).

____, *The British Military Presence in East and Central Africa* (Oxford: ODRP Report 2, 1986).

____, and Savage, Donald, *Government and Labour in Kenya 1895–1963* (London: Frank Cass, 1974).

Clifford, Bede, *Proconsul: Being Incidents in the Life and Career of The Honourable Sir Bede Clifford* (London: Evans Brothers, 1964).

Clothier, Norman, *Black Valour: the South African Native Labour Contingent*

1916–18 and the Sinking of the Mendi (Pietermaritzburg: University of Natal Press, 1987).

Cohen Michael, *Fighting World War Three From the Middle East: Allied Contingency Plans, 1945–54* (London: Frank Cass, 1997).

Cohen, Robin (ed.) *African Islands and Enclaves* (London: Sage Publications, 1983).

Cole, D. H. *Imperial Military Geography: General Characteristics of the Empire Relating to Defence* (London: Sifton Praed, 1928).

Creveld, Martin Van, *Supplying War: Logistics From Wallenstein to Patton* (Cambridge: Cambridge University Press, 1977).

Crew, Graeme, *Royal Army Service Corps* (London: Leo Cooper, 1970).

Darby, Philip, *British Defence Policy East of Suez, 1947–1960* (London: Oxford University Press, 1973).

Davis, Lance and Huttenback, Robert, *Mammon and the Pursuit of Empire: the Economics of Imperialism* (Cambridge: Cambridge University Press, 1988).

Dear, I. C. B. (ed.), *The Oxford Companion to the Second World War* (Oxford: Oxford University Press, 1995).

Dockrill, Suki (ed.) *From Pearl Harbor to Hiroshima: the Second World War in Asia and the Pacific, 1941–45* (London: Macmillan Press – now Palgrave, 1994).

Domingo, F. R. *Les Mauriciens dans la Deuxième Guerre Mondiale: La 8eme Armée au Moyen-Orient et en Italie (1941–45)* (Moka: Editions de l'Ocean Indien, 1983).

Dumett, Raymond (ed.) *Gentlemanly Capitalism and British Imperialism: The New Debate on Empire* (London: Longman, 1999).

D'Unienville, France, *Dialogues D'un Temps Trouble* (Port Louis: General Printing, 1943).

Edward-Hart, Robert, *Les Volontaires Mauriciens aux Armées 1914–18* (Port Louis: General Printing and Stationery Company, 1919).

Elliott, E. R. *Royal Pioneers 1945–1993* (Worcestershire: Self Publishing Association, 1993).

Emrith, Moomtaz, *History of the Muslims of Mauritius* (Port Louis: The Regent Press, 1967).

Eppstein, John (ed.) *Mauritius*, British Survey Popular Series, No. 146 (London: British Society for International Understanding, 1956).

Escaplon, P. *Roll of Honour: Mauritians Who Gave Their Lives 1939–45* (Port Louis: Escaplon, 1957).

Farrar-Hockley, Anthony, *The War in the Desert* (London: Faber & Faber, 1969).

Foot, M. R. D. *SOE in France: an Account of the Work of the British Special Operations Executive in France, 1940–44* (London: HMSO, 1966).

Forty, George, *British Army Handbook 1939–1945* (Stroud: Sutton Publishing, 1998).

Gallagher, John, *The Decline, Revival, and Fall of the British Empire: the Ford Lectures and Other Essays*, ed. Anil Seal (Cambridge: Cambridge University Press, 1982).

____, and Robinson, Ronald, *Africa and the Victorians: the Official Mind of Imperialism* (London: Macmillan Press – now Palgrave, 1961).

Gleeson, Ian, *The Unknown Force: Black, Indian, and Coloured Soldiers Through Two World Wars* (Johannesburg: Rivonia, 1994).

Grafftey-Smith, Laurence, *Hands to Play* (London: Routledge and Keegan Paul, 1975).

Graham, Gerald, *Great Britain in the Indian Ocean, 1810–1850: a Study in Maritime Enterprise* (Oxford: Clarendon Press, 1967).
——, *The Politics of Naval Supremacy: Studies in British Maritime Ascendancy* (Cambridge: Cambridge University Press, 1965).
Grove, Eric, *From Vanguard to Trident: British Naval Policy Since World War Two* (London: Bodley Head, 1987).
——, *Sea Battles In Close Up, World War Two*, two volumes (Surrey: Ian Allan, 1993).
Grundlingh, Albert, *Fighting Their Own War: South African Blacks and the First World War* (Johannesburg: Ravan Press, 1987).
Haggie, Paul, *Britannia at Bay: the Defence of the British Empire Against Japan, 1931–1941* (Oxford: Clarendon Press, 1981).
Hall, Richard, *Empires of the Monsoon: a History of the Indian Ocean and its Invaders* (London: HarperCollins, 1996).
Hamill, Ian, *The Strategic Illusion: the Singapore Strategy and the Defence of Australia and New Zealand* (Singapore: Singapore University Press, 1981).
Harrison, Frank, *Tobruk: the Great Siege Reassessed* (London: Arms & Armour, 1997).
Harrison, John, *Scholarship Boy: a Personal History of the Twentieth Century* (London: Rivers Oram Press, 1995).
Havinden, Michael and Meredith, David, *Colonial Development: Britain and its Tropical Colonies, 1850–1960* (London: Routledge, 1993).
Haywood, A. and Clarke, F. A. S. *The History of the Royal West African Frontier Force* (Aldershot: Gale & Polden, 1964).
Hazareesingh, K. (ed.) *Selected Speeches of Sir Seewoosagur Ramgoolam* (London: Macmillan Press – now Palgrave, 1979).
——, *The Story of the 1945 Cyclones* (Port Louis: Government Printer, 1948).
Hearnshaw, F. C. J. *Sea Power and Empire* (London: Harrap, 1940).
Hevesi, Eugene, *Hitler's Plan for Madagascar* (New York: American Jewish Committee, 1941).
Hezlet, Arthur, *The Electron and Sea Power* (London: Peter Davies, 1975).
Hinsley, F. H. *British Intelligence in the Second World War* (London: HMSO, 1993).
——, *Command of the Sea: the Naval Side of British History from the Eighteenth Century to the End of the Second World War* (London: Christophers, 1950).
——, and Stripp, Alan (eds) *Code-Breakers: the Inside Story of Bletchley Park* (Oxford: Oxford University Press, 1993).
Hough, Richard, *The Longest Battle: the War At Sea 1939–45* (London: Weidenfeld & Nicolson, 1986).
Ireland, Bernard, *Naval History of World War Two* (London: HarperCollins, 1998).
Jackson, Ashley, *Botswana 1939–45: an African Country at War* (Oxford: Clarendon Press, 1999).
James, Lawrence, *Mutiny: Mutinies in British and Commonwealth Forces 1797–1950* (London: Buchan & Enright, 1987).
——, *Raj: the Making and Unmaking of British India* (London: Abacus, 1997).
Jawatkhar, K. S. *Diego Garcia in International Diplomacy* (New Delhi: Sangam Books, 1983).
Johnson, Kate (ed.) *The SOE Sound Archive Oral History Recordings* (London:

Imperial War Museum, 1998).

Joslen, H. F. *Orders of Battle: The Second World War 1939–45*, two volumes (London: HMSO, 1960).

Keegan, John, *The Price of Admiralty: the Evolution of Naval Warfare* (London: Penguin, 1990).

——, *The Second World War* (London: Pimlico, 1988).

Kent, Marian, *Moguls and Mandarins: Oil, Imperialism, and the Middle East in British Foreign Policy, 1900–1940* (London: Frank Cass, 1993).

Killingray, David and Rathbone, Richard (eds) *Africa and the Second World War* (London, 1986).

——, and Omissi, David, *Guardians of Empire: the Armed Forces and the Colonial Powers* (Manchester: Manchester University Press, 1999).

Kilson, Robin and King, Robert (eds) *The Statecraft of British Imperialism: Essays in Honour of Wm Roger Louis* (London: Frank Cass, 1999).

King, Gillian, *Imperial Outpost – Aden: Its Place in British Strategic Policy* (London: Chatham House, 1964).

Kirk-Greene, Anthony, *On Crown Service: a History of HM Colonial and Overseas Civil Service, 1837–1997* (London: I. B. Tauris, 1999).

Kolinsky, Martin, *Britain's War in the Middle East: Strategy and Diplomacy 1936–42* (London: Macmillan Press – now Palgrave, 1999).

Lalouviere, Philippe La Hausse de (ed.) *Coastal Fortifications: Proceedings of an International Conference on Coastal Fortifications Held in Mauritius 18–21 June 1996* (Mauritius: Heritage, 1998).

Langford, Paul, *Modern British Foreign Policy: the Eighteenth Century 1688–1815* (London: Adam & Charles Black, 1976).

Lawrence, Joseph, *The Observers Book of Aircraft* (London: Frederick Warne & Coy, 1949).

Lee, J. M. and Petter, Martin, *The Colonial Office, War and Development Policy: Organization and Planning of a Metropolitan Initiative 1939–45* (London: Institute of Commonwealth Studies, 1982)

Lee Ready, J. *Forgotten Allies: the Military Contribution of the Colonies, Exiled Governments, and Lesser Powers to the Allied Victory in World War Two*, two volumes, (Jefferson, NC: McFarland & Company, 1985).

——, *World War Two Nation by Nation* (London: Arms & Armour, 1995).

Lenton, H. T. *British and Empire Warships of the Second World War* (London: Greenhill, 1998).

Lewin, Ronald, *Slim: the Standard Bearer. A Biography of Field-Marshal Viscount Slim* (Hertfordshire: Wordsworth Editions, 1999).

——, *The Other Ultra* (London: Hutchinson, 1982).

Lingayah, Sam, *A Comparative Study of Mauritian Immigrants in Two European Cities (London and Paris): an Investigation into the Process of Adaptation* (London: Mauritius Welfare Association, 1991).

Low, D. A. *Eclipse of Empire* (Cambridge: Cambridge University Press, 1991).

Lucas, Charles, *The Empire at War, Volume IV: Africa* (London: Oxford University Press, 1924).

Lucas, James, *War in the Desert: the Eighth Army at El Alamein* (London: Arms & Armour, 1982).

Lunt, James, *Imperial Sunset: Frontier Soldiering in the Twentieth Century* (London: Macdonald Futura, 1981).

McIntyre, W. David, *Rise and Fall of the Singapore Naval Base, 1919–1942* (London: Macmillan Press – now Palgrave, 1979).

MacIntyre, Donald, *Fighting Admiral: the Life of Admiral of the Fleet Sir James Somerville* (London: Evans Brothers, 1961).

Mackenzie, S. P., *The Home Guard: the Real Story of 'Dad's Army'* (Oxford: Oxford University Press, 1996).

Mackenzie, William, *The Secret History of SOE: the Special Operatons Executive, 1940–1945* (London: St Ermin's Press, 2000).

Macmillan, Allister, *Mauritius Illustrated: History and Descriptive, Commercial and Industrial Facts, Figures, and Resources* (London: W. H. & L. Collingridge, 1914).

Malim, Michael, *Island of the Swan: Mauritius* (London: Longman, 1952).

Mannick, A. R., *Mauritius: the Development of a Plural Society* (Nottingham: Spokesman, 1979).

Mansergh, Nicholas, *Survey of British Commonwealth Affairs: Problems of War-Time Co-operation and Post-War Change, 1939–1952* (London: Oxford University Press, 1958).

Marder, Arthur, *Old Friends, New Enemies: the Royal Navy and the Imperial Japanese Navy* (Oxford: Clarendon Press, 1981).

——, *Operation Menace: the Dakar Expedition and the Dudley North Affair* (London: Oxford University Press, 1976).

Mauritius and the War (Port Louis: Indian Cultural Association, 1940).

McCue, Paul, *SAS Operation Bulbasket: Behind the Lines in Occupied France* (London: Leo Cooper, 1996).

McIntyre, W. David, *The Rise and Fall of the Singapore Naval Base 1919–42* (London: Macmillan Press – now Palgrave, 1979).

Mehta, S. R. *Social Development in Mauritius: A Study on Rural Modernization in an Island Community* (New Delhi: Wiley Eastern Ltd, 1981).

Metz, Helen, (ed.) *Area Handbook: the Indian Ocean – Five Islands* (Washington, DC: Library of Congress, 1995).

Minns, Raynes, *Bombers and Mash: the Domestic Front 1939–45* (London: Virago Press, 1980).

Mitchinson, K. W. *Pioneer Battalions of the Great War: Organized and Intelligent Labour* (London: Leo Cooper, 1997).

Mockford, Julian, *Pursuit of an Island* (London: Staples Press, 1950).

Mohr, Ulrich, *Atlantis: the Story of a German Surface Raider* (London: Werner Laurie, 1955).

Moore, Bob and Fedorowich, K. (eds) *Prisoners of War and Their Captors in World War Two* (Oxford: Berg, 1996).

Mordal, Jacques, *Twenty Five Centuries of Sea Warfare* (London: Abbey Library, 1970).

——, and Auphan, Paul, *The French Navy in World War Two* (Annapolis, Maryland: US Naval Institute, 1952).

Muggeridge, Malcolm, *Chronicle of Wasted Time II: the Infernal Grove* (London: Collins, 1973).

Mulloo, Anand, *The Road to Independence* (Port Louis: Standard Printing, 1968).

Murray, Williamson (ed.) *The Emerging Strategic Environment: Challenges of the Twenty-First Century* (Westport, CT: Praeger, 1999).

Nagapel, Amedee, *Histoire de la Colonie: Isle de France-Ile Maurice, 1721–1968*

(Port Louis: Diocese de Port Louis, 1996).

Nairac, Edouard, *Causeries du Mercredi* (Port Louis: General Printing, 1943).

——, *Deuxième Série des Causeries Radiodiffusees de Sir Edouard Nairac* (Port Louis: Government Printer, 1942).

Naval Staff History of the Second World War, four volumes (London: Admiralty Historical Section, 1954–1957).

Neidpath, James, *The Singapore Naval Base and the Defence of Britain's Far Eastern Empire, 1919–1941* (Oxford: Clarendon, 1981).

North-Coombes, Alfred, *The Island of Rodrigues* (Port Louis: Mauritius Advertising Bureau, 1971).

Northcote Parkinson, C. *War in the Eastern Seas, 1793–1815* (London: Allen & Unwin, 1954).

O'Brine, Manning, *Dodos Don't Duck* (London: Hammond & Hammond, 1953).

Omissi, David, *Air Power and Colonial Control: the Royal Air Force, 1919–1939* (Manchester: Manchester University Press, 1990).

——, *The Sepoy and the Raj: the Indian Army, 1860–1940* (London: Macmillan Press – now Palgrave, 1994).

Ommanney, F. D. *The Shoals of Capricorn* (London: Longmans, Green and Company, 1952).

O'Neill, M. C. (ed.) *The History of the Second World War,* two volumes (London: Odhams, 1951).

Ovendale, Richie, *British Defence Policy Since 1945* (Manchester: Manchester University Press, 1994).

Page, Malcolm, *KAR: a History of the King's African Rifles* (London: Leo Cooper, 1998).

Parkinson, Roger, *The War in the Desert* (London: Hart-Davis, MacGibbon, 1976).

Parsons, Timothy, *The African Rank-and-File: Social Implications of Colonial Military Service in the King's African Rifles, 1902–1964* (Oxford: James Currey, 1999).

Patience, Kevin, *Konigsberg: a German East African Raider* (Bahrain: Dar Akhbar, 1994).

——, *Zanzibar and the Loss of HMS Pegasus, 20 September 1914* (Bahrain: Dar Akhbar, 1996).

Paturau, J. Maurice, *Histoire Economique de l'Ile Maurice* (Port Louis: Les Pailles, 1988).

Pearce, Robert, *The Turning Point in Africa: British Colonial Policy, 1938–48* (London: Frank Cass, 1982).

Perry, F. W. *The Commonwealth Armies: Manpower and Organization in Two World Wars* (Manchester: Manchester University Press, 1988).

Piggot, Juliet, *Queen Alexandra's Royal Army Nursing Corps* (London: Leo Cooper, 1975).

Pillet, J. R. *Entre Nous: Bulletins de Propagande du Poste Radio St Denis (November 1940 – February 1942)* (St Denis: Editions du Bureau de la Presse, 1942).

Pimlott, John, (ed.) *British Military Operations, 1945–1984* (London: Hamlyn, 1984).

Pitt, Barry, *Crucible of War: Western Desert 1941* (London: Jonathan Cape, 1980).

——, *Crucible of War: Year of Alamein 1942* (London: Jonathan Cape, 1982).

Playfair, I. S. O., Malony, C. J. C. and Jackson, W. *The Mediterranean and Middle*

East, six volumes (London: HMSO, 1954–88).

Porter, Andrew (ed.) *The Oxford History of the British Empire, Volume III: The Nineteenth Century* (Oxford: Oxford University Press, 1999).

Ramsurrun, P. *The Arya Samaj Movement in Mauritius* (Port Louis, 1970).

Rault, Maurice, *Navigateur D'Occasion* (Port Louis: Athevre D'Imprimer, 1985).

Rhodes-Wood, E. H. *A War History of the Royal Pioneer Corps 1939–45* (Aldershot: Gale & Polden, 1960).

Rich, Paul, *Race and Empire in British Politics* (Cambridge: Cambridge University Press, 1986).

Roger Louis, Wm, *Great Britain and Germany's Lost Colonies* (Oxford: Oxford University Press, 1967).

——, and Blake, Robert (eds) *Churchill* (Oxford: Oxford University Press, 1993).

Rogge, Bernhard, *Under Ten Flags: the Story of the German Commerce Raider Atlantis* (London: Weidenfeld & Nicolson, 1955).

Roskill, Stephen, *The War At Sea 1939–1945*, three volumes (London: HMSO, 1954–60).

Rohwer, Jurgen and Hummelchen, G. *Chronicle of the War at Sea 1939-45: the Naval History of World War Two* (London: Greenhill, 1992).

Rolfe, Mel, *To Hell and Back* (London: Grub Street, 1998).

Rosenthal, Eric, *Japan's Bid for Africa: Including the Story of the Madagascar Campaign* (South Africa: Central News Agency, 1944).

Salisbury Woods, Rex, *Cambridge Doctor* (London: Robert Hale, 1962).

Schofield, B. B. *British Sea Power: Naval Policy in the Twentieth Century* (London: B. T. Batsford, 1967).

Scott, Robert, *Limuria: the Lesser Dependencies of Mauritius* (Oxford: Oxford University Press, 1961).

Selvon, Sydney, *Ramgoolam* (Rose Hill: Editions de l'Océan Indien, 1986).

——, *Historical Dictionary of Mauritius* (London: Scarecrow Press, 1991).

Seton-Watson, Hugh, *The Decline of Imperial Russia 1855–1914* (London: Methuen, 1952).

Simmons, Adele, *Modern Mauritius: the Politics of Decolonization* (Bloomington: Indiana University Press, 1982).

Simpson, Michael (ed.) with Somerville, John, *The Somerville Papers: Selections from the Private and Official Correspondence of Admiral of the Fleet Sir James Somerville* (Aldershot: Scolar Press for the Naval Records Society, 1995).

Smith, Michael, *Station X: the Codebreakers of Bletchley Park* (London: Macmillan Press – now Palgrave, 1998).

——, *The Emperor's Codes: Bletchley Park and the Breaking of Japan's Secret Ciphers* (London: Bantam Press, 2000).

Somerville, Christopher, *Our War: How the British Commonwealth Fought the Second World War* (London: Weidenfeld & Nicolson, 1998).

Stafford, David, *Secret Agent* (London: BBC Worldwide, 2000).

Stamberg, Arthur, *Footprints on a Winding Road: Recollections of an Old Jerseyman* (Jersey: La Haule, 1998).

St John Barclay, Glen, *The Empire is Marching: a Study of the Military Effort of the British Empire, 1800–1945* (London: Weidenfeld & Nicolson, 1976).

Steiner, Erich Gershon, *The Story of the Patria* (New York: Holocaust Library, 1982).

Stripp, Alan, *Codebreaker in the Far East: How the British Cracked Japan's Top Secret*

Military Codes (Oxford: Oxford University Press, 1995).

Summerskill, Michael, *China on the Western Front: Britain's Chinese Workforce in the First World War* (London: M. Summerskill, 1982).

Tarling, Nicholas, *The Fall of Imperial Britain in South East Asia* (Singapore: Oxford University Press, 1993).

——, *British South East Asia and the Onset of the Pacific War* (Cambridge: Cambridge University Press, 1996).

——, *British South East Asia and the Onset of the Cold War, 1945–50* (Cambridge: Cambridge University Press, 1998).

Thomas, Martin, *The French Empire at War 1940–45* (Manchester: Manchester University Press, 1998).

Thompson, Julian, *The Lifeblood of War: Logistics in Armed Conflict* (London: Brassey's, 1991).

Tio-Fane Pineo, Huguette-Ly, *Chinese Diaspora in Western Indian Ocean* (Rose Hill: Editions de l'Océan Indien, 1985).

Titmuss, Richard and Abel-Smith, B. *Social Policies and Population Growth in Mauritius: Report to the Government of Mauritius* (London: Methuen, 1960).

Toussaint, A. *Select Bibliography of Mauritius* (Port Louis: Henry & Cie, 1951).

——, *History of the Indian Ocean* (London: Routledge & Keegan Paul, 1966).

——, *History of Mauritius* (London: Macmillan Education, 1977).

Turner, L. C. F., Gordon-Cumming, H. R., and Beltzer, J. E., *War in the Southern Oceans, 1939–45* (Cape Town: Oxford University Press, 1961).

Tyack, L. A. M. *Treasures of the Indian Ocean: Mauritius and its Dependencies* (Lausanne: France Inter Press, 1965).

Van Creveld, M. *Supplying War: Logistics From Wallenstein to Patton* (Cambridge: Cambridge University Press, 1977).

Villiers, Allan, *The Indian Ocean* (London: Museum Press, 1952).

Warlow, Ben, *Shore Establishments of the Royal Navy: Being a List of the Static Ships and Establishments of the Royal Navy* (Liskeard: Maritime Books, 1992).

Weinberg, Gerhard, *A World At Arms: a Global History of World War Two* (Cambridge: Cambridge University Press, 1994).

Whitley, M. J. *Cruisers of World War Two: an International Encyclopaedia* (London: Arms & Armour, 1995).

Willmott, H. P. *Grave of a Dozen Schemes: British Naval Planning and the War Against Japan, 1943–45* (London: Airlife, 1996).

Winchester, Simon, *Outposts* (London: Hodder & Stoughton, 1985).

Winterbotham, F. W. *The Ultra Secret: the Inside Story of Operation Ultra, Bletchley Park, and Enigma* (London: Weidenfeld & Nicolson, 1974).

Winton, John, *Ultra at Sea* (London: Leo Cooper, 1988).

Woodburn Kirby, S. *The War Against Japan*, three volumes (London: HMSO, 1957–60).

Journal articles

Allen, Richard, 'The Slender, Sweet Thread: Sugar, Capitalism, and Dependency in Mauritius, 1860–1936', *Journal of Imperial and Commonwealth History*, XVI (1988).

Babajee, E. 'Indian Troops in Mauritius', *United Empire: Journal of the Royal Empire Society*, VXLV, 5 (1954).

Burroughs, Peter, 'The Mauritius Rebellion of 1832 and the Abolition of British Colonial Slavery', *Journal of Imperial and Commonwealth History*, IV (1976).

Butler, L. J. 'Reconstruction, Development, and the Entrepreneurial State: the British Colonial Model, 1939–51', *Contemporary British History*, 13, 4 (1999).

Dowling, M. A. C. 'The Malaria Eradication Scheme', *Corona: Journal of His Majesty's Colonial Service*, II, 2 (1950).

Elcoat, Geoffrey, 'Some Memories of a War-Time KAR Officer', *Rhino Link: Newsletter of the King's African Rifles and East African Forces Dinner Club*, 12 (1997).

Harrison, Ted, 'British Subversion in French East Africa, 1941–42: SOE's Todd Mission', *English Historical Review* (April 1999).

Herchenroder, M. V. M. 'High-Lights of Mauritius Economy 1946–56', *Revue Agricole et Sucrière de l'Ile Maurice*, 36, 1 (February 1957).

Higginson, Tom, 'Mutiny in Madagascar', *Rhino Link: Newsletter of the King's African Rifles and East African Forces Dinner Club*, 15 (1998).

Hinds, Allister, 'Imperial Policy and Colonial Sterling Balances, 1943–56', *Journal of Imperial and Commonwealth History*, XIX, 19 (1991).

——, 'Sterling and Imperial Policy, 1945–51', *Journal of Imperial and Commonwealth History*, XV, 2 (1987).

Jackson, Ashley, 'African Soldiers and Imperial Authorities: Tensions and Unrest During the Service of HCT Soldiers in the British Army, 1941–46', *Journal of Southern African Studies*, 25, 4 (1999).

——, 'Supplying War: The HCT Military-Logistical Contribution in the Second World War', *Journal of Military History*, forthcoming.

Kennedy, P. M. 'Imperial Cable Communications and Strategy, 1870–1914', *English Historical Review* (October 1971).

Killingray, David, 'The Idea of a British Imperial African Army', *Journal of African History*, XX (1979).

——, 'Labour Exploitation for Military Campaigns in British Colonial Africa, 1870–1945', *Journal of Contemporary History*, 24, 3 (1989).

Krozewski, G. 'Sterling, the "Minor" Territories, and the End of Formal Empire, 1939–58', *Economic History Review*, 46, 2 (1993).

Larus, Joel, 'Diego Garcia: Political Clouds Over a Vital US Base', *Strategic Review*, 10 (1982).

——, 'Negotiating Independence? Mauritius and Diego Garcia', *The Round Table*, 294 (1985).

Lee, J. M. '"Forward Thinking" and War: the Colonial Office During the 1940s', *Journal of Imperial and Commonwealth History*, VI (1977).

Lynch, Timothy, 'Diego Garcia: Competing Claims to a Strategic Isle', *Case Western Reserve Journal of International Law*, 16 (1984).

Pearce, Robert, 'The Colonial Office and Planned Decolonization in Africa', *African Affairs*, 83, 330 (1984).

Platt, William, 'Studies in War-Time Organization: East Africa Command', *African Affairs* (January 1946).

Smyth, Rosaleen, 'Britain's African Colonies and British Propaganda During the Second World War', *Journal of Imperial and Commonwealth History*, XIV (1985).

Thomas, Martin, 'Imperial Backwater or Strategic Outpost? The British Take-over of Vichy Madagascar in 1942', *Historical Journal*, 39, 4 (1996).

Twining, William, 'R. G. Collingwood's Autobiography: One Reader's Response', *Journal of Law and Society*, 25, 4 (1998).

Willan, Brian, 'The South African Native Labour Contingent, 1916–18', *Journal of African History*, 19, 1 (1978).

Zwergbaum, Aaron, 'Exile in Mauritius', *Yad Washem: Studies on the European Jewish Catastrophe and Resistance*, IV (1960).

Unpublished works

Bell, A. S. and Kirk-Greene, A. H. M. 'Summary of KAR Papers and Contributors'.

Brown, John, 'Admiralty House and the Royal Navy 1810–1957' (1980).

Deutsch, Josef, 'A Free World? No Concentration Camp but Behind Prison Walls: the Story of the Refugees on the Fever Island Mauritius' (Beau Bassin, July 1945).

Domingue, Jean-Michel, 'The Experiences of the Mauritian and Seychellois Pioneers in, and Contribution to, the Egyptian and Western Desert Campaigns, 1940–43', MA Thesis (SOAS: University of London, 1994).

Foot, M. R. D. 'The Commonwealth's Input into SOE', conference paper (Oxford, 1998).

Grundlingh, Louis, 'The Role of Black South African Soldiers in the Second World War: A Contested Contribution', conference paper (Oxford, 1998).

Jackson, Ashley, 'Franco-Mauritians as Intermediaries of Empire', seminar paper (Oxford, 2000).

Kilson, Robin, 'Calling Up The Empire: The British Military Use of Non-White Labour in France, 1916–1929', PhD Thesis (Harvard University, 1990).

Mathieu, Alain, 'The Failure of the Mauritian Spies and the Taking of Reunion in 1942', Mauritius History Society (1992).

Sauzier, Guy, 'The Events Which Marked the Arrival of the Mauritian Battalion at Diego Suarez 1943', Mauritius History Society paper (1995).

Shuckburgh, John, 'Colonial Civil History of the Second World War' (London: Colonial Office 1949).

Walter, A. 'Echoes of a Vanishing Empire: the Memoirs of a Meteorologist and Civil Servant in the Colonial Empire, 1897–1947', two volumes.

Index

Abercromby barracks, Vacoas 62, 70, 72, 106, 181
Aborigines Protection Society 9
Adams, Capt. M. C. 74
Aden 17, 29, 30, 32, 183
Addu Atoll 11, 33, 36, 37, 42, 43, 56
Admiral Scheer 47
Admiralty 4, 16, 27, 38, 48, 50, 51, 56, 61, 67, 75, 77, 137
African Pioneer Corps (APC) 3, 103
Agalega islands 17, 43, 166
Aikoku Maru 48
Air Raid Precautions (ARP) 3, 9, 63, 64, 65
Alamein 2, 93
Americans 3, 13, 14, 16, 29, 31, 38, 39, 79, 133, 183
Andaman islands 43
Anglicization 87
Arab Native Labour Corps 82
Artisan Works Company, Royal Engineers 87, 126
Atlantis 47, 48
Australia 1, 7, 11, 18, 29, 34, 44, 134, 141, 182
Auxiliary Territorial Service (ATS) 3, 66

Bell, Sir Hesketh 24
Bell Village 83–4, 88, 177
Benghazi 81, 91, 98
Bissoondoyal, Bassdeo 157, 158
Bletchley Park 13, 18, 40, 131, 133, 135, 137
Brake 45, 47, 49
British Indian Ocean Territory (BIOT) 13, 17, 181, 183
Brooke-Popham, Admiral Sir Robert 31
Burma 2, 7, 9, 11, 33, 34, 56, 59, 105, 117, 125, 133, 164
Burns, Sir Alan 1

Cable and Wireless 51, 135
Cables 7, 16, 18, 40, 51, 52, 131, 132, 135, 141
Cassino 94
Catalina 11, 41, 43, 48, 49
Censorship 7, 131, 132, 136–51
Central Mediterranean Forces (CMF) 79, 93–5
Ceylon 8, 11, 18, 21, 23, 33, 36, 37, 38, 39, 40, 42, 44, 45, 49, 60, 61, 64, 96, 134, 140, 141, 165, 182
Ceylon Defence Force 104
Charles Louis Dreyfus 50
Charlotte Schleimann 45, 47, 48
Chesor 134
Chief Censor 52, 134, 136
Chinese 8, 53
Chinese Labour Corps 63, 81
Churchill, Sir Winston 3, 5, 6, 13, 32, 35, 53, 60, 160
Civil Defence Service 63
Civil Labour Corps 62, 66–8, 107
Clifford, Sir Bede xiii, 15, 58, 63, 74, 107, 109, 110, 138, 156, 160
Coastal Defence Squadron 12, 60, 64, 65, 72, 77
Cocos-Keeling islands 1, 18, 104, 182
Cold War 15, 16, 30, 181
Colombo 4, 36, 37, 131, 132, 133, 141
Colonial Development and Welfare 67, 168–71
Committee of Imperial Defence 58
Council of Government 10, 25, 65, 69, 75, 108, 109, 156, 157, 158, 159, 176
Creech Jones, Arthur 109, 153, 154, 157, 159, 178
Crete 79, 82
Cyclones 167, 177
Cyprus 30, 82, 98